# Windows NT Applications: Measuring and Optimizing Performance

Paul Hinsberg

MACMILLAN
TECHNICAL
PUBLISHING
U·S·A

# Windows NT Applications: Measuring and Optimizing Performance

By Paul Hinsberg

Published by:
Macmillan Technical Publishing
201 West 103rd Street
Indianapolis, Indiana 46290 USA

International Standard Book Number: 1-57870-176-7

Library of Congress Catalog Card Number: 99-61520

03 02 01 00 99  7 6 5 4 3 2 1

Interpretation of the printing code: The rightmost double-digit number is the year of the book's printing; the rightmost single-digit number is the number of the book's printing. For example, the printing code 99-1 shows that the first printing of the book occurred in 1999.

*Composed in Quark 4.04 and MCPdigital by Macmillan Technical Publishing*

*Printed in the United States of America*

## Trademark Acknowledgments

All terms mentioned in this book that are known to be trademarks or service marks have been appropriately capitalized. Macmillan Technical Publishing cannot attest to the accuracy of this information. Use of a term in this book should not be regarded as affecting the validity of any trademark or service mark. Windows is a registered trademark of Microsoft Corporation.

## Warning and Disclaimer

This book is designed to provide information about Windows NT. Every effort has been made to make this book as complete and as accurate as possible, but no warranty or fitness is implied.

The information is provided on an as-is basis. The authors and Macmillan Technical Publishing shall have neither liability nor responsibility to any person or entity with respect to any loss or damages arising from the information contained in this book or from the use of the discs or programs that may accompany it.

## Feedback Information

At Macmillan Technical Publishing, our goal is to create in-depth technical books of the highest quality and value. Each book is crafted with care and precision, undergoing rigorous development that involves the unique expertise of members from the professional technical community.

Readers' feedback is a natural continuation of this process. If you have any comments regarding how we could improve the quality of this book, or otherwise alter it to better suit your needs, you can contact us at `networktech@mcp.com`. Please make sure to include the book title and ISBN in your message.

We greatly appreciate your assistance.

**Publisher**
*David Dwyer*

**Executive Editor**
*Linda Ratts Engelman*

**Managing Editor**
*Gina Brown*

**Acquisitions Editor**
*Karen Wachs*

**Development Editor**
*Leah Williams*

**Project Editor**
*Alissa Cayton*

**Copy Editors**
*Kelli Brooks*
*Jennifer Mahern*

**Indexers**
*Nadia Ibrahim*
*Joy Dean Lee*

**Team Coordinator**
*Jennifer Garrett*

**Manufacturing Manager**
*Brook Farling*

**Book Designer**
*Louisa Klucznik*

**Cover Designer**
*Aren Howell*

**Compositor**
*Amy Parker*

## About the Author

**Paul Hinsberg, MBA, MCSE,** is the owner and operator of CRSD Inc., a computer consulting company in the Silicon Valley region. Paul also serves as a senior consultant with CRSD, and has fourteen years of experience with PC networking and enterprise systems, including Windows NT and Microsoft's BackOffice® suite of products. Paul also works as a software developer designing tools and utilities to augment his network consulting efforts. Some of these tools are included in commercial products. In addition to consulting, Paul has developed technical training courseware and served as the author/co-author of other books such as *Windows NT Performance: Monitoring, Benchmarking, and Tuning*, New Riders, 1998 (ISBN: 1-56205-942-4). He also works as an instructor for Learning Tree International. An enthusiastic sports participant, Paul can be found playing Roller Hockey or coaching one of his four kids in his free time. Paul can be contacted at `paulhins@home.com`.

## About the Technical Reviewers

These reviewers contributed their considerable practical, hands-on expertise to the entire development process for *Windows NT Applications: Measuring and Optimizing Performance*. As the book was being written, these folks reviewed all the material for technical content, organization, and flow. Their feedback was critical to ensuring that *Windows NT Applications: Measuring and Optimizing Performance* fits our reader's need for the highest quality technical information.

**Warren Emens** is a software consultant working throughout California. His work over the last fourteen years includes application development on a variety of platforms, including Microsoft Windows NT and Sun Solaris. His recent work in application development on Windows NT involved building the trading system software used by Bank of America's derivatives traders. He has been working this year with an Internet start-up company on the architecture and implementation of a Windows NT–based Web server system and a personalized Web browser client. His pet projects are MP3 applications and hardware and mastering the piano works of Robert Schumann.

**William McLuskie** is a Senior Consultant with Advanced Technology Systems, Inc. (http://www.advtechsys.com). He specializes in the development of n-tiered, Web-based applications for national and international clients. Most of his development work is done on the Microsoft Windows platforms using IIS, MTS, ASP, and Visual Studio. Additionally, he has taught object-oriented design, component development, and various programming languages at several universities, as well as in the corporate sector. He holds a B.S. in Computer Science and a M.S. in Computer Information Systems. William lives in Charlotte, North Carolina with his wife Brenda. When he is not coding, he is an avid student of Japanese martial arts and currently teaches at Aikido of Charlotte. He can be contacted at william@mcluskie.com or through http://www.mcluskie.com/william/.

# Overview

# Table of Contents

## Dedication

For my wife Priscilla and newborn daughter Madison who remind me that everything important in life can be seen in the twinkle of a loved one's eye.

## Acknowledgments

The author wishes to acknowledge the valiant efforts of the technical editors and Macmillan Technical Publishing editorial staff. Without your energy and compassion this book would not have been possible.
Thank you.

# *Introduction*

In case you have just picked up this book from the shelf and are considering reading it (or better, buying it), I would like to clarify its intent. For several years I have been working as an administrator as well as a programmer. As an administrator, I am always looking for ways to improve the performance of my network and NT systems. I analyze traffic patterns, examine memory and processor utilization, experiment with various configurations of Windows NT, and learn everything that I can about the internal operation of the system. As a programmer, I try to get my programs to run as smoothly and efficiently as possible. I am always looking for "elegant" code. To me, elegant code takes the fewest lines to accomplish a task of any degree of complexity, while using the least amount of resources. Having learned much along the way, I have embarked on a quest to share it with others. I have been writing and teaching about performance monitoring and tuning for years now. During my teaching and writing, primarily for system and network administrators, I have found that I often end up saying something to the effect of, "and this is the best we can tune the machine unless we are the developer of the code." The idea is that if you had developed the code, you could alter its behavior and make it more elegant. So, finally, I decided to take performance monitoring and tuning a step further.

Thus, this book is written for the developers who want to learn how to analyze the performance of their code. You will learn techniques for using a myriad of tools, which are most likely already at your disposal. You will learn techniques for testing and analysis. Throughout the book you will get glimpses of the internal NT architecture and how all the pieces work together. I will share my own experiences along the way and go into some in-depth examples of particular situations, like SQL front-end programming and Web development. Be clear on one point: I am not going to show you how to code. This book is about analyzing and testing. Using the information here, you will be able to tell how efficiently your code is interacting with the operating system. You will see what kind of resource requirements your system will need and how to best configure a system to run your code. You may find memory leaks, processor abuses, or networking inefficiencies in your code by using the knowledge found in these pages. It will not matter if you are programming in VC++, Visual Basic, DOS Batch File, Java, or Visual COBOL. Whichever language you use, the tools and techniques found here will still ferret out the bottlenecks and problems. As a developer you will have to fix them based on your knowledge of the development environment that you have selected. I myself am partial to Visual Basic for its readability, quick development cycle, and its widespread integration throughout the Microsoft family of products.

You won't find a lot of theory in this book, although it is unavoidable at times. I like to take a more practical approach. I always try to make the information I pass on immediately applicable, so I try to present it in a ready-to-use fashion. If that is what you are looking for, you are sure to find this book informative and immediately beneficial.

The first part of the book deals primarily with the tools that we are going to be using throughout the remainder of the book. As I said, I try to keep to the freebies that are included with things like the Windows NT Resource Kits, TechNet, and MSDN as well as shareware. I am not saying that expensive tools aren't worthy of your attention. I am simply trying to stick to my philosophy of information in the book being immediately applicable. Nothing is more frustrating than reading 20 pages about a tool that you don't have and your boss is not about to cough up the $5,000 for. If you are one of the lucky ones, who works for a company committed to the doing some major performance analysis, great! Most of us have to do with what we have or can download for free. You will find this section good for learning about the tools, or learning some new techniques and tricks in utilizing the tools that you are already familiar with. In addition, you will find some detailed discussions about the NT architecture. Don't worry—you won't find yourself buried in discussions of mutexes, mutants, semaphores, or discussions about the exacting processes NT uses to detail virtual memory pages. You will learn, however, how the many components of the NT architecture inter-operate. This will provide you with some insight into how and why certain programs and user actions generate particular types of activity on Windows NT.

The second part of the book is dedicated to discovery. In Part I, you are given a map, a pick, and a shovel. In Part II, you are sent into the world to search for gold. Using the tools at your disposal, you will see how to unmask the problems plaguing applications' performance and general NT performance. Detailed examples will provide you with the exact steps for analyzing a program and isolating the problem. Much of what you will learn here will have general applicability to any programming language. You will see how to determine if a memory-intensive program's resource cravings are really warranted or just excessive hoarding of resources. Every resource that a system might use will be examined so that no stone is left unturned.

Part III of this book takes you to the dark tangled world of complex applications with multiple servers and entangled resource requirements. Here the examples turn to the extravagant as we detail system processes and interaction with other servers across networks. Web servers, database systems, and applications that push the limits of NT performance will be covered. If you've got a weak stomach, perhaps you should find another career.

## Conventions Used

Typographical conventions you should be aware of when reading this book are as follows:

| Element | Style |
| --- | --- |
| Utilities, programs, Registry keys, filenames, and folders | ALL CAPS |
| Performance objects, counters, commands, parameters, and Web addresses | Monospaced font |
| New terms | *Italic* |
| Errors | "in quotes" |

# Part I

## Arm Yourselves!: Tools for Performance Monitoring

# Introduction to Performance Monitor

While Microsoft Windows NT was being written, the developers took special care to try to make the operating system as efficient as possible. Yes, a few of you might chuckle or even sneer at this remark, but for the complexity and diversity of Windows NT, it performs remarkably well. Certainly, there is always room for improvement. So the Microsoft developers wrote a tool to track the performance of the various components of Windows NT. The tool was built to have a small footprint and work with a minimum of influence on the performance. (You can't have the tool for monitoring performance messing up performance.) This tool was improved in operation and appearance so that it could be passed on to the general consumer. The tool is called the Windows NT Performance Monitor.

After you are done with this chapter, you will not only know how to work the Performance Monitor's variety of data collection and display methods, but you will also understand how the Performance Monitor internals work. Such knowledge will prepare you for the chapters that lay ahead. Throughout the rest of the book, you will be using the Performance Monitor to gain intimate knowledge about what your program is doing and how the Windows NT operating system is responding to your commands. In addition, when you are considering writing your own counters for the Performance Monitor, you will understand how counters will fit in the Performance Monitor Architecture.

# The Basics

The *Performance Monitor* is a tool for viewing information about your system. To understand the Performance Monitor, first you should consider the construction of the tool. After this is understood, you can begin to review the operation of the tool's various interfaces. Along the way, you might need to review the way that Windows NT operates.

Generally, I feel that reviewing how NT operates is a good practice. The development of applications has become very easy these days. Quick and easy graphical development tools allow people to create applications quickly, though not always efficiently. These tools speed the process, without the developer having to stop and think about the coding process or the platform.

The problems that lack of planning and forethought create are quite evident on the Web, which offers a new and diverse set of programming circumstances, which even seasoned programmers have sometimes neglected to take the time to understand. I am sure that all of you have run across a cool Web site that has all sorts of amazing graphics and cool applets. Too bad the developer never considered doing the simple test across a 56KB line to see if the page would load in a reasonable time. Certainly the new technology has within its grasp the ability to deliver rich and dazzling displays of creativity and ingenuity—if only the developer takes the time to understand the circumstances of the delivery.

The importance of understanding the basic architecture of the system before building on that architecture will be a recurring theme throughout this book. Although you might have used the Performance Monitor already, you might not be familiar with all the features and various implementations. You will see implementations of each of the views along with the good and bad aspects. You will also be exposed to Registry entries and DLL architectures used in the development and implementation of the Performance Monitor.

## Performance Monitor Architecture

Above all else, the Performance Monitor is a tool for analyzing data. The Performance Monitor generally consists of a set of DLLs for collecting information, primarily from the Windows NT Executive Services. The information is written to the Registry where it can be organized and viewed through the interface (see Figure 1.1).

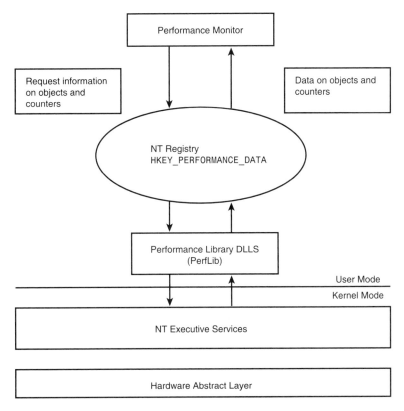

**Figure 1.1**  *The Performance Monitor is a collection of DLLs that passes performance data to the Registry to be viewed by the interactive program.*

The Windows NT Architecture consists of two primary modes of operation, the *Kernel mode* and the *User mode*. Kernel mode is where most of the operating system functions run, including the hardware drivers. The Performance Monitor's DLLs, or PerfLibs, interact with the operating system to collect data as quickly as possible. The objective of any measuring tool is to collect the data while interfering as little as possible with the object that you are trying to measure. Thus, the Performance Monitor must try to move information in the most efficient manner possible. The Registry was selected as the intermediate location for the data for this reason. Generally, the Registry is held in memory, and memory clearly has much lower access times. So, if you want information to be moved as quickly as possible through a system, you want it to stay in memory and not go to the hard drive.

The Performance Monitor Data is in the HKEY_PERFORMANCE_DATA section of the Registry. Don't bother opening the REGEDT32.EXE looking for it, or even the REGEDIT.EXE. Both of the tools offer views of the major Registry keys, but do not show the performance information. For performance information use the Windows NT APIs.

### Note

*When using the REGEDIT.EXE Registry editor tool you will see a Registry key called KEY_DYN_DATA or HKEY_DYN_DATA, depending on the version of the tool. This is not the same as the aforementioned HKEY_PERFORMANCE_DATA. The HKEY_DYN_DATA is used only in Windows 95/98. The key is displayed in NT as well, but any attempt to open the key to examine data will result in an error. If you are accessing the keys programmatically through one of the Microsoft APIs, you will need to access the keys differently. Generally, Microsoft supplies constants that translate to values, which in turn reference the actual objects—in this case Registry trees. In Windows NT/2000, you will need to use a declaration such as:*

```
Public Const HKEY_PERFORMANCE_DATA = &H80000004
```

*This constant differs from the one in Windows 95/98, as seen here:*

```
Public Const HKEY_DYN_DATA = &H80000006 ◆
```

The Performance Monitor will activate the collection of the data via the Registry, then it is up to the DLLs to communicate with the operating system. The communication is primarily with the component called the *Hardware Abstract Layer* (HAL); however, other components could be involved, depending on the objects that you are attempting to monitor. Within the Registry, the information on the objects and counters is stored in the following:

```
HKEY_LOCAL_MACHINE\Software\Microsoft\Windows NT\CurrentVersion\PerfLib\Language Code
```

This information is associated with the default language of the system via a language code (see Figure 1.2). In this example, the language code is 009, Western English. Generally, the code is evident, as it will be the only subkey underneath the PerfLib section. These entries can be expanded. The extra entries are referred to as extended objects. Using information that Microsoft supplies in a variety of places, you can create your own performance objects. Later in this section, the process is reviewed in detail.

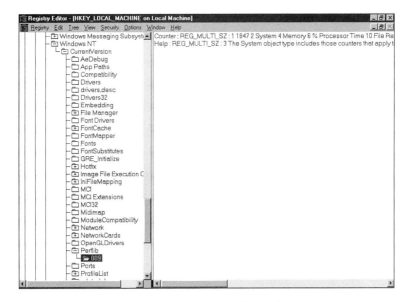

**Figure 1.2**  *A view of the objects that the Performance Monitor will be able to collect from the NT machine.*

Now you have a general understanding of the Performance Monitor Architecture. After this tool captures data via the Performance Library DLLs and passes it to the NT Registry, the information is read using the Performance Monitor interface.

**Note**

*See Chapter 2, "Windows NT Kernel Debugger, " for a more detailed review of how Performance Monitor Architecture works. The goal is to become proficient enough to write Performance Library DLLs for our applications. ◆*

## The Performance Monitor Interface

Now that you have a taste for what goes on behind the scenes, let's see how we can view the information. Recall that the Performance Monitor interface is going to retrieve the information from the Registry and display it in one of four different formats, called views. Before discussing the different types of views, let's discuss the common method each view has for selecting items for measurement. In selecting what you would like to see, you must decide upon which objects, counters, and instances will be used during the data-gathering process.

To begin, launch the Performance Monitor by selecting Start, Administrative Tools, Performance Monitor. (The executable is called PERFMON.EXE for those of you who like to click Start, Run and type in a command.) The Performance Monitor will launch a blank chart. Your first inclination will be to tell the Performance Monitor to start collecting some information. This can easily be done by clicking the plus sign on the toolbar at the top of the Performance Monitor. A common selection screen will display, which is where you can view the statistics.

### Note

*Releases of Windows past NT 4.0 place the Performance Monitor within the Microsoft Management Console (MMC). Thus, opening the MMC and then adding the Performance SnapIn enables you to begin collecting Performance Data. This book focuses primarily on NT 4.0.* ◆

In the Counter Selection dialog box, make your selections of objects, counters, and instances. Your selections determine the types of information that are displayed. Selecting objects, counters, and instances makes the difference between time well spent on analysis and a fruitless wild-goose chase.

### Objects

*Objects* are the basis for what you want to measure. It is easiest to think of an object as a computer component. The processor is an object, and there is a Processor object in Performance Monitor. Memory is an object on a computer, and there is a Memory object in Performance Monitor.

However, life is full of complexities, and so is the Performance Monitor. Other objects refer to more ambiguous items, such as TCP or SQL Server. Objects in Performance Monitor are handy ways of grouping the performance items that you want to measure. The two types of objects are *core* and *extended*.

Core objects are chiefly installed when you install Windows NT. The following are examples of core objects:

Processor

Process

Thread

Memory

Physical Disk

Logical Disk

Extended objects are added when you install additional software or software components. (Extended objects can also include ones that you write.) The following are examples of extended objects:

SQL Server

RAS Port

Internet Information Services Global

Active Server Pages

Exchange

Any number of these are installed when the corresponding software is installed. Generally, core and extended objects are treated the same. However, additional objects do require slightly more overhead. In order for extended objects to send data to the Registry so that the Performance Monitor can display properly, additional data-generating DLLs must be loaded. (This is explained more later in this chapter.) This process translates to additional overhead.

### Counters

After you have selected an object, you will then be able to select any number of counters from the listing below the object. The three basic types of counters are instantaneous (or raw), averaging (or rate), and difference. These counters are explained in the following:

- **Instantaneous (Raw)**

  Provides data on the current value of a measurable quantity. The Current Number of Logged in Users, Processor Queue Length, and Disk Queue Length are examples of raw counters.

- **Averaging (Rate)**

  Any counter with an average, percentage, or flow feel to it. Bytes Received/Sec or Frames Sent/Sec are good rate counters.

- **Difference**

  Displays a value if the difference between the current result and the previous measure is greater than 0. If the difference is 0 or less than 0, a value of 0 is displayed. Microsoft has not developed a counter of this type. One use for this counter would be to receive information on changes to counters that in the past have been simply total counters. This would be useful for checking the number of new connections made to a system since the last data sample. Another use would be to receive the number of network errors reported by the server service since the last sample. Such values would have special significance when performing controlled testing.

Microsoft has changed the names of the counters through the years, hence the titles in parentheses. Generally, I use the old terminology, which is rate and raw. The difference category was added in NT 4.0, but to date no counters are in this category. Although you might not be preparing for a Microsoft Certification exam, it is important to understand the terminology of the tools that you are using. Chances are that you will encounter other text which makes reference to Performance Monitor counters. Understanding the meanings will give you just that much more understanding of how to interpret the data. Microsoft seems to have adjusted the terminology to describe the nature of how the various counters are collected. The old terminology, rate and raw, was more descriptive of the type of data.

For example, *instantaneous* describes the collection of a value at a particular point in time. The old term, *raw*, describes the type of value. (Raw is how many people can you stuff into a Volkswagen.) The term *averaging* lets you know that the counter is being collected over a period of time, and a small calculation is performed to determine a value. The old term, *rate*, is again more descriptive of the type of value that you are getting. (Rate is how much water can be pushed through a garden hose per second.)

**Instances**

After you have selected the objects and the counters, you have one more selection, instances. You have probably figured this one out. An instance is an occurrence of an object on a system. You might have more than one processor (yeah, dream on), in which case processor 0 will be the first processor and processor 1 will be the second. Other objects have similar multiple instances—hard drives, for example. Instances can sometimes be a little deceiving. You might select the Network Interface object, for example. You have only one network card, yet there are multiple instances, as you can see in Figure 1.3.

In Figure 1.3, a single network card is installed on the machine, yet three instances of the network interface appear in the Instances box of the Performance Monitor dialog box. This particular machine has some extras installed, which result in the extra instances. The TCP/IP protocol is installed. In addition, the Microsoft WINs Client is running. This constitutes two interfaces. The third instance is the RAS client, which is installed. If you do not have a RAS connection and have copied some data across the network while examining the Bytes/Sec on each of the interfaces, only the second (TCP/IP) interface would display any activity. If you have a RAS connection and repeat the activity, the reported activity would change. The point is to remember that an instance does not always need to be a physical occurrence; it can be a virtual occurrence or a software object.

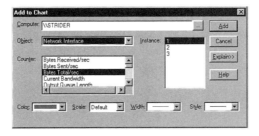

**Figure 1.3** *Instances can be deceiving, as seen when examining the Network Interface object in Performance Monitor.*

## Utilizing Performance Monitor Views

The Performance Monitor interface is a collection of data-examining methods, called views. The term *view* was coined in Microsoft documentation, and is as good as any, to collectively refer to the methods used to display information about system performance. Each view has its purpose, strengths, and weaknesses. The following is a list of views:

Chart view

Report view

Alert view

Log view

### Chart View

*Chart view* is the most common view for the Performance Monitor, and is the default view when the Performance Monitor is launched. Chart view is easy to see graphically and displays the information numerically for comparison or tracking purposes. In Chart view, you should be concerned with several sections of the display. In Figure 1.4 the sections are highlighted.

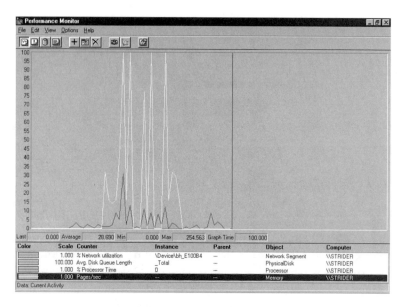

**Figure 1.4**    *Chart view's various sections represent data in a variety of ways, thus, aiding in the proper interpretation of data.*

The primary section of Chart view is the graph portion of the interface. The graph typically is displayed in a line graph format. However, if you select Options, Chart from the drop-down menu you will see some options for altering the display. Some of the options are to add the horizontal and vertical lines. These lines are quite useful when you are trying to make some comparisons between values displayed along the screen. The vertical maximum option can be used to increase the overall maximum value that is displayed on the graph.

Remember that the data points, which make up the line in Chart view's Graph Mode, are adjusted based on the scale that is displayed in Chart view's legend section. The scale is adjustable. When you are adding a counter, you can adjust the scale to display the values on the graph. Note that the numeric values, located in the Value Bar, are NOT adjusted based on this scale. Do not jump to conclusions about values that you see in the graphical portion of the display because they might be adjusted to a scale that is not suitable for the 100 maximum vertical value of the chart. Although it is possible to increase the vertical maximum of the chart through the Options menu, it is better to adjust the individual scale of the counter. This allows you to keep the rest of the counters in proper perspective. Keep in mind that if you are comparing various counters graphically, you need to have them at appropriate scales for comparison.

Let's look at the Chart Options dialog box (see Figure 1.5) a little more closely. As you can see, one of the options is to display the chart in a Histogram format as opposed to the graph format.

**Figure 1.5**   *The Chart Options dialog box allows you to alter the chart's display to suit your data analysis objectives and tastes.*

The Histogram option is an excellent method for quickly comparing similar items. This would be used with items like the %Processor Time or Working Set (which is the amount of memory that a process is taking). Say you are having a problem with a repetitive memory shortage. You can use the Histogram option to display the Working Set of each of the processes on the system. This allows you to smoke out the thief that is stealing all the memory for its own greedy little processes and threads.

Another exceptionally useful option is Update Time. This option determines how often a sampling of data will be taken and added to the overall data set that is being displayed. The default for the chart's Update Time is one second when viewing interactively. (Also notice the Manual Update option.)

You should take note that in Chart view, items will disappear if you simply let them go. As you look at activity, Chart view's Update Line marches across the display. Just when you think you have the issue clear in your head, the data is erased. Instead of racing against the Chart view clock, go into the Chart Options dialog box and set the update interval to Manual Update. In Manual Update mode Chart view only updates when you instruct it to do so. To instruct Chart view to update, click the Camera icon on the toolbar. Manual Update mode gives you the chance to review the interactive data at a more leisurely pace. If you need to examine data in a more thorough manner, you should use Log view.

Overall, Chart view is used when you want to examine the details of logged data or get a quick view of what is currently happening in the system. In addition, if you are looking for quick graphical comparisons of values, Chart view is very useful. When you need to compare actual values or perform further calculations of values, Report view will be more suitable.

### Report View

*Report view* does not print information, despite its name. Report view displays numerical information in a row and column format. For example, Figure 1.6 illustrates a processor utilization on a Windows NT Workstation.

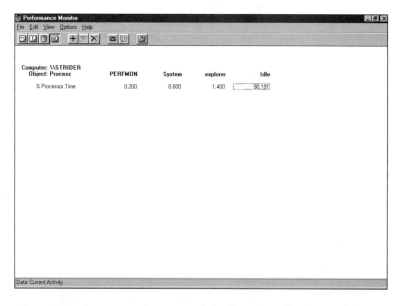

**Figure 1.6**   *Report view's numerical display is beneficial in performing minor calculations and recording exact numerical values.*

Adding counters and instances to Report view is identical to adding them in Chart view, with the exception that certain options are absent from the dialog box. The items for scale, line color, and line width do not apply to Report view. The options for Report view are limited to the Update Interval. You might adjust how often the data is collected or you can switch to Manual Update, which has its individual use in the Report view as well. If you notice a particularly interesting set of data, you can switch to Manual Update and the data will remain until you instruct the Performance Monitor to update.

Notice that the default update interval for Report view is five seconds, as opposed to the one second for Chart view. Thus, you can expect to see some differences between Report view's numbers and Chart view's numbers. This will also be true when you are looking at logged data.

Report view's strengths lie in being able to display numerical data in an effective manner. Whenever you need to make numeric calculations, such as `Input Pages/sec / Page Faults/sec`, to get the number of hard page faults on a system, you should use Report view. If you are attempting to measure raw throughput, you should use Report view as well. For example, determining the `Bytes Read/sec` for a hard drive configuration would best be measured and recorded using Report view.

### Alert View

Although Chart and Report views are primarily for displaying information, Alert view is more for reacting to conditions. You can use alerts in a variety of ways, several of which you will be exposed to in the following sections. The concept of the alert is that some event is generated based on a set threshold of a particular counter. You are allowed to set the object, instance, and counter. The difference between Alert view and other views is that you also select a value and a course of action to be taken based on the threshold (see Figure 1.7).

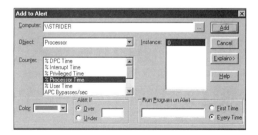

**Figure 1.7**  *Setting alerts is much like adding counters, except that you have a few additional parameters that are very powerful configuration items.*

When setting the threshold, decide if you want the alert to be triggered. If the value is less than or greater than a particular number, then enter the number. The Performance Monitor will not be checking your numbers for scale consistency; that is left to you. When setting the threshold, you need to know the scale of the counter that you are using with the alert. For example, the Memory object's Available Bytes counter is in units of bytes. Thus, if you want to keep an eye out for the critical 4MB of available memory, you should set the alert's threshold value to 4000000. After you have decided on the value, you can instruct the program to perform a particular action. The action can be launched the first time or every time the alert is triggered. The action can be any appropriate program. The following is a list of some actions that I have used in the past:

- Launching a batch file with NET SEND broadcast notifications, so that I know what is happening no matter where I am logged in

- Launching another Performance Monitor with specific settings to capture particular information based on the alert

- Launching the Network Monitor, a software network sniffer, to capture network traffic when utilization becomes high

- Launching specialized programs to diagnose or resolve specific issues

Alerts make almost anything possible. After you have a program, you will need to decide whether you want the program to run every time or the first time. Every time is just as it seems—each time a value is found to meet the criteria, the designated action is performed. If you are testing, be careful about the value that you set.

CASE STUDY    **Alerts Gone Wild**

As an instructor, I was teaching a class on NT Optimization. I had a student who wanted to experiment with alerts in the Performance Monitor and the launching of programs. He selected NOTEPAD.EXE as the program to launch. Note that this was an exceptionally useful choice; he would certainly be able to tell that the program executed, because it would pop up on his desktop. Next he used the %Process Time as the value to check. He selected a threshold of above ten percent. He wanted to make sure that the alert would fire and he would be able to see NOTEPAD.EXE pop up on the screen. After he hit OK, the alert caused NOTEPAD.EXE to launch.

What the student had neglected to do was alter the Every Time selection to First Time. Well, because every time the alert was checked the processor was more than ten percent busy, another NOTEPAD.EXE was launched. Soon he found it hard to keep up with closing the Notepads as they were launching from the alert. The lesson for the day was to make sure that you really want the alert to perform the action every time. The alternative is to have the alert fire only the first time the criteria is met.

Here is what actually happens when an alert is triggered:

1. The alert is checked and the criterion is met.
2. The designated program is executed.
3. The alert is checked again at the next interval.
4. If the criterion is still met, no action is taken. However, if the criterion is NOT met, the flag is reset.
5. The alert is checked again at the next interval.
6. If the flag has been reset and the criterion is met, the designated program is executed again.

So, despite having set the action to be taken only the first time that the criterion is met, you have the potential for the action to be executed several times.

Some additional options can be set for the alerts by using the Options menu (see Figure 1.8).

In the dialog box shown in Figure 1.8, you can set the interval time for checking the alerts. Again notice that the default is five seconds. Also, you can set the alerts to send notifications or put information into the Windows NT Event Viewer's application log. Both are useful when you are monitoring a long process and do not want to hang around waiting for something to happen.

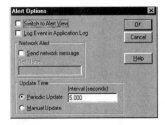

**Figure 1.8**    *Alert Options can add additional notification actions to the alert results as well as adjust the sampling interval.*

## Log View

Log view is not so much a view as it is a method for setting up how to log information to disk. To get the information that you need, you will need to set the following option in Log view:

The location and name of the log file

The interval for data collection

The objects to be collected

When setting up to collect data, set the objects that you want to collect. Unlike other views, in Log view you add entire objects with all their associated instances and counters. (In other Performance Monitor views, you would select specific instances and counters that you wanted to examine.) After you select all the objects, choose Options, Log from the drop-down menu to set the remaining items for data collection.

The first item you should consider is the location of the log file. You might need a lot of space, so select a drive with a lot of room. Also, if you are going to be tracking disk performance in the log, avoid putting the log on the same drive whose performance you are attempting to track. Next, set the interval for logging. The default is 15 seconds. Depending on what you are tracking, you might want to reduce this number to collect data more frequently. Consider that more frequent data collections result in a larger log file. Finally, click the Start Log button. If you want to stop the log, return to the Options, Log screen. The data will be collected to the file you have selected. In the Log view, you will see some basic information about the options that you have selected. In Figure 1.9 you can see a Log session in action.

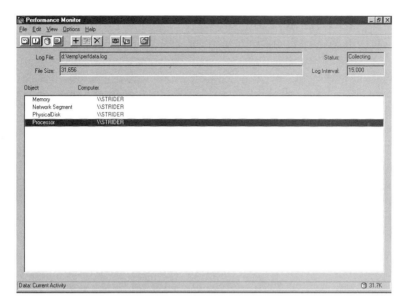

**Figure 1.9**  *After you have logged the desired amount of data, you can review it using any one of the Performance Monitor views, even Log view.*

You will see information about the name of the file, the size, the status of collection, and the objects being collected. You will not see any of the data, nor will you be able to open the log file until you have stopped the collection process, such as you see in Figure 1.9.

### Note

*Relogging of data is a useful exercise for reducing the size of the log file for easier transport or for removing some of the data that you do not find interesting. You might have collected numerous objects, resulting in an expansive log file on the order of hundreds of megabytes in size. After you have done some preliminary analysis and determine that only a few objects contain interesting data, relog the data to another log file. This results in a smaller file that is easier to move across the network, as well as taking up less room on your hard drive.*

*Another way to reduce the size of the log file is to reduce the collection interval. You might have originally collected data into a log at one-second intervals. After some analysis, you learn that collecting disk activity at one-second intervals was not much more enlightening than collecting disk activity at 15 second intervals. Relogging the data at a 15-second interval reduces the size of the file.* ◆

# Logging and Analyzing Data

You now have an understanding of the basics of the Performance Monitor tool. In the following sections you will be using the information you learned about in the previous pages as well as obtaining some more information on how to use the Performance Monitor. You will be guided through a session of data collection and analysis using some of the standard performance monitoring techniques. We will start with some simple goal setting.

Having an objective to your collection efforts allows you to remain focused. After you have the objectives down, you will need to make some preparations for collecting data. Figuring out which objects to collect and how much disk space you might need is key to the success of the data collection process. After you are ready to log the data, you will have yet a couple more choices. You can select the method of logging that best suits the situation. Lastly, you will want to have a look at the data. With the immense amount of data that can be quickly collected, having a few good methods for weeding out the interesting data points is a crucial time saver.

## Creating the Log

This section isn't simply a bunch of steps on how to log data. You will learn why to log data, a point often lost when instructing users. Logging data involves the following:

> Developing a goal or purpose
>
> Preparing to log data
>
> Logging data

After you've completed logging, you should analyze the data you've collected, which will be discussed in the next section.

### Developing a Goal or Purpose

Creating a Performance Log file doesn't start with kicking off the utility and generating great heaps of data to be analyzed. The log file starts with a purpose. You will need to have a clear objective for creating a log file.

One important objective is that developing code using a log file allows you to execute a complex series of instructions, while the Performance Monitor is collecting information on resource utilization of the machine. For example, let's say that you have written an application which updates/reports information from a database on a remote server somewhere else in the network. You want to replicate a standard user's data entry session and a report printout. There might be numerous screens and fields that you need to fill in to do the data entry correctly. In addition, you might have conditional programming that will run, only if you enter certain values into the data entry screen. In this case, you would want to run through the data entry process several times to test the performance of all the code.

Although you are performing all these tasks, the Performance Monitor is expected to collect the data. Using Log view will allow you to collect every bit of data and sort it in a log file, so that you can examine it at your leisure after the session is complete.

## Note

*If you are using Chart view or Report view, you have to be watching as information goes by the screen. Remember that the Chart and Report view information is transient. After 100 data points, the Chart view begins redrawing the screen and the data that you want to examine is gone.* ◆

## The Glories of Scripted Testing

*Most developers aren't really the greatest testers. Let's face it, our joy in life is writing elegant code to do really cool stuff, not running repeated scenarios through our new application. Most of us run through the code a few times to make sure that it executes without an error when you put the correct data in. You are always thinking that you can recursively test the application later. Well, it's later. Performance testing will often require repeated tests utilizing a variety of functions. Even if you have a Quality Assurance (QA) Testing department, they will be as excited as you would be about running through your application screens 100 times. In these cases a decent script program is worth the money.*

*Scripted-test software allows you to enter values in and have it run through the software's screens repeatedly while you have the Performance Monitor running in the background. This alleviates the need for a developer or QA tester to be present the entire time, which means labor cost savings to your boss. You will want to make sure he knows that so he will cough up the money to pay for a decent testing package. Some freebies are out there—Microsoft ScriptIt! is one that comes to mind. In any case, having repeated testing of a variety of variables against any application is worth the time and effort. Using the Performance Monitor in conjunction with such testing allows for an excellent overview of the performance of the system.* ◆

Keep the objectives of your data collection and the nature of the application that you are examining in mind. Let's consider the client/server database application. The client application performance is only half of the puzzle. You will also want to monitor the server components. You might have a database server, Web server, or some type of middleware business logic server working to respond to the client-side applications requests. You will want to examine the performance of the server, in addition to examining the performance of the workstation application. They directly affect each other! If you examine only one side of the communication, you might spend a lot of time working out performance issues that are related to the code on the other system. In this situation, you would set up the Performance Monitor on the remote system to log data.

Another application might have a completely different objective for the testing and data-collection process. You might have written a major enterprise class application that is expected to be concurrently used by hundreds or thousands of people at the same time. You will need to make accurate recommendations for the server and workstation configurations. Guessing at the best hardware to buy when installing a major application is begging for trouble. Always remember that the best-written application installed and configured poorly is no better than the worst-written application installed and configured correctly.

To avoid such hazards, use the Performance Monitor to examine the application while put under stress. There is a variety of ways to accomplish this and sometimes you will want to use more than one, depending on the stages of your development and deployment. You might be thinking, "What's the big deal? I will just recommend a nice big system that couldn't possibly have a problem servicing thousands of users." Unfortunately, you have to stop and think like a marketing person for a moment. Yes, I know it makes me queasy too. However, the idea is eventually to sell your application. If you require huge hardware costs, those costs will raise the client's overall cost. This might make your beautiful application less competitive and thus less likely to be purchased. What's the point in writing great applications if no one will be able to afford to use them?

## The Importance of Load Testing

*When you have prepared a major application for deployment, you will want to endurance test or stress test the applications client and server components. This involves the Performance Monitor and a scripted utility. Some of the scripted utilities have features to simulate multiple users per individual workstation. Therefore, you could use 5 workstations to simulate 20 users each and thus have a 100-user test case. Of course, these are not completely representative of 1000 individual workstations.*

*Another method for testing systems, especially server-side components, is to put a load on the system before running your test scenario against it. For example, you might have only two workstations for testing. Your preliminary testing indicates a 4% processor load on the server per client. You can put an NT Resource Kit utility on the server to force the processor to 40% utilization to represent 40 users. Then, use your two workstations to run the actual application and test the performance on the workstations. Again, this is not the most accurate method, but you will get a good idea of the effects of various system loads on the workstations and servers. Knowing anything about your application's load capacity is better than making blind recommendations.* ♦

Here are a few additional goals for using the Performance Monitor Log:

- **Network load testing**

  If your application communicates across the network, you know someone is going to ask the bandwidth requirements.

- **Troubleshooting system crashes**

  A number of server crashes and workstation-hung situations can be figured out with the Performance Monitor and other tools that will be introduced later.

- **Internal development server requirements**

  You don't want to be developing a large application using a weak server and workstation for testing. Using the Performance Monitor can give you ammunition for making the budget request for a new server.

- **Recommendations to clients**

  Anything that you do to help your clients' systems run faster and better will be well received. Instructing clients how to monitor their applications performance can help them find problems before they become critical or help them plan for their next upgrade, which of course benefits your company as well.

After you begin thinking in the Performance-Testing way, I am sure you will find other goals and uses for performance monitoring methods.

**Preparing to Log Data**

Now that you have decided why you are going to use the log file, you can begin to plan how you are going to do it. This will be, in part, dependent on what and why you are monitoring performance. In preparation for performance monitoring, you will need to decide the following:

What you are going to monitor.

How you are going to monitor (local versus remote).

What performance objects you need to monitor.

How long you are going to monitor.

What interval you are going to monitor.

If you have a self-contained application that sits on a desktop, you will want to monitor the one workstation. If, however, you have an application that involves several systems over a network you will want to monitor all the systems at the same time. Of course, you might decide to monitor only a workstation or server if you are certain that the problem is localized on one of the systems. This would usually fall into the troubleshooting category of the Performance Monitor goals that were previously mentioned. In most other cases, you are concerned with the overall performance of the application, which would involve the workstation, network, and server components. Thus, in any thorough testing you will need to monitor all of these.

*Monitoring Local and Remote Systems*

When monitoring a  system, you will have a couple of choices on where you want to monitor, local or remote. In *local* monitoring, the Performance Monitor is run locally on the system that it is going to be monitoring. In this case the hard drive will be the most affected by the Performance Monitoring activity. If you are monitoring remotely using the Performance Monitor from another machine to look at the data from a remote system on the network, the network will be affected. This can also affect the Processor of the remote machine, which will be explained in Chapter 5, "General Resource Consumption."

**Note**

*As we will see in Chapters 5 and 6, many components of a system will affect one another. Often, perceived performance problems in one area will be masking problems in another area. Thus, a cautious and scientific approach to examination of performance issues must be maintained.* ◆

Recall that when performance monitoring, we will want to avoid affecting the performance of the system we are trying to test. Thus, when deciding how to monitor the system, you will want to determine what component your application uses the least. For example, say you developed an application in Java that accesses a document review system that you have developed on a Web server. You are using Windows NT with IIS as your Web server. In this case, using the Performance Monitor to examine the system remotely would not be advised. A Web server is expected to have high network generated activity as its normal mode of operation. Because the network is a key component to monitor, you would not want to further affect the performance by having the Performance Monitor moving lots of data from the machine to a remote workstation. Conversely, if you have a workstation application that uses the disk intensely, you would not want to use the Performance Monitor locally because it would store its data on the hard drive, generating more disk activity. So, when selecting a method for monitoring performance, remember the following:

- Monitoring locally primarily affects the disk performance. (The processor and memory are potentially affected as well, but can be worked out with configuration changes.)
- Monitoring remotely affects the network and to a lesser extent, the processor.

*Choosing What to Monitor*

Now that you have considered whether you will be monitoring remotely or locally, you will want to consider what to monitor. When you are getting your first insights into a problem or just starting to evaluate the performance of a system, you should start with the basic four:

```
Processor: %Processor Time

Memory: Pages/sec

Physical Disk: Disk Queue Length

Network Segment: %Network Utilization
```

Consider these the four basic food groups for any application on a system: processor, memory, disk, and network. These represent the total of the systems hardware resources. After you have done some initial performance monitoring with these counters, you will have a clear understanding of what the next step for your monitoring process should be. For example, if you notice excessive processor utilization, you will want to begin to examine the processor in greater detail.

### Note

*See Chapters 5 and 6 for more detailed examples of monitoring that will assist you in the determination of problems with particular components. In Chapter 8, "Monitoring Database Systems," and Chapter 9, "Pushing the Limits," the examples and techniques will be expanded to focus on major software systems such as IIS and SQL Server. ♦*

At this point, you will want to stick with the basic four counters. As you build experience with different types of applications and situations, you will be able to add a couple more counters to jump ahead in your analysis, but you should never exclude any of the basic four counters. Of course, if you have a stand-alone computer that is not connected to the network, you could safely exclude the network component. But, this is a different situation than if you are working with a computer that is on a network and an application that is operating locally only. Network connectivity can affect other resources on the system.

### Timing

In preparation for monitoring, you will need to determine how long to monitor and at what interval. Both of these will work to determine the size of the logged file. When you are setting up a logging session in the Performance Monitor, the sample interval will default to 15 seconds. So, you get one sampling of data every 15 seconds. Normally this will be sufficient. However, it is important for you to recognize when it is not. There are a couple of cases where you want to watch the activity of the system a little more often:

Processor Intensive applications

Real Time applications

These types of applications can have high spikes with very short lifespans. The Real Time application is a special case more suitable with discussions of drivers, which are covered in Chapter 9. Real Time applications present a problem because the Performance Monitor will often not have the priority settings to regularly retrieve data. This will usually cause errors that Performance Monitor might or might not report, depending on the settings. In these cases, you will need to take the error values into account in your analysis of the data. Again, this will be covered in more detail Chapter 2, "Windows NT Kernal Debugger."

The other case, which was referred to previously, has to do with an application that is processor intensive. The processor is operating in a time zone where nanoseconds of operation are commonplace. Humans generally think of time as progressing on the order of seconds. Thus 60 second or even 15 second samples might seem to be plenty; but if you are deep into the exact performance of your applications' use of the processor, you might want the interval to be more frequent. Although it is possible to set the Performance Monitor collection interval to a fraction of a single second, this will more often lead to errors from the collection components.

After you have the collection time, you will need to turn your attention to the duration of the testing. This is dependent  on what you want to test. If you are testing particular interactions, you might only log data for a limited amount of time, such as 15 minutes while you run through some of your applications screens. On the other hand, you might have arranged for an extended examination of a client/server application's performance. This would involve multiple machines potentially running for hours to ensure an adequate sampling of data.

Now that you have all this information figured out, you might want to calculate the disk space that is going to be required to collect the data. This will be exceptionally crucial if you are going to be logging information over an extended period of time. For example, you might have arranged several computers to act as Internet clients running against your Web server with a database backend built on to it. You would like to know what the performance of the machine and software will be over a period of hours given various types and degrees of access. You might run the test for 24 hours, which is appropriate because the system would probably be open for use 24 hours a day after it is put in production. Data can pile up quickly and you will need to be able to anticipate the storage space needed to hold the information. To calculate the disk space required, you can use this simple formula:

```
Log File Size = Sample Size x (Duration/Log Interval)
```

For example, say we have a Sample Size equal to 3KB. Continuing with the Web server example from earlier, you are going to log data for 24 hours. In this case, the Log Interval of 15 seconds will be sufficient. We must convert the units properly. You know—60 minutes in an hour, 60 seconds in a minute. So your log space calculation example becomes:

```
3KB x(86400 sec/15 secs) = 17280KB or about 17MB
```

So in this case, you would need 17MB of free space on the hard drive where the data will be logged. The only piece of the puzzle missing is how to figure out how big the sample size will be. This will become clear in the next section, where you will learn how to set up Log view in the Performance Monitor.

**Logging Data**

You have now completed the initial planning for the data collection of your application's performance. You will need to set up the Performance Monitor to log data and figure out the sample size before continuing with the actual logging process.

1. Start the Performance Monitor.

   The Performance Monitor will appear in the Administrative Tools section of the Start menu.

2. Switch to Log view.

   True to Microsoft form, there are several ways to accomplish the same task. These consist of the toolbar icons, drop-down menus, and hotkeys. You should take the time to figure out which method you like and stick with it no matter which method is demonstrated in this text. In the case of the log, you might hit the cylinder on the toolbar or select View, Log from the drop-down menu, or select CTRL-L.

3. Click the plus sign on the toolbar to add items.

   When adding objects you will notice a spot for the computer name. You should select the computer name prior to attempting to select the objects that you want to collect.

You might select objects from multiple computers. However, use caution, as combining too many collections into one file can lead to confusion when you are analyzing data later. If you really want to collect data from multiple computers, start several sessions of the Performance Monitor.

Configure the various Log views to save data to different files. This will make it easy to determine which data goes with what machine. When you select a different computer, you might see different objects show up. Recall that some Performance Monitor objects are extended objects that are added when you install software or other operating system components. Because some systems might have IIS or SQL installed, counters for these major software components will be listed with the core objects.

Notice that the dialog box lists only objects. When you are logging data, the Performance Monitor will log all counters associated with the selected objects. Later, when you are reviewing the log, you will have all the counters for the selected objects available to you.

---

### Note

*When selecting objects you might use methods of highlighting objects that are similar to selecting files in Explorer. You might use CTRL in conjunction with a mouse click to select multiple objects. If you hold down the Shift key while selecting two objects, those objects and all objects in between will be highlighted.* ◆

---

4. Select the items that you are interested in collecting.

   Following our examples in this section, start with the four basic objects: processor, network segment, memory, and physical disk. Highlight the objects, click Add, and then click Done when you are finished.

5. Adjust the capturing options for the log.

   The dialog box can be opened by pressing CTRL-O.

6. Enter in the location and name of the log file in the dialog box in Figure 1.10.

   The location can be anywhere on the local computer. However, if you are doing some disk analysis on a particular drive, you will want to avoid putting the log data on that drive. After the log filename is in place, you can select the update interval. For the time being you should select Manual Update. Recall that you need to calculate the resulting size of the log file after you are done collecting information. You need the sample size to make this calculation. You would then click the Start Log button.

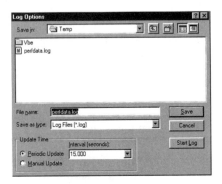

**Figure 1.10**  *The Log view's Options dialog box is the controlling point for logging. It is easy to forget that this is where you turn logging off and on.*

7. Record the size of the log file.

Completing Step 6 resulted in the dialog box it appears as in Figure 1.11. The information here displays the name of the log file, logging interval, whether the system is currently set to collect data, the objects collecting, and finally the size of the log file. In this example, the log file's size is 31,656 bytes. You will also notice a misleading value for the log interval. Despite the fact that we have set the log to Manual Update, a numerical value is being displayed as the logging interval. After watching the size of the log file for a few seconds, you should be assured that the system is not adding data to the log file.

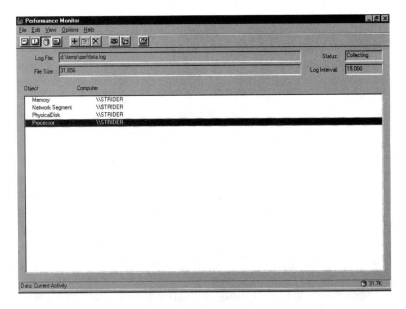

**Figure 1.11**  *In Log view's default appearance, you will see all the configuration information and the current size of the log file.*

8. To perform a manual collection, click the Camera icon on the toolbar or hit CTRL-U.

Make a note of the new size of the log file. Then, subtract the initial size from this new size and you have the sample size. In this example the sample size is

```
35836 bytes-31656 bytes = 4180 bytes
```

If you were collecting the data for 24 hours at an interval of 15 seconds as in the previous example, you would have a log file size of:

```
4180 bytes x (86400 secs/15 secs)= 24MB (approximately)
```

Thus, you will need 24MB of free space on your hard drive to execute this performance examination. You have ensured that you have the space and are ready to begin the testing.

9. Return to the Log Options dialog box (CTRL-O).

First, stop the log by clicking the Stop Log button. Re-enter the Log Options dialog box and select Periodic Update. Make sure the value is the one that you want. The default is 15 seconds, which in this case is fine. Then, click the Start Log button. If you examine the screen for 15 seconds, you will see an increase in the size of the log file, which is to be expected. You might run your other applications now to generate activity.

## Note

*In many cases you will want to re-run the test repeatedly. You will probably want to capture the same performance data as well. This process can be made easier by saving the log settings to a file. The log settings will include the computer name, objects, and interval of collection for the log. By selecting File and Save Log Settings, you will save this information for easy retrieval. This is true of the other Performance Monitor views too.*

*In Log view, the file will have a file extension of .PML. You might also save all the Chart, Report, Alert, and Log settings at once by saving the Performance Monitor's workspace to a file that has a default file extension of .PMW. In your log file's settings, the Performance Monitor will be opened up and the logging of data will begin immediately. (In Explorer double-click on a .PML file to start this process.) The data logging will use the log options contained in the .PML file. ◆*

10. After the test is over, stop the log by returning to the Log Options dialog box and clicking the Stop Log Button.

During the course of your data collection, you might want to enter in time stamps of when particular events occurred. For example, you might start a particular batch process. This would create a different situation than if there were standard user activity. So, you should make a note of it. The Performance Monitor allows you to place comments with time stamps in the log. This is done using bookmarks. A bookmark can be generated while in Log view and actively collecting data. You can either click the Open Book icon on the toolbar or press CTRL-B. A dialog box will appear that allows comments to be entered.

After the information has been added, a time stamp is associated with the comment and it is added to the Log file's data set. Later, you can view these time stamps and use them as markers to view data. The Performance Monitor will also set administrative bookmarks. These are placed in the log file whenever the log stops or starts collecting data. An administrative book-mark will also be entered when the computer whose performance objects are being examined drops off of the network. All these bookmarks will be visible when examining the data later.

## Analyzing Data

Now that you have collected all the data, you will want to analyze it. In this section, you will learn how to examine the data in the log files and find the interesting parts of the data quickly. You will also see how the bookmarks are used in analysis. You will see how to use charts and reports, as well as how to export data to other systems. The process of analysis will start with learning how to find the interesting portions of the data using alerts. After you have the interesting points of the data identified, you will need to examine the regions of data around those points. Using bookmarks and Time windows, you will be able to accurately zero-in on the critical data. Finally, you will want to examine the data with the charts and reports that have already been introduced to you. Thus, a process for analysis is defined:

1. Define alerts to identify critical points.

2. Use bookmarks and Time windows to isolate regions of related data around the critical points.

3. Use charts and reports to analyze the isolated regions.

To begin, when you open the Performance Monitor you will want to tell it to retrieve the data for display from a log file as opposed to collecting data interactively and displaying it, as you see in Figure 1.12.

**Figure 1.12**    *Setting the Data From will affect ALL views during that session. Changing views will not change where the data is coming from.*

To load a previously logged set of data, do the following:

1. Click the Options menu from the drop-down menu.
2. Click Data From.
3. Select a log file and click OK.

If you want to return to an interactive collection of data in any of the Performance Monitor views, repeat the preceding process and select Current Activity. This in no way affects the contents of the logged data.

After you have set the Performance Monitor to read the data from the log file, you will want to set some alerts.

### Alerts

Recall that the logging process can lead to a great deal of data. In our simple 24 hours example, you would end up with almost 6000 data points to consider. You could go through each one looking for information or you could use the Performance Monitor's Alert view to find the critical cases where the data displays alarming results.

To set up an alert in Performance Monitor, first select Alerts view (the Exclamation icon on the toolbar).

1. Click the plus sign on the toolbar. This brings up the Add to Alert dialog box.
2. Select the computer, object, and counters that you want to examine.

   You will notice that when you are looking at previously logged data, you will be allowed to add only computers and objects that were previously selected in the logging session. So, if you logged only the basic four objects, you shouldn't expect to see the SQL Server object or TCP object.

3. In the Alert If section of the  dialog box, enter a value that you want to know about.

   You must also indicate if you want to know if the data point is more or less than the value. Note that the Run Program on Alert section of the dialog box is disabled. You will be able to display only the time stamps for the Alert points, but not perform any automated action. After you click Add, a listing of the data points that meet the criterion you selected will be displayed. Each alert is assigned a different color so discerning between various alerts is easy. Table 1.1 describes the basic critical points for the four basic  counters.

*Table 1.1*    *The Basic Counters and Thresholds for Initial*
           *Analysis of Logged Data*

| Performance Monitor Counter | Critical Value |
|---|---|
| Processor:%Processor Time | > 80% |
| Memory:Pages/Sec | > 16 |
| Physical Disk:Average Disk Queue Length | > 2 |
| Network Segment:%Network utilization | > 67% |

When you look at these values, you should keep a few things in mind. First, every system is different. These values should be considered general guidelines—not hard and fast rules. These values can fluctuate based on the purpose of the system and the type of software. Also, every system will have its peaks in resource consumption. The values described in Table 1.1 are not generally a problem unless they are sustained over time. You might have a system whose Average Disk Queue Length jumps to 6 occasionally. But, overall it hovers around 1.6. This is acceptable. When performance monitoring, you must always consider the circumstances of the test when examining the data.

If you see areas of concern brought to light by the alerts, you will want to examine the data around the critical points. Generally, you will be using either the Chart or Report view to do this. But, you will first want to narrow your scope.

### Bookmarks and Time Windows

Just a few short sections back, you were introduced to the bookmark when creating logged data. The bookmark allows you to enter in a comment, but it also places a time stamp in the performance log so that you could enter in some data. You might use the bookmark to adjust the Time window within the Performance Monitor. The Time window allows you to focus the display of the Performance Monitor views to a specific section of the data. To open the Input Log file Timeframe, or Time window adjustment dialog box (see Figure 1.13), click the Edit drop-down menu and then Time window, or press CTRL-E.

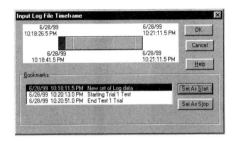

**Figure 1.13**   *Adjusting the Time windows when examining data from a log file is an important step in getting the right amount of detail from logged data.*

In the Input Log File Timeframe dialog box, you can see that the entire time the logging of data is displayed as a solid, gray bar. You might adjust the time to any time interval by using the mouse to click and hold on either end of the bar and dragging to a desired position. You might also use the bookmarks, which are listed in the Bookmarks section. The bookmarks will appear in the order that they appear within the log file. To reset the start of the Time window to a bookmark, click the desired bookmark and then click the Set as Start button to the right. To set the end of the Time window, repeat the procedure, but click the Set as Stop button instead. After you have set the Time window, it will apply to all views of the Performance Monitor. The Time window's importance is evident when you begin to examine data using the Chart or Report Views.

**Charts and Reports**

Performance Monitor charts and reports are the primary method for displaying data for interpretation. At this point in the process, you should have focused your Time window to examine particular events. When considering the Chart view, recall that the chart will display only 100 data points across. In our example we had about 6000 data points. They all will not fit in Chart view's display. So, the Performance Monitor takes every 60th data point (6000/100) and displays it.

This pattern is a little contrary to intuition. You would normally expect to see the first 100 data points in full detail; however, this is not the case. The Performance Monitor examines the entire set and displays data points from evenly spaced intervals based on the number of data points divided by the maximum number of data points that will fit in the display, which is 100. So, now the importance of the Time window should be evident. If the chart displays only every 60th data point in our sample data, there will be a loss of detail. You will see only some of the data points on the screen. So, if you adjust the Time window to include a smaller time interval of the entire data collection period, you are also reducing the overall number of data points that the Performance Monitor must consider when displaying a chart. If the Time window is reduced to a period representing 100 data points, the full detail of the data will be displayed for that interval as all the data points will fit within Chart view.

Another issue is that Chart view requires your careful consideration when displaying logged data and adjusting Time windows. When you examine a particular process, select that process from the Instance section of the Add to Chart dialog box. If the process is not running at the beginning of the current Time window, the instance will not be displayed in the Instance section.

Consider that you started logging data at 9:00.00. Thirty seconds later you started your application—for example, PWRVWR.EXE. You ran your application for a while as you logged performance data. After you are finished, you stopped logging and opened Chart view to examine the data. One of the objects that you were logging was the Process object, which contains information on all the individual processes running on an NT machine. Without adjusting the Time window, you attempt to add the Process: %Process Time to see how much of the processor time your application was consuming during your testing session. You are puzzled when you don't find the PWRVWR.EXE in the instance box in the Add to Chart dialog box.

Recall that when you started the data logging process, the PWRVWR.EXE was not running. Thus, the Performance Monitor does not consider it a valid selection for viewing within the given Time window. So, you adjust the start time of the Time window to be 9:00.31, a time just after you started your PWRVWR.EXE. Now, you open the Add to Chart dialog box and notice that the PWRVWR.EXE is in the list and you can examine the measurements of the application's resource usage. This again, brings up the importance of the bookmark. You might start and stop various components during a single logging session. You might need to find the locations within the log file while these applications are running to focus in on them. If you add bookmarks to the log when you are starting and stopping various applications, you will be able to locate these times in the logged data easily.

After you have your Time window adjusted, you can add counters to your Chart view. This is done the same way as the Log and the Alert views. Click the plus sign on the toolbar and select the items that you want to examine.

Notice that when you are examining logged data, you will be allowed to select only the machines, objects, and counters that you had designated in Log view when you originally collected the data to the log file. The logged data can be read from any machine. You might copy log files from the servers where the data was collected to the workstation for analysis.

> **Note**
>
> *One of the functions not available to you when examining logged data is the Explain button. The Explain button appears on the Add to dialog box when adding counters to charts, alerts, and reports. When you click the Explain button, it will display additional information on the objects and counters that you have selected. This information ranges from the obvious to suggestions on critical values and problem resolution. When looking at the logged data you will not be able to use the Explain button. ✦*

You might display data in a couple of different formats, charts and reports. The two do differ. The chart will display only 100 data points. However, when you are looking at counters in Report view, counters that are averages will be averaged over the entire Time window, not just 100 evenly spaced data points. This allows you to adjust the Time window and examine the various values over a time period. So, in the case of averages, Report view will have the advantage. If you are examining instantaneous counters (or raw counters), Report view will display the last value presented at the end of the Time window. Thus, if you move the end point of the Time window, the values in Report view will change. The chart has the advantage in this case as multiple data points are being displayed over a range. Adding objects and counters to Report view is done the same way that you add objects and counters to the other views.

Notice that in all the views, a particular functionality is missing, the capability to print the data. The Performance Monitor does not include any method for creating charts, graphs, or detailed statistics that can be formatted and put into a printed form. This functionality is left to other applications. The Performance Monitor does contain an Export function just for this purpose.

**Exporting Data**

The Performance Monitor's chief functional goals appear to have been to collect information, store it, and display it for interpretation. Clearly, the formatting and printing of such information was not one of the designers' goals. So, you must export your data to another application that is suited for such efforts. The Performance Monitor will export the data in the form of a *Tab Delimited* (.TSV) or *Comma Delimited* (.CSV) file. Once in this form, you can import the information into another application for analysis or formatting. Follow these steps:

1. Open the Performance Monitor.

2. Select Options, Data From to read the data from a log file.

3. Adjust the Time window.

4. Go to the Chart or Report view and add the objects and counters that you want to export.

   Although you are permitted to export any number of objects and counters, you will not be allowed to do so until they have been selected into a chart or report.

5. Select File, Export Chart or Export Report.

   You will be prompted for the name of the file and the format (.TSV or .CSV).

6. The data that is in the current display is then copied to the file you indicated.

7. Open another application. (I generally use Excel.)

   Then go to that application's File and Open or Import functions to move the data into the application.

After the data is in the application, you can perform any number of statistics on it, or format it for attractive reporting. If you are going to use a statistical package, be aware that the exported data file contains some header information that you might need to clean up before importing into your statistic program (see Figure 1.14).

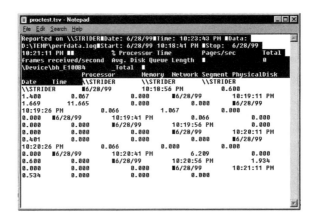

**Figure 1.14**   *The highlighted data represents the typical amount of data that will need to be deleted for use with external statistic packages.*

Any simple text editor or spreadsheet program can be used to remove the header information and resave the file in a cleaner format.

## Summary

This chapter has introduced you to the Performance Monitor. You should now have a working knowledge of the Performance Monitor and all the various views. You should be capable of creating log files and examining the data with an understanding of the capabilities and limitations of the various views. The step-by-step instructions serve as a guide to creating log files and preparing for interpretation. After learning about a few more tools, you will learn how to interpret the data in Chapters 5 & 6 of this book.

When learning about any software you should not limit yourself to reading a book. Any examples or step-by-step instructions should be attempted on at least a workstation. This will improve your retention of knowledge, and improve your understanding of the new topics. So, please wedge open the pages of the book on your desk and try to run through the examples.

# 2

# *Windows NT Kernel Debugger*

In Chapter 1, "Introduction to Performance Monitor," you learned about the Windows NT Performance Monitor, a tool for direct analysis of various resources being utilized by the Kernel as well as by User mode applications. Repeatedly, we mentioned the need to know as much as possible about the Windows NT operating system operations. The Performance Monitor, while an excellent tool, can sometimes lack the grueling details you might desire in order to figure out how and why the operating system is behaving the way that it is.

This chapter offers you a tool called the Windows NT Kernel Debugger, which can give you a view of NT operations that can't be seen through performance analysis. Clearly in this chapter, you will learn a lot more about the Windows NT Kernel Debugger. From its name, you might think you need to be a kernel programmer or device driver developer to have any practical use for it. However, this chapter will take much of the mystery out of the Kernel Debugger tool and a couple of similar tools. You will see how to install and configure the tool both for general investigation and kernel troubleshooting. You will see how the Debugger can be used with memory dump files, which are created when Windows NT kernel–level errors occur. Overall, you will see how the Kernel Debugger can often offer the developer or curious person some real insight into what is going on in the operating system.

Recall that user applications or User mode operations are a series of requests to the Windows NT Executive Services. Investigation of the operation of the Executive Processes will demonstrate the effects of the code that you write.

The Kernel Debugger most certainly also has its place as a troubleshooting tool. On Windows NT, the blue screen represents errors in the memory access or incorrect use of APIs in the Kernel mode processes. The processes that are described in this chapter will certainly be useful in diagnosing such problems as unhandled kernel exceptions and IRQL_LESS_THAN errors. Both of these errors are types of kernel-level errors that cause the machine to halt operations and display a blue screen with listings of loaded DLLs and processor stack information. These problems are not the focus of this text, although they will be useful as examples in this chapter and others.

We'll start with a discussion on how the tool actually works and what is required for its installation. Then, we will develop the installation discussions to include more details, as well as some tips on being prepared for particular types of analysis. Finally, we will walk through a sample installation, bringing all the concepts together into a thorough step-by-step process.

## How the Tool Works

The *Windows NT Kernel Debugger* is a piece of software that monitors and records information about kernel and executive-service activity. The Kernel Debugger program serves as your interface into the Windows NT kernel–level programs. To achieve this communication, the kernel will need to have access to information that is not normally available using Windows NT. In such cases, a special series of files called *symbol files* can be used. The Kernel Debugger uses the symbol files to decode the communication between the various services. In addition, it allows commands to be issued to extract other information, such as CPU stacks, loaded drivers, and memory details. To begin, let's learn what the symbol files really are and how they fit into kernel debugging and general Microsoft software.

Windows NT actually comes in two flavors. The first is the standard *retail build*. This is what most users install on their everyday machines. Then there is the *checked build*. The checked build can also be called the debug version. In this version of the NT operating system, the debug code is still embedded as part of the standard running code. Debug code, of course, makes the programs larger and slower. Thus, it is not an option for most installations of Windows NT.

The introduction of the symbol files allows the Kernel Debugger to run the code and produce the same type of output that would be available on the checked build of the NT operating system code. Symbol files are located on the Windows NT CD in the \SUPPORT folder. When utilizing the symbol files it is important to realize that the symbol files are matched to the build version of the code. Thus, when you are considering using the Kernel Debugger, you will need to take into consideration the use of service packs. The installation of the symbol files will be considered in the next section as part of the overall installation of the NT Kernel Debugger.

## Installation

The installation of the Kernel Debugger has five primary steps:

1. Prepare the source machine by installing the symbol files.
2. Select a communication method and prepare the hardware (if required).
3. Prepare the source machine by installing the Kernel Debugger.
4. Configure the Kernel Debugger for the type of connection that will be made. Other configuration options are set.
5. Prepare the target machine to connect the Kernel Debugger.

Kernel debugging must be done with two machines. The first machine is considered to be the *target*. This would be the machine that is either having some type of problem, usually a blue screen issue, or running the code that you are attempting to investigate. The symbol files will be installed on the machine that will be running the Kernel Debugger, which is called the *source machine*. The source machine will be the one that you sit in front of while issuing various commands via the interactive Kernel Debugger program.

### Debuggers Other Than the Kernel

*There are certainly other debuggers besides the Kernel. Visual C++, Visual Studio, Borland C++, Delphi, and many others come with some sort of debugger. These debuggers, as well as third-party debuggers that are built to assist the developer, certainly have their place in the diagnosis of problems with code.*

*However, these are User mode debuggers, as are the NTSD.EXE and the CDB.EXE, that are part of the Windows NT CD. Thus, they are not used to debug device drivers or the Kernel mode operations that you will see here. Also, recall that we intend to discuss performance improvement techniques that are independent of the programming language used to build the software. In addition, the NT Kernel Debugger is free with the purchase of Windows NT. By looking at the www.microsoft.com Web site, MS TechNet, or MSDN, you can obtain a list of third-party debuggers that work with Microsoft Windows NT.* ◆

## Installing the Symbol Files

You must start with the symbol files that are part of the original NT installation. These are on the Windows NT original CD in a folder called the \SUPPORT\DEBUG\I386 for the Intel platform. The other supported NT platforms are represented in other subfolders, such as PPC and ALPHA. Microsoft has provided a program called EXPNDSYM.CMD to make the expansion of the symbol files easier. The EXPNDSYM.CMD will determine which operating system you are using and then select the appropriate symbol files. To run the program, it is best to open a Command window. The program has the following syntax: `EXPNDSYM [source drive] [target path]`. The source drive will be the drive containing the Windows NT CD. The target path will be the path where you want the Windows NT symbol files to end up.

> ### Note
>
> *Although not specified as necessary, some other utilities seem to expect the symbol files to be in a particular folder, the %SYSTEMROOT%\SYSTEM32\SYMBOLS folder. To install the symbol files in this manner, execute the command like this:*
> `EXPNDSYM E:\ C:\WINNT`
>
> *Of course, this assumes that the CD-ROM drive is E: and the folder where you have installed Windows NT is the C:\WINNT folder. Although intended for use with Microsoft's interactive Kernel Debugger, the symbol files can be installed anywhere.* ◆

> ### Note
>
> *%SYSTEMROOT% is basically shorthand for "the directory where the Windows NT operating system was installed." The default folder for Windows NT 4.0 is C:\WINNT. You might have selected a different folder at the time of installation. If you are curious, open a command prompt and type "Set" or "Set S." A listing of the environment variables will be displayed, and %SYSTEMROOT% will be among them.* ◆

The expansion of the symbol files will take several minutes and will display abundant information on the screen, none of which is exceptionally interesting. Therefore, you may get your coffee refilled at this point. After the symbol files have been expanded, you will need to install the symbol files for the Windows NT release that is on the target machine. The target machine and the source machine should be on the same NT build and service pack revision, if possible. This is not altogether critical, but unusual results might occur if the builds and revisions are different. Thus, if you are on Windows NT 4.0 *United States Service Pack* (USSP) 4 on the target machine, your source machine should be on Windows NT 4.0 USSP 4.

To install the service pack version of the symbol files, you simply expand the service pack and copy the \SYMBOLS folder on top of the symbols folder that you had just created with the EXPNDSYM.CMD utility. Note that expanding the service pack symbol files without first installing the original symbol files from the Windows NT CD is insufficient. Service packs do not replace all the operating system code—only parts of it.

Also, the service packs are cumulative. Applying the symbol files from service pack 4 does not require you to apply the symbol files from service packs 1, 2, and 3 first. They will all be present.

### How to Acquire the Symbol Files for Service Packs

*Windows NT 4.0 USSP 4.0 and later are distributed without the symbol files. Thus, you will need to make sure that you download the symbol file distribution separately from the service pack distribution. In the past, MS TechNet subscribers have enjoyed the luxury of having the service packs symbol files promptly delivered to them on CD as part of the monthly subscription CDs. Since USSP 4.0, these distributions have been out of sync with the general distribution of the service packs. Thus, you might need to go to the Microsoft FTP site or a suitable mirror site to acquire the files.*

*The Microsoft FTP site is* ftp.microsoft.com. *Windows NT distributions are found under the BUSSYS folder. When selecting a symbol file, make sure that you have selected the appropriate folder. Of late, the folders have been organized by version as well as language. Certainly, downloading the Japanese version of the service pack to apply to an English version installation of Windows NT will do you little good. Also, within the US there are two versions of the service packs. One is the 40-bit encryption version and the other is the 128-bit encryption version. Select the appropriate service pack according to the potential security-component differences, as well as version and language differences, to ensure proper operation. For the USA/English version of the 128-bit Service Pack 4, download the following file: SP4CSYMI.EXE.*

*This file is found at the following path on the Microsoft FTP site:*

```
/bussys/winnt/winnt-public/
fixes/usa/nt40/ussp4/checked/i386
```

*Note that the above line is a single-path statement.* ◆

Once you have properly applied the symbol files to the source machine, you will need to connect the two computers. You will need to decide how to connect the two computers together so that one can debug the other. The connection will have some minor hardware requirements.

## Choosing a Connection Type

As previously stated, the Windows NT Kernel Debugger requires two machines. One is considered the target and the other is considered the source. The source machine runs the kernel debugging software. The two are connected in one of two ways—by serial connection or modem.

The first selection, via serial cable, is the more common for development personnel. The serial cable is called a NULL MODEM cable. Generally, this will be a 9-pin cable with female connectors on both ends. This cable can be acquired from any computer store. Sometimes the cable is called a "Direct Connect" or "PC Connection" cable. Essentially, the configuration of the cable has a couple of pins reversed on one end, which allows the two PCs to talk and listen on the same cable.

The second method is to connect a modem to each machine and have the source dial into the target machine. Often this will be the method used if you are working with a third-party vendor or Microsoft Support. In such situations, you are usually working on a machine that is crashing for some unknown reason. Microsoft will want to dial in if the problem has not been reported before and they are having difficulty reproducing the problem with their local hardware. In either case, the concept is the same—you will want to specify the port and the baud rate for communication. These parameters must be set on both machines.

Now that you have selected the communication method and acquired the appropriate cable and peripheral equipment (as the case might be), you are ready to begin the configuration of the Kernel Debugger.

## Installing the Kernel Debugger

The Kernel Debugger program, as well as some of the supporting files you will use, will depend on the hardware architecture of the machine that you are working with. Table 2.1 lists the information you will need.

*Table 2.1    Required Kernel Debugger Files*

| | Support Platforms | | | |
|---|---|---|---|---|
| Description | Intel | Alpha | PPC | MIPS |
| Kernel Debugger Executable | I386KD.EXE | ALPHAKD.EXE | PPCKD.EXE | MIPSKD.EXE |
| Kernel Debugger Extensions DLLs | KDEXTX86.DLL | KDEXTALP.DLL | KDEXTPPC.DLL | KDEXTMIP.DLL |
| Help Files | IMAGEHLP.DLL | IMAGEHLP.DLL | IMAGEHLP.DLL | IMAGEHLP.DLL |
| Platform Support Status | Continued | Continued | Discontinued | Discontinued |

In most cases, you will be copying the files for the Intel-based machines. You will need the I386KD.EXE, KDEXTX86.DLL, and the IMAGEHLP.DLL. These may be copied to any folder on the source machine.

I prefer to create a separate folder on the C:\DEBUGGER and put the programs, along with a configuration batch file, in the folder. After the Kernel Debugger is in place, you will need to configure how the Debugger will work and tell it how you have arranged for communications between source and target machines.

## Configuring the Kernel Debugger

The various parameters for the communications method are set in the environment variables on the source machine. In addition, other environment variables control when the Kernel Debugger will become active, where the symbol files are, whether a log file for the session will be created, and where the log file will be placed. The environment variables are read when the Kernel Debugger first starts up. However, on the source machine you will use environment variables primarily to set up the communication ports and speed. This is done by setting the _NT_DEBUG_PORT variable to the COM port that the modem or serial cable is connected to—for example, _NT_DEBUG_PORT=COMx. You will also need to set the _NT_DEBUG_BAUD_RATE to the speed of communications. Then, when you run the Kernel Debugger, the program will set up communications based on these parameters. The other parameters are covered in the section, "A Sample Installation," later in this chapter.

## Configuring the Target Machine

On the target machine, the environment is often not established when the system experiences a blue screen. You aren't able to use environment variables for parameters, as we did in the source machine configuration for the Kernel Debugger. Thus, Microsoft had to use a different method for instructing the Kernel mode services to operate in debug mode. For the target machine, the options are set in the BOOT.INI file. The BOOT.INI file is a hidden, read-only file that exists on the root folder of the C-drive on any Windows NT machine, regardless of the hardware architecture. You must modify the file and place the parameters on the end of the line that describes the installation that you would like to start.

For the target machine, you will need to edit the BOOT.INI file and use the command line switch on the end of one of the options. The primary parameters will be the /DEBUGPORT and the /BAUDRATE. You will set the /DEBUGPORT=COMx, where x will be 1 or 2. The /BAUDRATE=xxx is the communication rate for the device. In the next section, you will walk through a sample installation and see exactly how this might appear. Once you have set these up, the machines are prepared to communicate with one another.

# A Sample Installation

In this section, we will walk through the installation and configuration of the Kernel Debugger. You might have just written an application that is giving you some problems. The code is not producing a Dr. Watson error, as a User mode problem would. Instead, a problem is occurring down in the Kernel mode, which generates a blue screen in some cases, but not all. Your program might be a device driver or an intensive multimedia application. Alternatively, it might be making extensive use of Win32 APIs. You would like to examine the process in more detail.

We will be taking the five general steps that we discussed earlier and expand on them. The steps to follow will include more information as well as offer example commands and settings. Let's review the five steps we will be running through:

1. Prepare the source machine by installing the symbol files.

2. Select a communication method and prepare the hardware (if required).

3. Prepare the source machine by installing the Kernel Debugger.

4. Configure the Kernel Debugger then for the type of connection that will be made. Other configuration options are set.

5. Prepare the target machine to connect the Kernel Debugger.

To start with, you will need two computers. The first, the source machine, will be running the Kernel Debugger, and the second, the target machine, will be running your program. Now that the formalities are complete, let's get started with the symbol file installation.

# Step 1: Preparing the Sample Installation's Symbol Files

Here, we are going to get the Symbol Files and expand them onto our source and target machines. Remember that matching the symbol files to the version of the system is going to be important. Matching the versions of the source and the target machine is also critical.

### Step 1a: Determining the Version of the Operating System

The information regarding the version and service pack revision can easily be obtained in the Windows NT Diagnostics utility. This utility is found in the Start Menu's Administrative Tools group. After it is acquired, you might need to install the source machine with a different version of the operating system so that it matches the target. The folder location of Windows NT on the source machine is irrelevant to the operation of the Kernel Debugger. That means you can use a single workstation, or even a laptop, with several copies of Windows NT installed on it. You just install the various versions in different folders. Usually during transition periods between versions, I will have at least two versions installed and sometimes another version with a particular service pack installed. For example, my laptop might have a folder structure such as:

| Folder | Description |
| --- | --- |
| D:\WINNT | Most recent NT version, such as Win2000 |
| D:\WINNT40 | Windows NT version 4.0, Service Pack 1 |
| D:\WINNT40SP5 | Windows NT version 4.0, USSP 5 Applied |

I simply have to adjust the BOOT.INI file to boot into any one of these versions. Incidentally, I usually use the D-drive because I have Windows 98 installed on C:.

### Step 1b: Installing the Symbol Files

You have already confirmed that the source machine is running the same version and service pack revision as the target machine. To install the symbol files, use the Windows NT Server (or Workstation) CD. Using the EXPNDSYM.CMD program, you can expand the symbol files onto the source machine. You will then want to apply the symbol files from the service pack that you had installed on the computer. In this example, the command that was run on the source machine was: EXPNDSYM.CMD E: D:\WINNT40.

This created a folder called D:\WINNT40\SYMBOLS and several sub-folders where it placed all the symbol files. In this example the E: drive is my CD-ROM.

On the target machine the command that was run was as follows: EXPNDSYM.CMD D: C:\WINNT. The difference is that the target machine is a workstation configured for a standard user. A standard NT user would use his first partition for the operating system—in this case, C:\WINNT. The folder is the default folder for a Windows NT installation. With no other hard drive partitions configured, this user's CD-ROM drive is given the designation of D. With the symbol files now installed, we are ready to move to the next major operation, selecting the communications method.

## Step 2: Selecting a Communication Method for the Sample Installation

You will need to decide how you plan to connect the machines in order to proceed. In this case, you would select the null modem cable connecting the serial ports. Using the modem connection would make more sense if you were soliciting outside assistance from another developer, or perhaps a vendor. So, run down to the local computer store and grab an appropriate cable. Get the computers in close proximity and plug them together.

## Step 3: Installing the Kernel Debugger on the Source Machine

This is relatively easy, as the Kernel Debugger installation is little more than selecting the appropriate files based on the operating system and then copying them to a folder. In our case, we are using an Intel-based machine. We create a folder—C:\DEBUGGER—and copy the files according to the information listed in Table 2.1. Now we are ready to configure the Kernel Debugger.

## Step 4: Configuring the Kernel Debugger Environment

This involves setting the appropriate environment variables. Variables aside from those for communications settings can be used. Because setting the environment each time is mundane, you will probably want to build a batch file that sets the variables and then launches the Kernel Debugger. The following is a sample batch file with some parameters that typical for the sample installation we are working our way through. For our communications, we have elected COM2 and will be using a connection of 9600 Baud, as follows:

```
: Kernel Debug
:: Use Com2 over serial connection 9600
::
SET _NT_DEBUG_PORT=COM1
SET _NT_DEBUG_BAUD_RATE=9600
SET _NT_SYMBOL_PATH=D:\WINNT40\SYMBOLS


C:\DEBUGGER\I386KD.EXE -v
```

## The Kernel Debugger Environment Parameters

*The following parameters are used to configure the Kernel Debugger. They are all environment variables that are set within a Command session (DOS Windows) prior to calling the Kernel Debugger. They are as follows:*

- **NT_DEBUG_PORT**

  *This is the COM port that will be used on the source machine to contact the target machine.*

- **NT_DEBUG_BAUD_RATE**

  *This is the baud rate for communications on the debug port. For Intel-based computers, the baud rate for modems is 9600 or 19200bps. For direct connections, the maximum baud rate is 19200bps. In the case of RISC-based computers, the baud rate is always 19200bps.*

- **NT_SYMBOL_PATH**

  *This is the full Path to the \SYMBOLS folder.*

- **NT_LOG_FILE_OPEN**

  *This is the name and path to a file that will be used to write the debug session to. It will write all commands and the results to a text file.*

- **NT_LOG_FILE_APPEND**

  *This is the name and path to a file to append the log output to, as opposed to overwriting.*

- **NT_CACHE_SIZE**

  *The NT CACHE SIZE is the size in bytes of memory the Debugger will use.* ✦

## Command Line Switches for the Debugger

*The Kernel Debugger, like any good program, comes with command line switches. Here is a list of the command line switches for the Kernel Debugger. Occasionally, you will hear about a switch or command that is not published. This appears to be most of them:*

- *-b*

  *Immediately starts the kernel on the remote machine for debugging. This option is used if you are interested in examining driver initialization at boot time.*

- *-c*

  *Resyncs the modem connection to make sure that the communications are being done correctly. This is not used with direct serial connections.*

- *-n*

  *Loads the symbols as soon as the Debugger loads, as opposed to waiting for a particular executable to be encountered. This uses more local memory and slows the startup some, but generally makes execution faster while actually debugging.*

- *-v*

  *Verbose mode.*

- *-m*

  *Useful option for modem connections if you need to issue additional modem commands or verify modem communications. Again, this is not usually the case with direct connections. In this option, the Debugger will be forced into terminal mode.*

- *-x*

  *Typically not necessary. The Debugger will break when an exception occurs, even before an application is given a chance to deal with the error. Thus, if error trapping is interfering, you can use this option.*

- *-y[PATH]*

  *Path to the symbol files.*

- *-z[PATH]*

  *Path to a crash dump file. As opposed to interactive debugging, the Kernel Debugger can be used to read files, called memory dump files, created during a blue screen.*

  *-v and -n are some typical choices. For modem debugging, you will usually use the -v and the -m. ♦*

## Step 5: Preparing the Target Machine to Be Monitored

To prepare the target machine, you must set up some parameters in the C:\BOOT.INI file. Recall that this file is a hidden file. To see the file, you will need to either adjust the parameters on the file or adjust the configuration of the NT Explorer. To adjust the parameters on the file, open an NT Command Prompt, go to the C:\ FOLDER, and then type:

```
C:\>ATTRIB -H -R BOOT.INI.
```

This will remove the hidden read-only DOS type attributes from the file and make it visible to the utilities available in Windows NT. To return the BOOT.INI file back to its normal DOS-attribute state, issue the following command:

```
C:\>ATTRIB H R BOOT.INI.
```

The BOOT.INI file is in a standard flat format, which can be viewed and edited with Notepad. Typically, you would want to take one of the entries and copy it to a new line, which is what we have done to achieve the file in Figure 2.1. You would add some of the parameters to the end of the line. The parameters will control the operation of Windows NT.

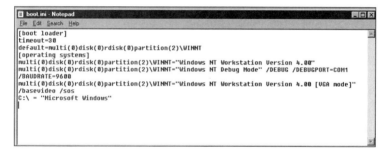

**Figure 2.1**   *The BOOT.INI file contains the basic information for finding and booting installations of Windows NT as well as parameters for setting various modes of operation for Windows NT.*

The following is a listing of the parameters that are used in conjunction with kernel debugging.

- **/CRASHDEBUG**

  This parameter will cause the target machine to start only the Debugger after the operating system has encountered a blue screen error. Normally, this would not be the option that you would select because you will want to be observing what is going on with the operating system in general. However, if you were only encountering a blue screen when a particular piece of code were running, you might select this option to avoid the delays caused by the Kernel Debugger running at startup.

- **/DEBUG**

  This parameter will allow kernel debugging as soon as the operating system begins initializing the drivers—before the actual user login screen. This is exceptionally useful if you are debugging drivers while they are initializing.

- **/DEBUGPORT=COMx**

  Here you specify the COM port that you will be using for communications between the two computers. COM1 or COM2 seem to work best.

- **/BAUDRATE= XXXXXX**

  This is the baud rate that you will be using. When connecting to another computer via a serial cable, it will be important for this rate to be consistent between the machines.

In this case, let's say that you are using the COM1 port operating at 9600. You will want the Kernel Debugger to start immediately so that you can track progress if you choose. The operating system might not actually be failing. If it never fails, the debugger on the target machine will never be prepared to accept the communication. Therefore, unless you are able to predictably reproduce the crash, you will want to watch the entire process.

You would then connect the cable to the system and reboot. When the machine reboots, make sure to select the option from the BOOT.INI menu that represents the startup options to start the Debugger. When you select the appropriate option and the cable is correctly connected to another machine or modem, the blue startup screen appears with extra detail:

```
                          CD        DSR SND RCV
Kernel Debugger Started Using: COM1 (0x3ef8, Baud Rate 9600)
Microsoft (R) Windows NT (TM) Operating System (Build 1381)
1 Systems Processor (128MB of Memory)
```

On the target machine, it is possible to interrupt even the boot process at this point. You could watch the loading of the drivers. After you have this working, you might want to reboot the target machine just to see the effect when you have the source machine running with the Kernel Debugger active.

At this point, the Kernel Debugger is ready for use. You would start the source machine, run the Kernel Debugger batch file, and then boot the target machine. Now you are ready to analyze the operating systems's core operations.

# Kernel Debugger Usage

You now are familiar with the typical set up and start-up of the Kernel Debugger. You will undoubtedly want to begin to use the tool to analyze the operations of the operating system.

## Debugging

When the Kernel Debugger first starts, you will be presented with a screen much like Figure 2.2, which displays information about the connection.

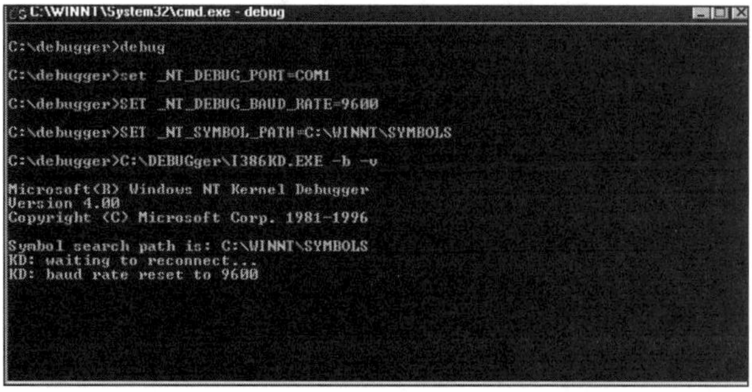

```
C:\WINNT\System32\cmd.exe - debug

C:\debugger>debug

C:\debugger>set _NT_DEBUG_PORT=COM1

C:\debugger>SET _NT_DEBUG_BAUD_RATE=9600

C:\debugger>SET _NT_SYMBOL_PATH=C:\WINNT\SYMBOLS

C:\debugger>C:\DEBUGger\I386KD.EXE -b -v

Microsoft(R) Windows NT Kernel Debugger
Version 4.00
Copyright (C) Microsoft Corp. 1981-1996

Symbol search path is: C:\WINNT\SYMBOLS
KD: waiting to reconnect...
KD: baud rate reset to 9600
```

**Figure 2.2**     *Initialization of the Kernel Debugger displays information about the configuration and connections.*

The Kernel Debugger starts by letting you know that it has succeeded in initial communications. A resync timeout would be a typical message indicating a failure.

Although the communications are in place, the Kernel Debugger is nothing more than a passive observer. If you connect during the boot phase, it will display messages about various DLLs and drivers being loaded, as displayed in Figure 2.3. The real fun starts when you break into the kernel and start looking around. When you do so, the target machine will appear to be unresponsive. The Kernel Debugger on the source machine is controlling the execution of code at this point. You have the full attention of the target machine.

**Figure 2.3**    *The Kernel Debugger displays the modules being loaded during system startup. This can aid in the troubleshooting startup problems with NT drivers, much like the use of /SOS in the BOOT.INI file.*

## Note

*The /SOS switch is used primarily for troubleshooting. The switch serves two purposes. First, it displays the names of the drivers as they are being loaded. Second, it instructs Windows NT to start the graphical interface with a base-video configuration. This saves users who have erroneously adjusted the screen parameters in such a way that the screen is incoherent.* ✦

## Warning: Be Careful Closing the Debug Window!

*If you abruptly close the debug window—for example, by clicking on the X or hitting CTRL-F4—you will terminate communications, but not control. The remote machine will appear hung. Reconnecting with the Kernel Debugger and issuing the go or resume command will allow the remote machine to resume normal operation.* ✦

When you first start out with the Kernel Debugger, you will want to issue one or more of the following signals:

- **Ctrl-C**

  Breaks into the kernel, stopping execution on the remote machine and giving you full control.

- **Ctrl-B**

  Gracefully terminates the debugger.

- **Ctrl-R**

  Resynchronizes the two machines.

- **Ctrl-V**

  Toggles Verbose mode.

- **Ctrl-D**

  Displays debugging information, which is useful when you are initially trying to set up debugging and having problems.

Each of the control signals listed, aside from Ctrl-C, must be followed by pressing the Enter key on the keyboard. Ctrl-C, the break command, will stop the execution of NT on the remote machine and present a dialog box.

The message is displayed in red. It lets you know that the kernel has been interrupted prior to any error occurring. Using the g command will continue normal operation.

## Running Commands

The Kernel Debugger is a tool that can display lots of information. Unfortunately, figuring out the commands to retrieve the available information is not always very clear. There are actually several different ways of communicating with the Kernel Debugger and the remote system. You have already witnessed the first, the use of the Control commands, such as CTRL-C. The other is to issue direct commands to the Kernel Debugger. These are entered directly at the "kd>" prompt. The last way is a series of commands preceded by the "!" symbol. Figure 2.4 shows a display of the various commands available in the standard mode.

A couple of the most useful commands are those that store information. The .logopen [filename] command will open a log file and begin to pipe all information typed and displayed in the Debugger to the file. Using the .logclose command will close the file. You can also issue the .logappend [filename] to append more information to an existing file. Also, the Q command is good for gracefully shutting down the Kernel Debugger; but don't forget to issue a g prior to closing to get the remote machines operating system running again. More information is collected using the ! commands. The list below was generated by issuing the !? command:

```
kd> !?
Built in ! commands:
  !reload [filename]
  !sympath [dir[;...]]
```

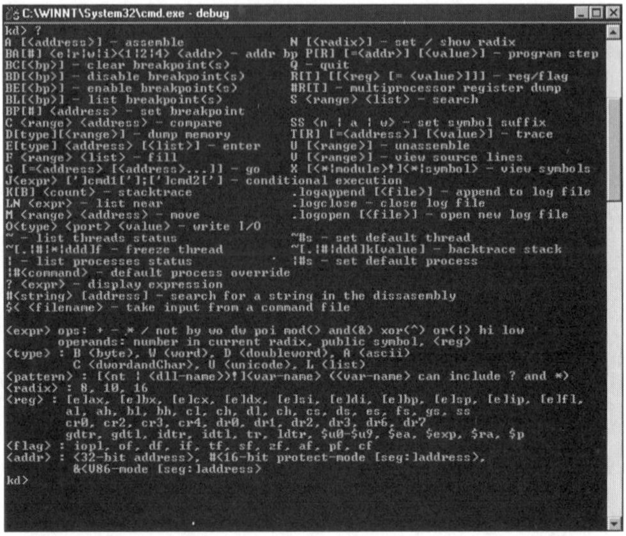

```
C:\WINNT\System32\cmd.exe - debug
kd> ?
A [<address>] - assemble                    N [<radix>] - set / show radix
BA[#] <e|r|w|i><1|2|4> <addr> - addr bp P[R] [=<addr>] [<value>] - program step
BC[<bp>] - clear breakpoint(s)              Q - quit
BD[<bp>] - disable breakpoint(s)            R[T] [[<reg> [= <value>]]] - reg/flag
BE[<bp>] - enable breakpoint(s)             #R[T] - multiprocessor register dump
BL[<bp>] - list breakpoint(s)               S <range> <list> - search
BP[#] <address> - set breakpoint
C <range> <address> - compare               SS <n | a | w> - set symbol suffix
D[type][<range>] - dump memory              T[R] [=<address>] [<value>] - trace
E[type] <address> [<list>] - enter          U [<range>] - unassemble
F <range> <list> - fill                     V [<range>] - view source lines
G [=<address> [<address>...]] - go          X [<*|module>!]<*|symbol> - view symbols
J<expr> [']cmd1[']:[']cmd2['] - conditional execution
K[B] <count> - stacktrace                   .logappend [<file>] - append to log file
LN <expr> - list near                       .logclose - close log file
M <range> <address> - move                  .logopen [<file>] - open new log file
O<type> <port> <value> - write I/O
~ - list threads status                     ~#s - set default thread
~[.|#|*|ddd]f - freeze thread               ~[.|#|ddd]k[value] - backtrace stack
| - list processes status                   |#s - set default process
|#<command> - default process override
? <expr> - display expression
#<string> [address] - search for a string in the dissasembly
$< <filename> - take input from a command file

<expr> ops: + - * / not by wo dw poi mod(<>) and(&) xor(^) or(|) hi low
       operands: number in current radix, public symbol, <reg>
<type> : B <byte>, W <word>, D <doubleword>, A <ascii>
         C <dwordandChar>, U <unicode>, L <list>
<pattern> : [<nt | <dll-name>>!]<var-name> (<var-name> can include ? and *)
<radix> : 8, 10, 16
<reg> : [e]ax, [e]bx, [e]cx, [e]dx, [e]si, [e]di, [e]bp, [e]sp, [e]ip, [e]fl,
        al, ah, bl, bh, cl, ch, dl, ch, cs, ds, es, fs, gs, ss
        cr0, cr2, cr3, cr4, dr0, dr1, dr2, dr3, dr6, dr7
        gdtr, gdtl, idtr, idtl, tr, ldtr, $u0-$u9, $ea, $exp, $ra, $p
<flag> : iopl, of, df, if, tf, sf, zf, af, pf, cf
<addr> : <32-bit address>, #<16-bit protect-mode [seg:]address>,
         &<V86-mode [seg:]address>
kd>
```

**Figure 2.4** *Issuing a "?" produces a display of standard commands that can be used to perform a variety of tasks associated with controlling the Debugger.*

The following are useful when developing extension libraries:

```
  !load <extlib>
  !unload
  !noversion
? - Displays this list
bugdump              - Display bug check dump data
calldata <table name>    - Dump call data hash table
db <physical address>    - Display physical memory
dd <physical address>    - Display physical memory
dblink <address> [count]  - Dumps a list via its blinks
devobj <device address>   - Dump the device object and Irp queue
drvobj <driver address>   - Dump the driver object and related information
drivers              - Display information about all loaded system modules
eb <physical address> <byte> <byte, byte ,...> - modify physical memory
ed <physical address> <dword> <dword,dword,...> - modify physical memory
errlog              - Dump the error log contents
exr <address>           - Dump exception record at specified address
filecache             - Dumps information about the file system cache
filelock <address>       - Dump a file lock structure
frag [flags]           - Kernel mode pool fragmentation
   flags: 1 - List all fragment information
       2 - List allocation information
       3 - both
handle <addr> <flags> <process> <TypeName> - Dumps handle for a process
    flags: -2 Dump non-paged object
heap <addr> [flags]       - Dumps heap for a process
    flags: -v Verbose
        -f Free List entries
```

```
               -a All entries
               -s Summary
               -x Force a dump even if the data is bad
          address: desired heap to dump or 0 for all
help                - Displays this list
ib <port>              - Read a byte from an I/O port
id <port>              - Read a double-word from an I/O port
iw <port>              - Read a word from an I/O port
irp <address>           - Dump Irp at specified address
irpfind            - Search non-paged pool for active Irps
locks [-v] <address>     - Dump Kernel mode resource locks
lookaside <address> <options> <depth> - Dump lookaside lists
     options - 1 Reset Counters
     options - 2 <depth> Set depth
lpc                 - Dump lpc ports and messages
memusage             - Dumps the page frame database table
ob <port>             - Write a byte to an I/O port
obja <TypeName>         - Dumps an object manager object's attributes
object <TypeName>        - Dumps an object manager object
od <port>             - Write a double-word to an I/O port
ow <port>             - Write a word to an I/O port
pfn                - Dumps the page frame database entry for the physical page
pool <address> [detail]    - Dump Kernel mode heap
    address: 0 or blank - Only the process heap
             -1 - All heaps in the process
         Otherwise for the heap address listed
    detail: 0 - Sumarry Information
           1 - Above + location/size of regions
           3 - Above + allocated/free blocks in committed regions
           4 - Above + free lists
poolfind Tag [pooltype] - - Finds occurrences of the specified Tag
   Tag is 4 character tag, * and ? are wild cards
   pooltype is 0 for nonpaged (default, and 1 for paged
  NOTE - this can take a long time!
poolused [flags]       - Dump usage by pool tag
     flags: 1 Verbose
     flags: 2 Sort by NonPagedPool Usage
     flags: 4 Sort by PagedPool Usage
process [flags]       - Dumps process at specified address
processfields        - Show offsets to all fields in a process
ptov PhysicalPageNumber   - Dump all valid physical<->virtual mappings
             for the given page directory
ready               - Dumps state of all READY system threads
regkcb             - Dump registry key-control-blocks
regpool [s|r]        - Dump registry allocated paged pool
    s - Save list of registry pages to temporary file
    r - Restore list of registry pages from temp. file
srb <address>          - Dump Srb at specified address
sysptes            - Dumps the system PTEs
thread [flags]         - Dump thread at specified address
threadfields          - Show offsets to all fields in a thread
time               - Reports PerformanceCounterRate and TimerDifference
timer               - Dumps timer tree
```

```
token [flags]          - Dump token at specified address
tokenfields            - Show offsets to all fields in a token
tunnel <address>        - Dump a file property tunneling cache
trap <address>          - Dump a trap frame
vad                  - Dumps VADs
version                - Version of extension dll
vm                   - Dumps virtual management values


X86-specific:

apic [base]            - Dump local apic
cxr                - Dump context record at specified address
ioapic [base]           - Dump io apic
mtrr               - Dumps MTTR
npx [base]             - Dumps NPX save area
pcr                - Dumps the PCR
pte                - Dumps the corresponding PDE and PTE for the entered address
sel [selector]          - Examine selector values
trap [base]            - Dump trap frame
tss [register]  - Dump TSS
```

The information from these commands will vary depending on the type of operating system. Generally, the following commands tend to be of the most use:

| Command | Description |
|---|---|
| !process | Displays process information details |
| !drivers | Lists all the loaded drivers |
| !trap | Used primarily for troubleshooting errors |
| !memusage | Displays detailed memory usage |
| ! bugdump | Displays the bug check codes if an error occurred |

### Note

*For more information on some of the kernel debugging commands, see David A. Solomon's* Inside Windows NT, *Second Edition, Microsoft Press (ISBN 1-57231-677-2).* ♦

In addition to monitoring a system interactively, the Kernel Debugger can be used to analyze a file from a blue screen.

## Memory Dump Files

The memory dump file is another way of collecting information about an error that has occurred on a system. The information in the memory dump file can be captured and analyzed using the Kernel Debugger.

## Creating Memory Dump Files

To create a memory dump file on a machine that is generating blue screens, you will need to adjust some parameters in the Control Panel, System applet. After the applet is open, click the Startup/Shutdown tab. You will need to make sure that the Write debugging information to: option is checked and that a filename is in the text box, as displayed in Figure 2.5. The default filename is the best choice.

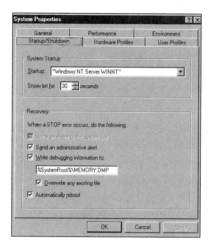

**Figure 2.5** *In the System Properties, you can configure the memory dump file, as well as control other potential alerts and whether the system will be rebooted automatically.*

You will need to verify of the following in order to configure the system in the way described in Figure 2.5:

- A PAGEFILE.SYS is on the same partition as the operating system.

- The PAGEFILE.SYS on the system partition is equal in size to the amount of RAM plus 1MB.

- Enough space is on the partition that the MEMORY.DMP is configured to be written to. The MEMORY.DMP will be approximately RAM plus 1MB in size.

Once this has been configured, the information will be saved in the PAGEFILE.SYS on the partition with the NT operating system installed on it the next time that the system produces a blue screen. When the system reboots, the PAGEFILE.SYS will be locked until the information can be copied to the memory dump file indicated in the System Properties in the Control Panel. As the PAGEFILE.SYS is locked, the system might likely report that the Virtual Memory is low. This is a temporary condition until the copying of the data is complete. Once complete, the system will return to normal operation. The system will run much slower until the virtual memory is released and accessible. After the memory dump file is written, you can then proceed with analyzing the dump file.

**Analysis Tools**

The Kernel Debugger is the first tool that you might consider for analyzing the information in the memory dump file. Recall that issuing the I386KD.EXE with the -z parameter will allow you to specify a memory dump file to analyze. After it is loaded, you can use all the regular commands to analyze the information. A typical command would be `i386kd.exe -z c:\winnt\memory.dmp`. This would load the MEMORY.DMP file into the Kernel Debugger. The same rules apply for the installation of the symbol files.

Another tool for looking at the MEMORY.DMP file is the DUMPEXAM.EXE from the Windows NT CD. The program will convert the MEMORY.DMP file into a flat text file for viewing. The command syntax would be `dumpexam-v -y %systemroot%\Symbols`. You would issue the command from a command prompt with your current directory set to the same directory where the MEMORY.DMP file is. The %SYSTEMROOT%\SYMBOLS is the location of the symbol files corresponding to the version and service pack level of the machine that created the dump file.

# Summary

In this chapter, we primarily examined the Windows NT Kernel Debugger. This particular tool, which is native to Windows NT and appears on the Windows NT CD, can be a very powerful aid when you are trying to examine the internals of the Windows NT operating system. It not only can be used for simple examination of another system, but also for troubleshooting the blue screen of death.

You should now understand the importance of the Windows NT symbol files and their inclusion in this particular process. You saw how to install the symbol files and understand now that you must install symbol files from the service pack revision that your Windows NT operating system is on.

You can modify the kernel debugging session through the BOOT.INI file on the target machine, which is the failing machine. You can adjust the Kernel Debugger's operation on the source machine or the machine used to examine the failing machine by utilizing environment variables. You've seen that in this particular process all the steps are very clear but can be complex, especially in the interpretation of the information being displayed.

At this point, I would suggest that you try this process with a couple machines of your own. The best thing to start with is of course the standard serial cable as opposed to trying to deal with the added complexities of a modem connection. However, if you're willing to try, you should also look at using a modem connection to do this kind of analysis. Recall that the modem connection will be the way that some other vendor, such as Microsoft, might want you to work with the Kernel Debugger. As always, getting your hands dirty with technology is usually the best way to learn.

# 3
## Windows NT Utilities

In this chapter, you will be exposed to many of the utilities that you can utilize from the Windows NT CD and the NT Resource Kit. The NT Resource Kit Tools are excellent for helping with management, troubleshooting, and development tasks. However, the documentation typically offers little in the way of applicable uses of the tools or interpretation of the output some of the tools produce. Here you will find that information.

In this chapter, we discuss case-oriented use of the tools. No one uses all of the tools all of the time. Typically, you will want to pick out a couple you find very helpful and use those regularly. The others you will want to be aware of so that, should a need arise, you will know you have a tool for the situation. You can always refer to the online help or this book when attempting to apply the tool for the first time.

Certainly, the tools mentioned here are not all of the tools in the NT Resource Kit, of which there are over 170. This chapter includes the ones I feel are the most useful. I would suggest that while you go through this chapter, as well as some of the others, you sit close to your computer so that you can have a look at some of the tools and techniques that are being utilized in the various sections of the book. In this chapter, being near a computer will help you determine exactly how the tools work, and whether you like how they work. Many of the performance tools that we will be discussing will make references to Windows NT memory and virtual memory processes and systems. Therefore, we will start the chapter with a review of Windows NT's memory model and how virtual memory is provided to applications and system processes. Then the chapter will proceed with a discussion of the command line tools for process analysis. These are primarily used to give you quick views of statistics, but in some cases offer insight not available in other tools.

*The tools here are from the NT Resource Kit Update 3. The Update 3 of the NT Resource Kit tools was not accompanied by the release of any books. Books that augmented the information in the original Resource Kit release accompanied previous versions of the Windows NT Resource Kit, including Update 1 and Update 2. You will need to acquire the tools from TechNet, a CD-based subscription service I mentioned before, or from the Microsoft Web site. You may also use the Microsoft FTP server at* ftp.microsoft.com *to acquire some of the utilities. The tools are usually found in an unsupported folder on the FTP site.*

*The tools are always being updated so you will want to keep tabs on the distribution points. Also, when you launch the tools or look at the help file, many give you the name and email address of the program author. If you are having a specific problem or have a suggestion, you might want to drop them an email.* ◆

Next you learn about some of the graphical tools for investigating processes, drivers, and various resources. You are then introduced to a couple of tools that enhance the operation of the NT Performance Monitor. These specifically resolve a couple of problems that you run in to when trying to monitor processes using the Performance Monitor. After that, you learn about some load simulators that give you a different aspect of performance tuning. Primarily, the other tools offer you insight into what is going on within the operating system. The simulators allow you to control the load on your system and test how it operates. This can be important for determining the best configuration on which to run your application. Lastly, you will see how to use some tools focused on application development, which can track process activity and the use of DLLs/APIs.

# Windows NT Virtual Memory Model

Before getting into these tools, you must understand the basics of virtual memory. In Figure 3.1, you can see the general depiction of the way Windows NT handles virtual memory. This is simplified, but suitable for the purpose of the page fault discussions here.

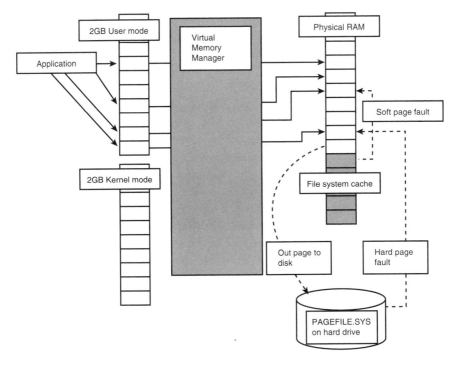

**Figure 3.1**   *The VMM works in cooperation with other systems in the NT Kernel, like the Cache Manager and I/O Manager, to swap data and code back and forth to a page file.*

Every application is offered the opportunity to use up to 4GB of memory. 2GB of this memory are allocated to Kernel mode operations—in other words, to program activities that involve Kernel mode processes. The other 2GB are dedicated to the User mode operations. In this section of memory, the program might store code or data. Each one is roughly treated the same. So no matter if you are loading another DLL or you are requesting another set of data from a data file, the operation of moving the information into memory is the same.

Certainly, most of us do not have 4GB of memory in our workstations or servers, let alone 4GB for every application that we are going to run. Thus, Windows NT must somehow simulate that amount of memory. This is done by offering a program's virtual address out of what is called the *virtual address space.* The Windows NT Virtual Memory Manager exposes the virtual address space to the applications. When a piece of code requests more information, it will request the information from a particular place in memory. This location is referred to by an address—in this case, a virtual address. The *Virtual Memory Manager* (VMM) will translate this virtual address to a physical address in RAM. *RAM* (Random Access Memory) always refers to physical memory chips installed on a computer and not any virtual memory being provided by the NT operating system. On occasion, the VMM will find that the information does not translate to a physical location in RAM, which the program has information in. Thus, it will need to put the appropriate information in that location. The first place that the VMM will look for the information is in the file system cache. The file system cache, or simply cache, is a dynamically sized section of RAM that Windows NT maintains for the temporary storage of information that is being written or read from various file systems.

---

**Note**

*The term file systems, although it accurately refers to hard drives, includes network drives as well. Network access is implemented as a file system controlled by many of the same Kernel mode processes as standard hard drive access. Thus, you will need to recall that the processes described take into account network activity as well as disk I/O.* ◆

---

The file system cache is controlled via a process called the Cache Manager. The Cache Manager is a component of the I/O Manager, a Windows NT kernel-level process. The I/O Manager, which you will become more familiar with later, is actually a collection of several components that work together to control the major I/O for the Windows NT operating system. These include networks, disks, and other I/Os implemented as file systems. If the VMM happens to find what it is looking for in the file system cache, a copy of the information is moved from the cache into the location in RAM where the VMM is expecting to find the information. For all of the complexity of this operation, it is relatively quick when compared to hard drive access.

So, what happens if the VMM does not find the information in the file system cache? Well, it will have to look on the hard drive. Periodically, Windows NT will look around in the RAM to see if there is anything that isn't being used. This information will be placed in the cache and eventually on the hard drive. This is done to try and conserve space in RAM that, as we all know, is a critical resource to the operating system as well as the programs running on the operating system. Windows NT attempts to conserve memory utilization, relative to the amount of physical RAM installed in the computer. This moving of information between the RAM, file system cache, and hard drive is called *paging*. The file on the hard drive is called the page file, PAGEFILE.SYS to be precise.

Returning to the program requesting data, consider that it does find the information in the file system cache. This movement from the file system cache to the physical location in RAM is called a *soft page fault*. A soft page fault is generally not disruptive to the operation of a program. Moving information back and forth inside the physical address space is a relatively quick operation. However, there are situations where excessive soft page faults can affect the operation of a system. These will be discussed in Part 3, "The Specialist: Analysis of Specific Application Scenarios." For now, you can consider the soft page fault to be relatively harmless to the performance of your application.

The *hard page fault* can become a real nuisance. Consider that the hard drive access time on any system is a hundred times slower than access to physical RAM. This can become a problem if your application is causing excessive hard page faults. Hard page faults can be indications of general RAM deficiency. However, a developer should always first consider not increasing RAM, but finding out if the program that they have written is too casual about its use of the precious memory resource. The definition of a hard page fault is generally considered to be an event that results in information being read from the hard drive since it is not readily available in RAM. Thus, when you first start a program or initialize data, you will see a spike in the number of hard page faults. This is because the application is requesting code or data pages that are not currently in RAM; thus a disk read is required. Again, this is a simplistic definition of a hard page fault. As well as being an indication of a general lack of memory, page faults can also:

Be the first indication of a memory leak

Show poor organization of DLLs and functions

Reveal poor data retrieval practices

### Note

*When reviewing page fault information, consider the initializing process for code and data. A hard page fault is generated when loading information from a hard drive. In some code, you will need to load functions from DLLs as well, which again will generate hard page faults. So, when trying to capture data regarding the page faults of your application, start the analysis after the application has started and is fully initialized. Then you will know that you are seeing information on hard page fault totals for running conditions and not start up.* ◆

A *memory leak* is a situation where a developer has inadvertently utilized memory space without letting go of it when he is done. Generally, creating handles to objects and not properly closing the handles when you are done working with the object creates memory leaks. If the functions are poorly organized, it can result in loading code from several DLLs throughout the operation of a program. Keeping a watchful eye on the page faults while you exercise various functions within your application will help you determine if you have done a good job of organizing the code. In some cases, it is a matter of whether the compiler has done a good job at optimizing the code. Many programs that you write will be retrieving information from a data file of some kind. This will often result in hard page faults. Especially in the case of database applications, the appropriate development of queries and data requests can make or break an application's performance.

### Note

*You can find additional information on tuning Windows NT for memory utilization in Windows NT Performance: Monitoring, Benchmarking, and Tuning, New Riders Publishing, (ISBN 1-56205-942-4). And if you are insanely curious about the twisted details of memory allocation and the process of aging try Inside Windows NT, Second Editionn, Microsoft Press, (ISBN 1-57231-677-2).*

*This second book is completely architecture; but the more you understand the internals, the better you will be able to predict operating system behavior.* ♦

We will be doing plenty of monitoring with the Performance Monitor later. For now, consider the PFMON.EXE utility and some of the others from the Resource Kit.

## Command Line Tools for Process Analysis

There are still some arguments about whether GUI or command line is the better interface. Personally, I find that they both have their place. The GUI makes life simple, but the command line is generally less intrusive to the operation of the system. In certain cases, the command line launches and displays information more quickly than GUI.

For example, the Performance Monitor is a wonderful tool. As you saw in Chapter 1, "Introduction to Performance Monitor," you can perform all sorts of gathering and displaying methods for performance data. But, when your system is really being tasked, it often is difficult to get the Performance Monitor to run quickly. Also, consider that the graphical display is one of the more time-consuming activities that a regular user can place on an NT system. So, you have command line tools to the rescue. It isn't all that dramatic, but in such cases it plays an important part in the analysis and general operation of Windows NT. In this section, we will discuss the following command line tools:

PFMON (Page Fault Monitor)

PMON (Process Monitor)

TLIST (Task List)

PULIST (Process User List)

The PFMON, Page Fault Monitor, is used to monitor the page faults associated with a particular application's operation. PMON, Process Monitor, is a quick way of reviewing general performance information in a numerical column format. The last two tools, TLIST and PULIST, will display lists of processes and security descriptors quickly and in a simple format.

### Note

*In many cases, you can receive assistance with an NT Resource Kit utility by typing "/?" after the program. If this doesn't work, try the command without any arguments. (A word of caution, however: You should have some idea about what the program does before you start trying to use the command switches. Often the name of the program gives you a clue.)*

*The file REGTOOL.HLP also contains information on the Resource Kit tools. Some of the tools can be disruptive to the operation of your machine if used incorrectly. One such tool is ROLLBACK.EXE. This tool will roll your installation of NT back to the graphical setup portion of the install. The tool does not accept the "/?" switch and does not give the user a warning about what is going to happen to their installation of Windows NT. This has caught many users off guard. I recall seeing the pleas for help in the newsgroups. The moral is to be careful about running programs when you are not sure about what the program does. You should always try a new utility on test workstations or servers before using it on a system that you care about. ◆*

## PFMON

*PFMON.EXE* (Page Fault Monitor) is a program that will display information about the page faults that a program is generating. Page faults are generally an indication of usage of the memory resources. There are several causes for such activity, which will be covered in the next section.

Here are the available options for the PFMON.EXE program:

```
PFMON [switches] application-command-line
       [-?] display this message
       [-n] don't display running faults, just log to pfmon.log
       [-l] log faults to pfmon.log
       [-c] only show code faults
       [-h] only show hard faults
       [-p pid] attach to existing process
       [-d] Database format (tab delimited)
format: pagefault number, Page Fault type (Hard or Soft),Program Counter's Module,
Symbol for PC, Decimal value of PC,Decimal value of PC, Module of the virtual address
accessed,Symbol for VA, value of VA
       [-k] Kernel mode page faults and User mode page faults
       [-K] Kernel mode page faults instead of User mode
```

Most of the options are self-explanatory. The ones used most often are the -n and the -p. The -n option will allow you to log the information out to a text file so that you can examine the information later at your leisure. Also, it will prevent the added cycles from displaying the information on the screen. (Remember, whenever you are monitoring anything, you want to remain as unobtrusive as possible.) The -p. option will attach to an established program.

Every program—rather, process—is identified on Windows NT by a unique process identifier. The process ID will remain unique to the program during the life of the execution of the process. Thus, you can safely track the activity of the process through the process ID. If you happen to be writing services for Windows NT or other operations that might not happen in the foreground, this option will be invaluable. To determine the process ID, you can use TLIST or PULIST, which are mentioned later in this chapter. The PFMON breaks down the page faults into several groups for your analysis (see Figure 3.2).

Figure 3.2 is only the tail end of all of the information that PFMON.EXE will display. The rest of the display is information on the faults as they are occurring. I would suggest running a simple command like:

```
PFMON NOTEPAD.EXE
```

or

```
PFMON NOTEPAD.EXE > Monitor.txt
```

**Figure 3.2**    *PFMON collects page fault information
and displays the totals in several categories.*

Using the second syntax, you will be able to view the full amount of data at your leisure by opening the MONITOR.TXT file in notepad. When you examine the output, you will see hard and soft page faults. Again, the hard page faults will be much more significant to the performance of the system. You will also see a breakdown of code, user and Kernel mode page faults. This helps to determine where the problems might be. Kernel mode operations might indicate problems with the way you are using APIs or the way your program is attempting to utilize Windows NT services. Excessive page faults due to code page requests might indicate poor program flow.

When possible, PFMON will also break down the calls to various NT components, as seen in Figure 3.2. Focus either on the data or code page faults. If you are attempting to streamline your code, use the -c option for the page fault monitor to be able to look only at code faults in the program. A general indicator of memory deficiency is a hard page fault over 50% of the total page faults. Should you encounter this situation, you might want to reconsider the usage of program memory as well as begin the search for memory leaks.

## PMON

PMON.EXE is the Process Resource Monitor. This tool offers an excellent view of all of the processing running on an NT system. Using this tool you will be able to examine the various processes running on your system and determine the type of resources being used. It focuses mainly on the CPU and memory utilization. The CPU and memory are after all the most sought after resources on a computer, so this makes sense. The tool has no command line options and displays in a text-based format, as seen in Figure 3.3.

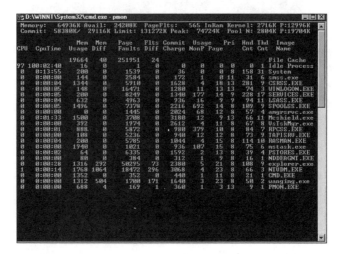

**Figure 3.3**    *PMON.EXE displays CPU and Memory usage on a per-process basis in a text-based format.*

In order to close the display, you might simply type a "Q" or press CTRL-C. Let's examine the output more closely.

### Note

*You will want to adjust the size of your Command Window before using PMON.EXE. The number of processes can scroll off of the screen. Adjust by opening a command prompt and clicking in the top left corner. Then click on Properties. Click on the Layout tab and adjust the screen buffer as well as the screen height. I find a buffer height of 100 and a screen height of 40 works with most tools and commands. ◆*

The top lines of the display summarize the condition of the system's overall memory resource at the time that you are looking at the display. The PMON.EXE will automatically refresh the information every five seconds. The first few items describe the amount of memory installed and the amount of free memory. From there you have the following:

- PageFlts indicates the total number of page faults since the last sample.
- InRAM Kernel indicates the amount of kernel code resident in physical memory. The value is an indication of the amount of the pageable memory pool that is currently resident, not paged out.
- The Commit values on the next line deal with committed memory. Memory is committed when it has secured backing or is ensured that it will not be paged out. Backing refers to whether page file space has been reserved for the memory.

  Alternatively, if there is sufficient free memory, the system will permit an application to exist without backing as long as the amount of free memory remains at a suitable level. This level is dependent on the amount of memory installed on the system. The first value for Commit is the amount of memory committed. The second is a sum of all of the values actually committed by each process or in use with the intent or possibility of being paged out.

- The Limit is the commit limit, which refers to the combination of all of the PAGEFILE.SYS and the physical RAM in the system. This value is the size of the PAGEFILE.SYS without expanding it. As you probably know, the page file is configured in the Control Panel's System applet as a range of values. The Limit only knows what the pagefile's size currently is, not what it could be expanded to.
- Peak shows the peak value of the committed memory.
- Pool N: displays a value for the nonpage pools physical size.
- Pool P: is a value, seen next to N:. It is the paged pool virtual size.

These give you an indication of how memory is looking on the system. Generally, memory pressures can take the form of committed memory approaching the commit limit, as well as a drastic increase in the amount of paging.

The data on each of the processes breaks down as follows:

- **CPU**

  This column refers to the percentage of CPU consumed by this process. You will notice a process called IDLE in the list. This is a process designed simply to keep the processor busy when nothing else is going on.

- **CPU Time**

  This is the amount of CPU time this process has consumed since the process was started. This will include all time prior to when the PMON.EXE utility was launched.

- **Memory Usage**

  This is basically the Working Set size of the processes. The Working Set refers to the total amount of memory being utilized by code and data during the process.

- **Memory Diff**

  This is the difference between samplings of the data.

- **Page Faults**

  This is the total number of page faults generated by the process. Notice that there is no distinction made between soft and hard page faults here. Thus, be cautious about interpreting the value incorrectly.

- **Flts Diff**

  This displays the changes in the Page Faults between the current and the previous reading.

- **Commit Charge**

  This is the amount of memory that the process has committed. Recall that committed memory either has backing in the form of reserved space on the PAGEFILE.SYS or a guarantee from the system that it will not be paged out of memory.

- **Usage NonP**

  This is the amount of the system's nonpageable memory pool that this particular process is utilizing. Primarily, you will see only kernel level (operating system) processes with usage of this type. Recall that even User mode processes like Word will use various Kernel mode processes to perform some actions.

- **Usage Page**

  This is the amount of the page file that is currently in use by this process.

- **Pri**

  This is the process's base priority from which any threads will get their priority. The priority of a process and threads basically determines how often the thread will be able to access the processor to complete its work.

- **Hnd Cnt**

  This is the number of open handles for this process.

- **Thd Cnt**

  This is the current number of threads that this process has created. A thread does not necessarily imply processor activity. However, threads do result in memory consumption and the potential for sending instructions to the processor. Every process consists of at least one thread.

- **Image Name**

  This is a name of the executable being run.

This quick tool will keep track of what is going in the system as your application is running. The idea is that you will want to watch the consumption of the various memory resources as you run your application. You will want to see how much of the application's Working Set is being paged out and how much is staying in memory.

Looking at the Memory Usage column, you get an idea of the size of the processes' total memory consumption. By comparing that to the Commit charge, you can see how much of the memory has actually been committed to the process. The difference between the values represents the reservations for memory that have not taken place. Also, you can see how much of the page pool your application is using. This will indicate the amount of code or data that has sat unused in memory until it was paged out. As always, when talking about observing memory, you will have to watch the page faults. They will let you know how often code is waiting for information stored elsewhere in RAM or hard drive files to be moved into the appropriate physical address space. The presence of applications with low values for page faults is a sign of a well-written program. Thus, monitoring your program's page faults will assist in designing efficient code.

# TLIST

TLIST.EXE provides you with process ID information and more. This program and the PULIST that you will see shortly are both command line tools, with slightly different takes on displaying information about running processes.

By running TLIST without any parameters, you will get a simple textual display of the processes that are running on your system, their names, and the *process id* (PID) associated with them (see Figure 3.4).

**Figure 3.4**    *The PID that TLIST.EXE displays is often the first step in tracking a program's activities. The PID is unique to the system and thus identifies a process from all other processes on the system.*

However, TLIST has more to offer than just the displaying of the PID. TLIST –T, for example, will produce the same display, but with the parent-child relationships suggested by indentation, as you can see in Figure 3.5.

**Figure 3.5**    *Seeing the parent-child relationship between various processes allows you to understand a process's behavior better.*

TLIST.EXE has other options that make it a very useful tool for the quick analysis of the status of a particular process. TLIST [PID] will display detailed information about a particular process. PID is the ID of the particular process that you would like to examine. If you supply a PID, then you will see the display as depicted in Figure 3.6.

**Figure 3.6**    *When supplying a PID in the TLIST command line, you will see detailed information on the memory usage and DLLs loaded by a process.*

This display starts with descriptive information on exactly where the process is run from. In the case of the previous example in Figure 3.6, you can see that the process starts from the D:\WINNT\SYSTEM32 folder and has a working directory (CWD) of D:\. The next couple of lines describe the state of the memory consumption for the process. The memory consumption for the process is described first in the Virtual Memory size and then by the Working Set size. The *Virtual Memory size* refers to the amount of information that the process is using that has been moved to the pagefile on the hard drive. The *Working Set size* refers to information that is currently loaded into active memory for the process. The Working Set peak term is evident from its title, but is very important in catching hints of memory leaks. If the Working Set size and the peak size are the same, the process is a candidate for containing a memory leak.

> ### Note
>
> *Remember that when a value of condition is mentioned, such as the previously mentioned value for the Working Set, you will want the statement to be considered over a sustained period of time. Certainly taking a single look at a particular process at a particular time and noting that the value of the Working Set size and the peak Working Set size is the same might actually be meaningless. However, if you examine the value over a period of several minutes, you might notice that the Working Set and the peak Working Set are the same number consistently. This is the real indication of a potential problem. Again, whenever such potential values are mentioned in this text, you should always consider that a single sample that matches the condition could never be considered conclusive evidence that there is a problem. Repeated observations strengthen the conclusion.* ◆

In the top portion of the display, you will see the number of threads that the process is running. All processes include at least one thread. Immediately below this is a listing of the threads. The display can get a little confusing at this point, as another listing appears below the thread listing. However, the thread listing has one to three digit numbers in the leftmost column. There will be as many listings as there are numbers of threads indicated in the previous line of the display. In our case, we had a single thread; thus we had a single item in the listing. The number in the column actually refers to a thread ID, not another process ID.

Just as there is a unique process ID for each individual process, there is a unique thread ID for each thread within a process. The *thread ID* (TID) can be used to track the thread in Performance Monitor and other processes. It is also how a programmer gains a handle on a thread to examine and change its properties. The other information on the thread indicates the address where the thread is loaded, any errors that might have been indicated, and the current state of the thread when the information on the process was captured. While the thread state and error are interesting values, they are generally of little use in this particular display. The problem is that these values change often and thus don't have a lot of value. Usually, you will catch a process in a waiting state. The *waiting state* is indication that the thread is waiting for some other process or hard component to give it something to do.

The remainder of the listing is a list of the DLLs that have been loaded on behalf of this process or have been called by the process. Some DLLs are not necessarily loaded and charged to this particular process's Working Set. Shared DLLs will be loaded and charged to the system as opposed to the individual process. The DLLs listed will have information about their versions and the location where they are actually loaded. It is unfortunate that the full path to the DLLs was not included in the display. However, this is still a quick way to check on the versions of the DLLs that the process is utilizing. Often, DLL conflicts present all sorts of problems, from poor performance to downright failures of the application or service. On Microsoft DLLs, and some other company's, you might see a "shp" which refers to the shipping or free build as opposed to a checked or debugged version of the code.

PULIST, on the other hand, offers the same type of initial view as the TLIST program, but also displays some security data.

## PULIST

The primary purpose of the PULIST program is to provide you with process information and some basic security information about the various processes (see Figure 3.7).

**Figure 3.7**  *Knowing the security context that a process is running in will help to diagnosis issues with access problems and user rights being utilized by the program.*

PULIST's display is simple. The first column shows the name of the executable, the second shows the PID, and the third shows the security context. Many of the processes will show as the NT AUTHORITY\SYSTEM. These are part of the Windows NT Executive Services or are being run under the local system. When you configure a service to run on Windows NT, you either give it a security context to run under or you take the default of allowing the software to run under the local system account. While PULIST will not offer you any further details than TLIST did, it does permit one action that TLIST does not. PULIST allows you to examine the process list and corresponding process IDs from another machine over the network. This is sometimes handy when you are troubleshooting process problems on a remote system. The syntax  for the command is simply:

```
Pulist \\[servername]
```

However, if the machines are not operating in a domain, the display of the PULIST might not show you all of the security information when you are examining a remote server. In such cases, you will still see a listing of the processes and the associated PIDs, just no security information.

Both TLIST and PULIST are quite handy and useful. For more detailed information you will want to have a look at one of the graphical tools that are available. These tools, while more intrusive in their operation on the system, provide far more  detailed information than TLIST or PULIST.

# Graphical Tools

Graphical tools give you the benefit of a pleasant interface and the opportunity to represent information in a graphical/pictorial manner. In addition, the graphical tools tend to have more detailed information than some of the command line tools discussed earlier. Here we review a couple of graphical tools that are very useful to the developer as well as the administrator. The first one is the Task Manager, which oddly enough is often overlooked as a method for analysis. Most folks use Task Manager's default views or just use it to kill a rouge process. However, the ability to quickly call upon Task Manager along with some of its good options makes it worthy of your attention. The other tool mentioned is the Process Explode, an NT Resource Kit tool, which details almost every aspect of a running process and its associated threads.

## Task Manager

The Task Manager utilizes the same information as the Performance Monitor but is faster and easier to launch. As far as detailed performance analysis, you will still need to return to the Performance Monitor; however, you can still do some rudimentary analysis in the Task Manager. The best feature of the Task Manager is that it can be launched using any one of the following three methods:

Right-clicking on the toolbar and selecting Task Manager

Pressing CTRL-ALT-DELETE and clicking on the Task Manager button

Pressing CTRL-SHIFT-ESC

The second and third methods are the real benefit. Say your system is caught up in some heavy background process like handling some excessive interrupts due to bogus network traffic. You might not be able to click on any portion of the desktop; thus, you don't have a way of analyzing the problem. However, you can launch the Task Manager since you can use a hardware interrupt, CTRL-ALT-DELETE. Unless your machine is completely hung up, you should be able to get the CTRL-ALT-DELETE screen to come up. Then you can launch the Task Manager and have a peek at what is going on.

Some of the other standard features of the Task Manager are very useful as well, like running a new task and killing a rouge process. One of the primary functions of the Task Manager is to provide performance information.

**Task Manager Performance Tab**
The Task Manager is able to display some rudimentary performance information. Recall that the memory and the processor are generally considered to be the most important resources to managers as far as performance is concerned. In the Task Manager, the memory and processor are generally the only two items that are analyzed. There are two very basic graphical screens displaying the processor utilization and the amount of memory being used. If you have multiple processors, you will see information displayed on a per-processor basis.

If you click View and Show Kernel Times, a red line will appear on the display which indicates the percentage of time the processor is spending on Kernel mode operations. If you see from the red line that the kernel is consuming almost all of the processing time consistently, and the processor is around or over 80% utilized, you will want to switch to the Performance Monitor to do some real analysis. Generally, 80% utilization should be an indicator that you need to watch how the processors are being used on a system.

The rest of the display is dedicated to memory. The Totals box, which lists the handles, threads, and processes, gives you a picture of how the system's memory is being used from a process perspective. Handles, threads, and processes all take up space on the system. Excessive numbers of open handles should make you think "memory leak?" as leaving open handles to objects is the leading cause of memory leaks in applications. The creation and breakdown of processes on the NT system is the most overall resource-intensive operation on the system. Should the number of threads and processes be fluctuating, you could have a rouge process—or more likely a service that is having some difficulty launching other processes (applications) or creating threads. Both situations can be caused by improper parameters and calling methods to APIs or automation functions.

The Physical Memory section should look familiar to you, at least the names of the various items. They are as follows:

- The **Total** is the total physical RAM in the system.
- The **Available** is the amount of memory that is neither reserved nor committed.

This value should not fall below 4MB. Windows NT likes to reserve about 4MB to perform swapping of items in memory and to handle sudden requests for memory. Should the value drop below 4MB, you should be considering memory shortage a problem.

- The **File Cache** refers to the File System Cache that is being controlled by the Cache Manager to buffer reads and writes to the various file systems, including the network.

   You can expect this value to fluctuate depending on the various operations that are occurring on your system. For example, if you are copying the latest service pack for NT down from an internal network server in your company, you can expect the File Cache value to increase as the I/O demands increase in an effort to copy the information.

### Controlling the File System Cache

*While you generally cannot control the size of the File System Cache without hacking the registry, you can control the preferences NT shows to resizing the Cache. This is controlled via the Network applet in the Windows NT Control Panel. You open the Network applet and click on the Services tab. There you will find a service called Server, which you select. Then you click on the Properties button. You will see a display like Figure 3.8.* ✦

**Figure 3.8**    *The properties of the Server service are located by opening the Network applet from the NT Control Panel.*

Here you have four choices. The first two will allow you to minimize the amount of memory used for servicing other users trying to reach your computer from the network. Here is the break down of the various choices, as depicted in Figure 3.8:

- **Minimize Memory Used**

   This choice is used when you are allowing no more than 10 users to connect to the system. This way the memory can be allocated to other processes.

- **Balance**

  This choice is good for 10 to 64 user connections to a system. Again, for a small memory conscious server this might be a good choice. For example, it would be good if you have an office of 30 people and the server is used for more than sharing files.

- **Maximize Throughput for File Sharing**

  This choice is for user connections more than 64. This is the default choice for Windows NT. For systems that are sharing files and printers, this is an excellent choice. This directs Windows NT to favor dynamically increasing the size of the File System Cache over reserving more memory for applications.

- **Maximize Throughput for Network Applications**

  This choice is used for application servers. Again, 64 or more user connections will be supported in this configuration. This would be the connection of choice to primary domain controllers, backup domain controllers, and application servers (like Microsoft SQL Servers). In this configuration, Windows NT favors giving more memory to the various applications over dynamically increasing the size of the File System Cache.

Under the Commit Charge section in the Task Manager's performance display, you will see the amount of memory and the pagefile that is being used:

- The **Total** represents all of the committed memory on the system. This includes memory that has space reserved in the pagefile and memory that is guaranteed not to be paged out.

- The **Limit** is the combination of the sizes of the pagefiles and the amount of physical RAM.

- The **Peak** displays the highest level of the Total Commit Charge since the system was last started. Should the Total value close in on the Limit, you should consider that you have a memory problem that needs to be investigated and corrected.

The Kernel Memory section describes how the Windows NT Kernel mode services are utilizing the memory allocated:

- The **Total** represents a combination of the paged and nonpaged memory pools. The kernel creates these two memory pools to utilize and perform various operations. Items in the nonpaged memory pool cannot be paged out on the pagefile, while code and data in the pagable memory pool can.

- **Paged** is an indication of just how much of the paged memory pool is being used.
- **Nonpaged** is of course the amount of memory used in the nonpageable memory pool.

You will generally find the important portions of the Windows NT Kernel in the nonpaged memory pool. Having the code in memory all of the time enhances performance and in some cases is a necessity. You certainly cannot have the microkernel, which handles scheduling of threads on the processor being paged out to disk. Overall, viewing this screen gives you a decent picture about the general health of your system.

**Task Manager Processes Tab**
Let's examine another section of the Task Manager, the Processes tab. Here you see a listing of the various processes on a system and the default values of PID, CPU (which is % CPU time), the RAW CPU time, and memory usage. These values give you a more detailed look at how resources are being used on your computer system.

Clicking on any one of the column headings automatically sorts that column in ascending order. Clicking the column a second time reverses the order. What is often missed is that you can click on View and then Select Columns. This will allow you to adjust the columns that are displayed in Task Manager, as in Figure 3.9.

**Figure 3.9**   *A wide variety of statistical values can be displayed right from the Task Manager for quick analysis.*

Many of these values have already been discussed previously in the last few sections. So, here we mention the ones that are new. The *USER Objects* represents objects created and being used by the process in User mode. *The GDI Objects* isolate those objects that have to do with the graphical display of data. *GDI* is the Graphical Device Interface. You can click any number of the columns in the list and have them displayed in the Task Manager.

### Note

*If you happen to be dealing with legacy 16-bit applications, you will want to keep an eye out for the NTVDM.EXE in the list of processes. These applications will need to run under the NT Virtual Dos Machine (NTVDM). All NTVDMs will appear the same except that the named threads that are running the various 16-bit applications will appear in the display indented from the NTVDM process. They will NOT have PIDs associated with them, as 16-bit applications actually run as threads within the NTVDM process.* ✦

## Process Explode

For even more detailed information about a process, you can turn to the Process Explode, PVIEW.EXE, from the NT Resource Kit. This bad boy has it all—PIDS, TIDs, Security Context for threads and processes, memory allocations in excruciating detail, and detailed information on each DLL being used. Figure 3.10 shows a sample display of the PVIEW.EXE examining the EXPLORER.EXE process.

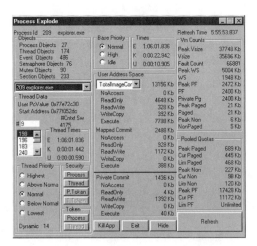

**Figure 3.10**    *PVIEW.EXE can display an incredible amount of information about any process running on a Windows NT system.*

After launching PVIEW.EXE, select the process in the leftmost combo box. The information in the rest of the display is updated immediately. Along the leftmost side, you will see the thread and security information. If you are having problems with threads or a process not being able to perform a particular task, or difficulty accessing a particular process, this is where you would look. You will also see a listing of the IDs for the various threads running within the process. When you highlight the individual threads, you will see detailed information on the run time for each one. You can observe the elapsed time ("E") as well as the user and kernel time that the thread has consumed during its existence. The center column focuses on the overall process. The process priority and the time counters appear near the top. This gives you an indication of whether the process is spending most of its time in user or Kernel mode.

Clicking the various priority buttons will indicate how much time the process is spending in the various priorities. A slow process with a lot of idle time can be an indication that you might want to reorganize the flow of data to keep the process generally occupied, as opposed to feast or famine. This depends in part on the type of application you are writing. Also down the middle column, you will see the user address space. You will find a second combo box here that allows you to select the various DLLs that the process has loaded. When you select one of the DLLs, the statistics for the DLL in that process are displayed. In this way, you can get very detailed in how memory is being used by your process.

The final column contains many of the now familiar counters. You will see information on the amount of memory and the number of page faults listed here. Overall this utility gives you a complete breakdown on most of the attributes and resource usage of your processes. These remain only descriptive statistics that allow you to tune the amount of memory that an application is using. You will still need to rely on the Performance Monitor to get a look at Performance Statistics and analyze trends or simulated loads. As I pointed out in Chapter 2, "Windows NT Kernel Debugger," the Performance Monitor is not the perfect tool. However, the Resource Kit provides some assistance.

# Performance Monitor Enhancements

The NT Resource Kit contains many tools for enhancing the abilities of the Performance Monitor. While there are several, the two presented here are the most useful: SETEDIT and the Monitor Service. As you will see shortly, these programs add to the functionality of the Performance Monitor. SETEDIT allows you to set up Performance Monitor to capture information on a process before that process has actually been started. The Monitor Service allows you to set up the Performance Monitor as a service, thus eliminating the requirement of a user being logged on to a system and recording data.

## SETEDIT

When you are using the Performance Monitor, you will sometimes want to monitor a process when it is first starting up. This is a problem since in the normal Performance Monitor Add to Chart dialog box, you must point and click on a particular object. You are not permitted to type in the value for an executable that you are looking for. For example, let's say you wanted to observe MS EXCEL.EXE when it is first starting. You go to the Performance Monitor Chart view and click on Edit and Add to Chart. You then select the Process Object. You soon realize that the EXCEL.EXE is not going to be in the list, but you have no way of specifying a process that isn't in the list of running processes.

You can use SETEDIT.EXE to compensate for this problem. SETEDIT appears like an odd combination of Chart and Log view of the Performance Monitor (see Figure 3.11). SETEDIT.EXE doesn't actually display any statistics. It gives you a method for preparing a Performance Monitor Chart Settings file—a *.PMC. This file can be read and used by the Performance Monitor to configure Chart view.

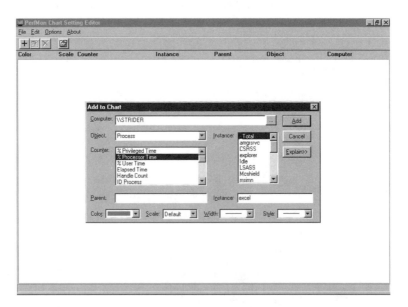

**Figure 3.11**    *The SETEDIT program looks much like the Performance Monitor; however, you will only be setting up a characteristics file and not doing any actual data capturing until you start the Performance Monitor.*

Let's walk through the process of using SETEDIT.EXE to specify a non-running process, usually called a Mortal Instance, as a target for analysis.

1. Open the SETEDIT.EXE.
2. Click on the "+" to open the Add to Chart dialog box.
3. Select the Process object.

   Notice that there are two Instance boxes. One is a listing of what is currently running on the system. The other is a text box that allows you to type in a value. Usually, it is better if you start your application and then select it from the List box. Then you won't have to worry about spelling the application's name correctly. Typically, you do not include the ".EXE" on the end of the executable's name.

4. Select a process or type a process name in the Instance text box.

   You are free to adjust the other parameters such as line style and color if you so desire. In our example, the Excel application's name was typed in and the EXPLORER.EXE name was selected from the list. Performing the steps above should result in a display similar to Figure 3.12.

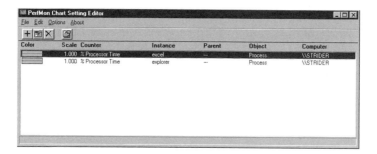

**Figure 3.12**   *SETEDIT is prepared to store information into a file for use by Performance Monitor to analyze the Excel or Explorer applications.*

5. Once you have the items that you wish to observe and have made any other configuration choices, click on File and Save Chart Settings.

   This will save the settings you have just configured to a *.PMC file.

6. Close SETEDIT and open the Performance Monitor.
7. Select File and Open from the Performance Monitor menu.
8. Select the file that you just saved in the SETEDIT.EXE program. As soon as you click on OK, the Performance Monitor will start displaying data. You will notice that the program isn't actually running yet and will have a value of zero for all of its data points. Figure 3.13 shows that once you start the application, the Performance Monitor will immediately begin collecting data.

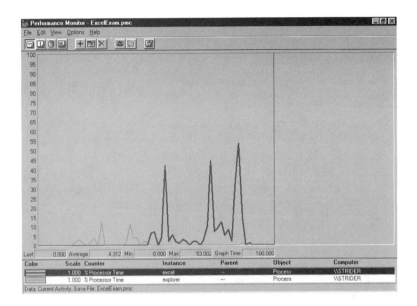

**Figure 3.13**    *Normally, you wouldn't even be able to achieve this type of analysis since the Performance Monitor wouldn't allow you to select the EXCEL.EXE of EXPLORER.EXE images unless they were already running.*

### Note

Whenever you are monitoring a process, remember to monitor the `ProcessID` counter. This is especially true in the case of the Mortal Instances that are being discussed in this section. If the process stops and starts repeatedly, strange results will appear in your reports and charts.

Tracking the `ProcessID` counter allows you to determine when a value is a legitimate peak or valley and the data point is simply due to the process stopping and starting. The `ProcessID` will fall to zero any time that a process stops. Extending the example above, if Excel were stopped, its `processID` would fall to zero and show up in the chart that way. The `%Processor Time` might also fall to zero, but it also might jump to 100%; both values are essentially erroneous. The process does not exist; therefore it is neither idle (processor usage at 0) nor is it consuming all of the processor. When you restart Excel, it might or might not receive the same PID. ◆

The SETEDIT program can also be used to modify the general settings for Performance Monitor's Chart view. With the SETEDIT.EXE program open, click on Options and Chart. The display will be identical to the information you see if you click on Options and Chart in the Performance Monitor. When you save the chart settings to a file, these options will be saved and later read  by the Performance Monitor.

## Performance Monitor Service

The Performance Monitor is an interactive tool. However, in some cases, the Performance Monitor needs to be running in the background, usually over extended periods of time. Usually programs you write do not run for hours, but you might actually have some type of batch process that does. Some heavy statistical packages run programs overnight, performing repeated regression mathematics. Examples might be of complex scientific data or financial forecasting information. You might not want to have an interactive process running on a locked workstation to monitor this process. For one, the interactive process is more intrusive, and might affect, to some extent, the processor and memory performance. Second, the potential for interruption is increased. You might be performing a test on a development server that any number of other developers could walk up to an interrupt by simply logging off. The NT Resource Kit contains a tool that allows you to configure and run the Performance Monitor as a service. This service is handy but has its pros and cons. Its characteristics are as follows:

- The service will run in the background as a real NT Service.
- Both logged data and alerts can be generated.
- There is a command line interface so the NT Schedule service can be used to configure the starting and stopping of the data collection.
- The service MUST be running on the same machine that is going to be the target of the data collection.
- You will need to log the data to a local hard drive.

Configuring this service involves a couple programs and a few steps. First, you will need the DATALOG.EXE and the MONITOR.EXE from the NT Resource Kit. The programs are found in the C:\NTRESKIT\PERFTOOL\ MEASTOOL folder if you have installed the NT Resource Kit to the C Drive. These two files should be copied to the %SystemRoot%\System32 folder of the machine that is going to be monitored. Here are the rest of the steps for installation and configuration:

1. Copy the MONITOR.EXE and DATALOG.EXE to the %SystemRoot%\System32 folder on the machine that will be the target of the analysis.

2. Open a command prompt and go to the %SystemRoot%\System32 folder.

3. Type the command MONITOR SETUP.

   A message will be displayed indicating a successful installation. It will also indicate that the service has been set to a manual startup mode. In other words, the service will not start when NT is rebooted. It will only start if specifically instructed to do so by user intervention.

   The MONITOR.EXE program is your interface to control the DATALOG.EXE service that you just installed. Before starting the service, you will need to tell it what you want it to collect. This is done through the Performance Monitor.

4. Open the Performance Monitor and create a *.PML or *.PMW file for the data logging service to use as a configuration file.

   This is done the same way you used the Performance Monitor to con-figure a regular log file back in Chapter 1—set the objects you want to collect, the interval for collecting samples, and the name of the log file. Make sure to point the Performance Monitor to the target machine. The easiest way to do this is to create the configuration file on the same machine you are eventually going to log the data to. Once you have your settings, click on File and Save in the Performance Monitor and save the log settings to a *.PML file in the %SystemRoot%\System32 folder. This ensures that the data logging service will be able to find the file. Alternatively, you can create a *.PMW, Performance Monitor Workspace, file. If you are going to use alerts along with logging, create a *.PMC file to make sure you get both sets of settings.

5. Now that you have the configuration file, you must notify the data log-ging service. Use the command MONITOR [configuration file]. This will inform the data logging service that it should use the configuration file mentioned to configure the Performance Monitor collection and alert process.

6. To start the process, type MONITOR START.

   When you are ready to stop the process, type MONITOR STOP at a com-mand prompt.

The actual MONITOR START and MONITOR STOP commands can be issued from any computer by including the computer name that you are addressing in the command, such as MONITOR \\STRIDER START where STRIDER is a machine name in my network that I am using the data logging service on.

You can use the NT Schedule service to issue the MONITOR commands. If you have repetitive testing going on over a few days, you can use the Schedule service to keep the log file from collecting information all the time and getting enormous. You might also want to use this same process if you are determining a baseline for the performance of your application. This would imply the use of some kind of simulation program, which is the topic of the next section. Consider using this process on a couple of your willing customers if your application is complex and has an enterprise-wide scope. This will help make sure you have configured the client's installation correctly and have improved recommendations for other clients down the road.

> *Note*
>
> *When using alerts, be cautious. If your alerts are configured to trigger an application to run, make sure that the application will never have any reason to interact with a user. This means ironclad error trapping, which rules out batch files. However, you can still use VBScript or JavaScript with the Windows Scripting Host (WSH) installed. This will allow for both error trapping and quick development. ◆*

# Simulators

Previously, you installed the Performance Monitor service for logging data. Now create a variety of situations that your application will need to run under. The Resource Kit comes in handy with a few tools for simulating various resource tensions on a machine.

## CPU Stress

CPUSTRES.EXE stresses out the processor (or processors as the case might be). Figure 3.14 displays the program's graphical interface that allows you to control up to four threads and their consumption of the processor's time.

Start by selecting the Process Priority Class. The process's threads will run with this as the base priority level. Within the base priority level, the threads can be adjusted to run above or below normal. Then you can adjust whether the CPU will stress to access shared memory. Shared memory essentially is controlled by the kernel-mode services; thus altering this setting will force more kernel-related CPU activity. In addition, it will simulate a certain amount of memory stress by forcing an increase in the File System Cache.

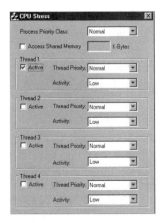

**Figure 3.14**    *CPUSTRES.EXE will launch up to four threads at a variety of priority and activity levels.*

Once that is set, click on the Active boxes next to the number of threads you want to be active. Then adjust the priority of each thread and how active or busy you want the thread to be. The result is a CPU that is as occupied as you would like it to be.

"Why do this?" you ask. Suppose you have targeted a production server as the recipient of your new enterprise SQL server-based application. The production server is already running MS SQL, so that is not a problem. However, using the Performance Monitor, you notice that the CPU is 68% busy already. This makes you stop and think about how your application might behave if the system were already under a great deal of stress. In addition, you wonder what your application might do to a system already at that level of CPU utilization. So, you get your test server and start up and configure CPUSTRES.EXE so that the system is about 68% busy. Then launch your application and observe the results in the Performance Monitor. While the simulation isn't exact, it is relatively quick and easy to do. Also, you now have some reassurance that your application will function well under situations when the CPU might be utilized by other machines.

## Memory Usage Simulations

Memory is clearly a valuable resource on any system. Simulating memory consumption is going to be valuable for application development and testing as well as general troubleshooting. The Windows NT Operating system provides a method for adjusting memory on its own through the manipulation of a boot file called BOOT.INI. The BOOT.INI file is a read-only, system file that is always located on the C:\ of an NT system. As we saw in Chapter 2, the BOOT.INI file is more than a simple listing for selecting which of the installed operating systems to boot. Parameters you supply can alter the way Windows NT operates. Chapter 2 demonstrated how parameters adjust the kernel debugger operations. The memory adjustments are similar.

The Windows NT Resource Kit contains valuable tools for simulating memory consumption with different goals and techniques. The first is CLEARMEM.EXE, which forces the applications to relinquish their hold on memory unless it is absolutely required. Here you will see how this helps diagnose problems as well as gives an excellent idea of how much memory your application is actually consuming. The LEAKAPP.EXE program slowly consumes memory and virtual memory. This tool allows you to see how your application reacts to containing memory shortages. It also serves as an excellent simulation of an application with a memory leak.

CLEARMEM.EXE and LEAKAPP.EXE are the NT Resource Kit tools that simulate memory consumption and assist in determining a minimum Working Set for applications. The minimum Working Set refers to the amount of memory that an application needs to load in physical RAM to continue to operate. When memory is extremely scarce, Windows NT will reduce the applications and services to their minimum Working Set allowing the entire system to continue to operate. Memory management is a key to the performance of the operating system as a whole. Controlling your applications' appetite for this cherished resource should be one of your top priorities when developing an elegant and efficient application.

### Adjusting Memory with BOOT.INI

Once a computer has completed its POST and has read the Master Boot Record, control is transferred to a program called NTLDR. This is the NT Loader program that controls the remainder of the boot sequence until the NTOSKRNL.EXE program assumes control. The C:\BOOT.INI file is the file that the NTLDR program reads, parses, and ultimately displays to the user. During the process, the NTLDR checks for any command line switches to be used or passed on to the NTOSKRNL.EXE. When your computer first starts to boot up the operating system, a text display on a black background lists your choices, typically something like:

```
Windows NT Workstation Version 4.00
Windows NT Workstation Version 4.00 [VGA mode]
```

This is followed by a countdown from 30 seconds, unless you have altered this value. As we saw in Chapter 2, the BOOT.INI has some command line options that can be used for troubleshooting. Here we can use a different conditional statement called MAXMEM to control the amount of memory that Windows NT will recognize on a system. Normally, Windows NT utilizes all memory available on the system. But, if you edit one of the lines in the BOOT.INI you can force NT to only recognize a subset of what is actually available. This can be used to simulate Windows NT running in various memory configurations without actually having to remove the chips from the system. The BOOT.INI file has the read-only and system DOS attributes set. You will need to alter the read-only attribute so you can edit the file. Once you have done that, open the file and copy the first line below the [operating systems] tag. Then, paste this line in somewhere else below the [operating system] tag. Edit this line, placing the /MAXMEM=[some value in MB] at the end. For example, if you want to test your workstation as if it only has 32MB of RAM as opposed to 96MB, alter your BOOT.INI to look similar to the one in Figure 3.15.

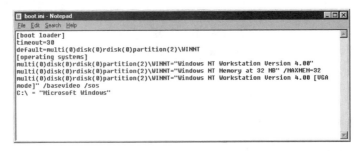

**Figure 3.15**    *This sample BOOT.INI has been modified so that a user can start NT with a configuration that recognizes only 32MB of RAM.*

The position of the line in the file determines the order in which it will be displayed when NT boots up. Be careful not to adjust the ARC commands, which tell the NTLDR where the NT operating system kernel files are.

### Note

*For more information on the ARC naming convention and its use with Windows NT, refer to the Windows NT Server Resource Kit, Volume 1—the Resource Guide.*

*As a suggestion, before you start altering the BOOT.INI file of a working machine, copy it to a floppy. You can then boot Windows NT from the floppy that contains a working copy of the BOOT.INI file if you run into a problem. Creating a boot floppy is easy. Just format a floppy on the Windows NT workstation or server. Then copy the following files:*

NTLDR

NTDETECT.COM

BOOTSECT.DOS

BOOT.INI

NTBOOTDD.SYS (only used on some systems)

*If you run into a problem with the BOOT.INI on the hard drive, pop the floppy in and boot the system.* ✦

Once you have made the adjustments to the BOOT.INI and saved them, you can boot the operating system and select the option you just created. The amount of memory, in our case 32MB, will appear on the blue screen that appears when the kernel is actually loading. Further, Windows NT will display in the diagnostics and other locations that it only has 32MB, despite the physical presence of more memory. Now you can test your system and applications as if they are running on a machine with only 32MB of RAM. This technique is primarily used as a method of benchmarking the performance of an application operating in restrictive memory conditions.

### Note

*The technique of reducing the memory that NT sees also comes in handy when you are having problems with a Blue Screen of Death, or kernel stop error. In such cases, a vendor or Microsoft might ask you to create a memory dump file for them to examine. The memory dump file is about the size of the amount of memory on your system. So if you have 128MB of RAM, the dump file will be at least that big. Sending that to Microsoft might be a bit of a problem depending on your Internet connectivity. If you tell Windows NT that it has only 32MB or RAM, you can create a memory dump file 32MB in size. This is a little more manageable.* ✦

## CLEARMEM.EXE

The BOOT.INI edit allows you to modify how much memory Windows NT sees, but it does not necessarily reduce the applications to their minimum Working Sets. In addition, it cannot be done dynamically. Although rebooting is easier than removing the cover and putting chips back in, it still is not the same as running a program. CLEARMEM.EXE will systematically force all of the applications and services to their minimum Working Set. This gives you a chance to see exactly how big the applications need to be under the very tightest memory conditions. This again helps you to make proper recommendations for the amount of memory required by your programs. Of course, your program's needs will change as various functions are executed.

Once you have used CLEARMEM.EXE to reduce the application down to its minimum size, you can observe it as you perform various functions to get an idea of how particular functions alter the program's Working Set size. This will help narrow down the features in your code that you need to work on. Another good use for the CLEARMEM.EXE is to help find applications with memory leaks. A memory leak is the plague of the developer as well as the scourge of the user. A memory leak slowly eats away at your precious stockpile of memory until nothing else can function and sometimes the entire system crashes. Some memory leaks can cause the Blue Screen of Death. Others, especially those in device drivers and Kernel mode services, can cause what I call the Black Screen of Oblivion. When this occurs, your system simply stops functioning, the screen goes black and the system reboots. No Blue Screens, no memory dump files, no event viewer messages—just a reboot. Whenever you find that you are rebooting your sever regularly once a month, a week, every few hours (yikes!), you should suspect a memory leak. Of course there are other causes of such problems. These problems usually involve faulty hardware, but the memory leak is by far the most common.

Running CLEARMEM.EXE is easy. You simply launch the application and wait. The tool will fill all of the memory that it can find on your system. Once allocated, it will attempt to access the memory as quickly as possible. This will force Windows NT to keep most of the CLEARMEM.EXE Working Set in physical RAM. Since CLEARMEM.EXE is consuming all of the RAM, all of the other processes on the system have to surrender all but the most critical portions of their memory. CLEARMEM.EXE will even access files and consume any left over memory dedicated to the file system cache. Once it has acquired all of the memory it can possibly get, it releases the memory. This will return the system to normal operation after a couple of minutes. During this whole process, you will want to be running the Windows NT Performance Monitor. When running the monitor, you generally should observe the following:

Process: Working Set for all process on the system

Memory: Available Memory

From these counters you will be able to tell when CLEARMEM.EXE has reached its peak and the other applications are at their minimum, as in Figure 3.16.

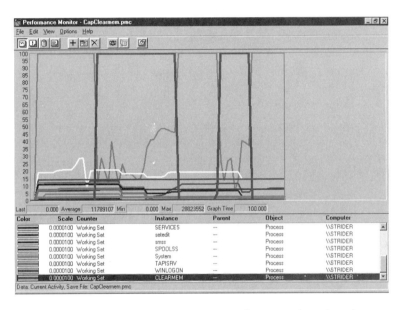

**Figure 3.16**   *CLEARMEM.EXE is working to reduce the other processes to their minimum Working Sets.*

Notice that the CLEARMEM.EXE's Working Set is increasing and eventually peaking. It is a good practice to run the CLEARMEM.EXE program twice in a row. The second run helps to stabilize CLEARMEM.EXE's hold on memory. At this time, the applications will be at their minimum. While using Performance Monitor's Chart view is nice for seeing what is going on in this case, you will most likely want to set up Performance Monitor to log the information. That way you can analyze step by step later. CLEARMEM.EXE's actions are best described as hostile. The consumption is quick and abruptly disruptive to the operating system and all processes. LEAKYAPP.EXE is more subtle and controlled in its approach, offering you other options in analysis.

### LEAKYAPP.EXE

This application takes a different approach to memory allocation than CLEARMEN.EXE. LEAKYAPP.EXE slowly consumes memory until it has stolen it all away. This is the typical behavior of an application that is experiencing a memory leak. The benefit of the LEAKYAPP.EXE is that you are allowed to watch the gradual reduction of memory and how your application might be reacting to this reduction. In addition, you can stop LEAKYAPP.EXE's consumption of memory at any point, so that you can perform any special analysis like exercising additional functions or waiting for your application to get used to its new restrictions. LEAKYAPP.EXE is a simple graphical application that displays a status line indicating the stage of memory consumption, and three buttons. Once started you can exit, start or stop leaking, or reset. Click on the Start Leaking button and away it goes.

When you first launch LEAKYAPP.EXE, you will notice that the status line already indicates a certain amount of memory in use. This is an indication of how much of the virtual memory the system has already allocated to other processes besides LEAKYAPP.EXE. The line will continue to increase once you have clicked on the Start Leaking button. During any point of the operation, you can click on the Stop Leaking button. This will stop the growth of the LEAKYAPP.EXE's Working Set, but will not release the memory it has already consumed. Clicking on the Start Leaking button will again start the process of consuming more and more memory. When you click on the Reset button or you close the application, LEAKYAPP.EXE will release all of the memory it has consumed up to that point. The system will return to normal operation. When you are looking at the LEAKYAPP.EXE and other processes on the system, you will again want to utilize the Performance Monitor. Below is a list of counters you will want to view when performing analysis:

```
Process: Private Bytes: leakyapp
Process: Working Set: for all instances of running processes
Memory: Available Bytes
Memory: Pages/sec
```

The Private Bytes will let you know how much memory LEAKYAPP.EXE has actually consumed. The Working Set counter for all of the processes will again tell you how much memory the processes are utilizing in their ever-constricting memory environment. The Pages/sec counter will give you a sampling of what a system looks like as far as paging is concerned when the memory availability is at its lowest. Figure 3.17 is a sample of what the Performance Monitor Chart view might look like when running LEAKYAPP.EXE.

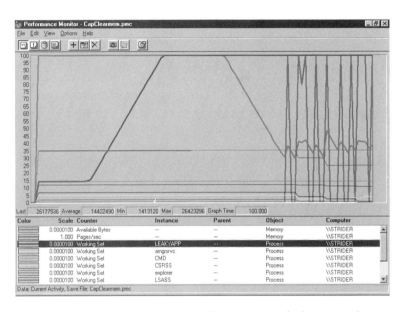

**Figure 3.17** *The LEAKYAPP.EXE offers a picture of what an application with a memory leak will look like. Keep in mind that a real leaky application's consumption of memory will typically be rather slow.*

Notice that when the Available memory closes in on 4MB, Windows NT's preferred minimum for available memory, the paging gets more frequent. The battle to maintain suitable available memory is being fought by the VMM. In this case, a click on the Reset button gives the victory to Windows NT. However, when it is a real application it is a little harder to find the leak to plug it.

*The Dark Side of LEAKYAPP.EXE*

*LEAKYAPP.EXE has the potential to cause the same problem as any other appli-
cation that is leaking memory. It can consume all of the memory until you finally
get erratic system behavior and potentially even a system crash. So, if you start it,
don't forget about it!* ◆

# Tracking Programs

In this final section, you are introduced to some utilities specifically geared
to track processes. The APIMON.EXE will allow you to trace applications
API calls and track their usage. The Heap Monitor will allow you to
observe the usage of memory heaps.

Before utilizing these tracking tools, you might need to modify some of
the Windows NT debugging flags. This is done by adjusting Global Flags
for the NT operating system.

## Global Flags

As programmers, you will usually put in some type of debug flag to be able
to run the program in a different mode or level of error reporting when you
are troubleshooting. Most often this is done through command line
switches. However, with NT another approach is taken—the Global Flags.
The Windows NT Registry has a section that specifically allows for the setting of flags that control many of the services and environmental subsystems
on Windows NT. Some of these switches have been incorporated into a
graphical tool as shown in Figure 3.18.

There is relatively little documentation on the Global Flags and not all of
them are included in this particular utility. The settings you will want to
generally make have to do with the Registry or the Kernel, as indicated by
the Radio button at the top of the display (see Figure 3.18).

After making any changes to the Global Flags, you generally need to
reboot the system. This is the safest way to make sure that settings are
applied. On some occasions, it is only necessary to stop and restart services
like the Server Service or Workstation Service, but it is simply easier to
reboot the server than try to keep clear which settings require what type of
action. Most of the Global Flags are required to be set when using another
tool like the Heap Monitor.

**Figure 3.18**    *The GFLAGS.EXE tool allows you to view and set some of the Global Flag values for the Kernel and other services.*

There are other tools from the *Software Development Kits* (SDK), *Device Driver Kits* (DDK), and other development environments that also require the use of Global Flags. In more detailed troubleshooting usually associated with the development of device drivers, you are required to install the check-build of the Windows NT operating system. The check-build will be larger and considerably slower than the normal retail-build of Windows NT. If you have ever run beta code for NT, you have experienced this behavior. Generally, it is best to use the Global Flags only when directed to do so when installing or using particular utilities. Many applications, like the API Monitor, are simply going to use APIs and some system permissions to do their troubleshooting.

### The Danger of Global Flags

*If you feel the need to experiment with Global Flags, make sure that you are doing it on a system that you can afford to crash. Global Flags generally enable debugging features within the operating system and its Kernel mode processes. Debugging can lead to instability as additional code and interference is being created by having to run through debug routines.* ◆

## APIMON

The APIMON.EXE, or API Monitor, allows you to track the activity of a particular application. It will detail the various calls to API functions. API Monitor will also show you the DLLs that have been loaded and which ones were actually utilized. It will track the amount of time your application has spent in various functions and DLLs. The API Monitor can trace the applications calls and display some information on the nature of the API call. In addition, it can display information on the page faults generated by the application.

You must first launch the API Monitor application. Then open a program to execute and start the monitor. As the program is executed, the API records the information to the screen.

Examine what is happening as the application is running or review the information afterward. This tool is used to profile how the application is running and the APIs/DLLs that it is utilizing to perform its operations. You will want to pay specific attention to the number of times a particular API is called and where it is loaded. This is important when trying to group functions within your code. Also, pay attention to calls to Kernel mode DLLs, since these have that added cost of transitioning to Kernel mode. To begin, let's walk through the use of an API Monitor:

1. Launch the APIMON.EXE, a graphical utility.

2. Click on File and Open to select the executable you will be running.

3. Click on ToolBox or Tools and Options from the menu.

   The Miscellaneous options are actually the most interesting. Here you will want to at least Enable Tracing and Enable Counters so that you can get some meaningful information. Tracing will allow API Monitor to track the actions of your program as they are happening. You might also wish to turn on the monitor page faults. That way you can observe which of the DLLs is most prone to issues of paging. Then click Apply or OK.

4. Start the monitoring by clicking the green arrow.

   While the system is monitoring data it will refresh the various screens as seen in Figure 3.19.

If you have enabled tracing, you can click on the magnifying glass icon on the toolbar. This will open Trace View window. In this window, you will see a listing of the API function calls in the order that they were made, along with the first four parameters that were used in the call.

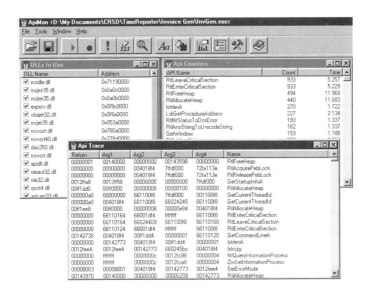

**Figure 3.19**  *The API Monitor will collect and display several types of statistics about the APIs and DLLs being used by your application.*

When you are done collecting information, close the application or stop monitoring. At this point, you will be able to view the information in the API Monitor display, save the data, or view some graphical representations of the data. You will usually end up with three windows of information: the API Counters, the API Trace, and the DLLs in Use. The API Trace has already been discussed. The API Counters window is a display of all the API function calls, along with the number of times that they were called and the overall time spent in the function. This is a method of deciphering how much time your application is spending executing various functions. This information can influence your decision to create groups of functions or code the flow of your program to improve its utilization of the APIs. The DLLs in Use window will list all of the DLLs that were loaded. A check mark will appear to the left of the DLLs that had functions that were utilized. Empty check boxes potentially mean DLLs were initialized but not utilized in the code. This will help identify DLLs that are not necessary for the proper execution of your application and can thus be removed from the declarations.

When you click on the Tools and Write Data to Log File, the API Monitor will record the information it has collected regarding the API calls, DLLs, and the API Trace to log files. By default, the log files are stored in the %windir% folder, usually C:\WINNT on a standard Windows NT installation. The file names are APIMON.LOG and APITRACE.LOG. The log files will contain more information than what was actually displayed, although the listing might be long. You can leisurely review the information to make a determination on the flow of your code.

## Heap Monitor

Windows NT controls various sections of committed memory for temporary storage of various objects. Applications are able to request pieces of this memory from a process heap that is created in a 10MB chunk for each process initially. The use of the various heaps on the system and especially those used by your applications are indicators of an efficient (or inefficient) use of memory. The Heap Monitor allows you to view information about the way that your program is using this memory. To monitor your application, start the application or service that you have written. Then find the PID by using either TLIST.EXE or PULIST.EXE as mentioned previously. Once you have your process's PID, issue the command HEAPMON.EXE –p [PID]and the Heap Monitor will begin tracing your application's usage of memory. The HEAPMON.EXE screen is a text-based screen as seen in Figure 3.20.

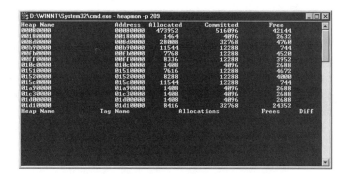

**Figure 3.20**    *HEAPMON.EXE is displaying information on a process utilization of memory.*

### Note

*Recall that the tools in the Resource Kit are separated in subfolders from the default C:\NTRESKIT. Most of the performance tools are in the \NTRESKIT\Perftool folder. In the case of HEAPMON.EXE, you will need to look in the NTRESKIT\Perftool\Meastool folder. This will also be true of the CPU Stress as well as LEAKYAPP.EXE. APIMON.EXE will be at the root of the NTRESKIT folder.* ◆

Generally, when working with the applications, the various heaps created for the process will not have a specific name. They will be designated, as seen in figure 3.20, by their location in memory. In some cases of Kernel mode processes, like the Win32 subsystem, the heaps will have specific names and purposes, like GDI Heap and the Desktop Heap. Each of these is utilized for specific functions within the process. In your case, you will simply want to watch for the changes in the allocation of the heaps as you perform various functions within your application. If you find that a particular heap is continuing to grow without returning the memory allocation back to the global or system heap, then you might have a memory leak.

# Summary

In this chapter, you were outfitted with an arsenal of tools and utilities to start some real investigative work into performance monitoring your applications. These tools, along with the Performance Monitor, offer a variety of methods for detailed and quick analysis of resource utilization and behind-the-scenes operation of applications and the operating system below them. Along the way, you were exposed to some of the NT architecture, which should prove useful as you move forward toward more advanced investigative techniques. Before launching into applying these tools more directly to application development issues, there are more tools that you need to add to your already impressive arsenal. These tools don't come from Microsoft, but they are very powerful and useful in performance analysis. We will look at these tools in the next chapter.

# 4

# Freeware/Shareware Tools

While Microsoft packs as much as they can into the operating systems, we will always say, "I wish I had a tool to…" Microsoft has attempted to grant our wishes with the Windows NT Resource Kit and the software tools included on the CD. However, it is foolish to think that a single company or group of individuals can provide all of the computing needs of the user community. Besides, there are more ways to do things, even in Windows NT, than the Microsoft way. This is where other programmers like you come in. You can find a large variety of tools and utilities on the Web today. Some are useful, others are not. Sometimes just finding these tools is the trick; other times trying to figure out how to use them is the real challenge. Many times, I have acquired a free tool only to find that there is zero documentation and poor help file. I know documentation is a hassle sometimes. After all, we are programmers not writers, for the most part. This section of the book is dedicated to providing you with information about some of tools that I have found exceptionally useful. I have focused on a set of tools that are easy to locate, consistently well done, and are usually accompanied by enough information to get you using them quickly. Of course, the fact that these tools are free is an attraction as well.

Because these tools are free, you don't need your boss's approval, a purchase requisition, or a note from your mother to use them. You just need an Internet connection to download the tools. For the purpose of this chapter, I will stick with the common industry terms of shareware and freeware. All of the utilities here are of the freeware type, but also usually have a shareware or even commercial version that includes more advanced features.

### A Word of Caution about "Free" Software

*Keep in mind that no matter where you get the software, you will find some good stuff and some bad stuff. For this reason, a certain amount of caution should be taken when trying out new software, especially the freeware and shareware varieties. In the case of freeware, you haven't even paid the developer, so why should they assume any of the risk? Therefore, when you crank up a new utility, do it on a workstation that you are not too worried about messing up. Costing you a half day of work while you rebuild your machine is one thing; but crippling the entire development staff because you loaded a nasty little program on the development server, is another. The tools here will not cause you any problems on Windows NT 4.0 through Windows 2000, no matter what service pack revision you are on. However, due to the nature of some of the APIs and other sneaky little actions these tools perform, using them on Windows 3.51 will produce unknown results.* ♦

Because the focus of this book is on performance monitoring, I stuck with the tools that can be used for monitoring a program's activities and performance. The first tools, FILEMON and REGMON, both monitor the system's access to particular types of objects. FILEMON monitors files and folders and REGMON monitors Registry accesses. Both of these tools have assisted me on numerous occasions when trying to figure out what a program is doing with all of its time. The next tool is WINOBJ. It basically displays, in an Explorer-type format, all of the objects in the system's namespace. This tool is useful when you are getting unusual errors about access to system resources. I have also included a tool that allows you to analyze open handles that any application on the system might have. Open handles are one of the leading causes of memory leaks and general memory resource utilization. Keeping tabs on what is being used on a system is always important.

While some of the tools have counterparts that must be paid for, I have stuck with the freebies. Generally, the purchased version of the utility includes a few added functions, which I will point out when applicable or useful. All of these tools come from a great Web site called www.sysinternals.com. They are constantly producing new tools and updating the old ones, so you might want to make this particular site a common stop while browsing the Internet.

### Note

*Systems Internals™ is run by Mark Russinovich and Bryce Cogswell. Both gentlemen have written articles for a number of technical magazines. Mark is a regular in the Windows NT Magazine™ publication. Bryce is a contributing editor for Dr Dobb's Journal. Both have a Ph.D. from Carnegie Mellon University. While their credentials and background are impressive, what is really important is that they have been producing quality tools and utilities for Windows and Windows NT for a number of years. At the www.sysinternals.com site, you will find a variety of white papers and other Windows internal information in addition to all of the cool utilities. A software company called Winternals Software produces copies of their tools for general sale. ◆*

# File Monitor

Sometimes you have the opportunity to create code from scratch. Many times you are either working on a program that was written by a previous developer, or is being written by a development team. As a result, you know your way around the code that controls the functionality you are responsible for, but not for the code of the other developers. Some applications are very complex, and/or have been developed and redeveloped over a period of time. Information about how the code performs certain functions can be lost. This can lead to problems in development, run time errors, and performance problems. Thus, investigative tools, such as FILEMON and the subsequent REGMON, have a purpose in life—to assist in determining how code is performing particular functions and where it is getting its information.

File Monitor has assisted me on several occasions when code produced errors such as "File Not Found," "Unexpected error: (2)," or "Unexpected error: (5)." These errors generally indicate that you are having a problem accessing something, usually a file, although there are many other types of objects in Windows that it can be. The File Monitor can assist you in figuring out exactly what file this program is trying to examine, which can help you resolve problems in access or corruption. In addition, FILEMON allows you to see what type of files are being accessed and how often. This can often assist in figuring out performance problems.

### File Monitor Put to Use

*I was once working with a group that was involved in writing code for collecting financial information and performing complex analysis. The program had been around for some time and was having several sections rewritten. The program collected data in the form of loosely formatted text files from multiple machines on a wide area network. The information was brought into a central server, where various mathematical calculations representing a series of "what-if" scenarios were performed on the data and then reported. The calculations were recursively run altering only select parameters each time. This produced the effect of trying to predict what would happen, should financial conditions in the United States change. This is a common sort of activity for any company managing mutual funds, large stocks, bonds, derivatives, or generally involved in high volume banking.*

*Due to the volume of information and the recursive nature of the calculations, the process took six hours to complete. Code rewriting was done in an attempt to consolidate common functions and resolve issues with the calculations. Consolidating the common functions, we hoped would result in a smaller footprint in memory, as well as faster running code.*

*One week before we were going to move the application to production, we were running some mock tests on the application to see if we had actually improved the performance of calculations. It was a standard test run against a copy of the production database. Much to our dismay, the application was taking more than twice as long as before to produce the information. We ran Performance Monitor on the system to see what was going on. During the calculations portion of the application, the disk activity was up to almost 85%. While we had a number of calculations to perform, the writes back to the database were done relatively serially at the end of the calculation sets. This generally produced a large memory requirement, but our hardware configuration had allotted for such a requirement. Repeated tests displayed the same activity. The old code was run and did not have the problem.*

*When we came across the FILEMON utility, we hoped to use it to gather information about what files were actually being accessed on the hard drive. We suspected the database, but the statistics on the database performance seemed to show nothing unusual. With the FILEMON utility loaded, we ran the application again. The utility displayed a series of files that were being created and populated with information regarding each calculation, the parameters, and the results. Given the number of the calculations and the recursive method that was calling them, the frequency the files were being written to was incredible and was clearly a strain on the overall system. With a little more investigation into the code, we found that one of the programmers had created a series of log files to trace the calculations' activity in an effort to debug the mathematics. In limited test runs, this did not produce a problem. On the production-level data, the problem was obvious.*

*This experience shows that the FILEMON tool has some immediate applications. It also demonstrates the point that when you are putting debug code in, it is best to have a trigger of some type associated with the debug code. At least if you have a debug switch that must be run, the debugging conditions in your code will produce a minimal amount of impact. Still the ultimate solution is to always remember to remove such calls from the code prior to delivering to production.* ◆

## How It Works

The FILEMON, as described by the developers, is implemented as a file system driver. In order for the FILEMON program to track the activity of all of the applications on the system, it is best to go to the source of where all of the File I/O must occur. The File I/O must occur within the I/O Manager, one of Windows NT's Executive Services. The I/O Manager is responsible for practically all of the input and output functions on the Windows NT. Essentially, the I/O Manager is a combination of device drivers and I/O queuing mechanisms that work together to perform efficient input and output operations. When considering the File I/O, there are basically two types of requests that need to be tracked, *I/O Request Packets* (IRPs) and Fast I/O requests.

### Note

*The FILEMON utility, as well as many of the others mentioned in this chapter, actually works on Windows 9x as well as Windows NT. Because we are primarily concerned with Windows NT here, it will be the focus of the explanation. In Windows 9x, the FILEMON utility will produce the same output; however, the method of acquiring the information is different than described here. The Web site of the developer of FILEMON offers more information on how FILEMON operates with Windows 9x.* ◆

### I/O Request Packets (IRPs)

When an application needs to move data from a file or to a file, a request is made to one of the I/O Manager's threads. The request is packaged into an I/O Request Packet and placed in a queue. An IRP is queued based on the priority of the request. Another thread of the I/O Manager is servicing the queued transactions by directing them to an appropriate driver for processing. The I/O Manager handles more than disk I/O; the various drivers can be fault tolerance drives, customized vendor drivers, CDFS drivers, or network drivers. In any case, once the transaction is written, the original application is notified that its particular I/O request has been satisfied. The I/O Manager will generally perform this activity synchronously with respect to the application. However, not all applications are written equally. If the application is designed specifically for synchronous I/O, the application will, prior to continuing with another task, wait until the I/O Manager has notified it that the transaction is complete.

### Fast I/O Requests

The other I/O activity is the Fast I/O Request. This is a method that applications or other Executive Services can use to bypass the I/O Manager in order to speed up the process of reading/writing data. Fast I/O is used when the needed information is found in the File System Cache, as opposed to the hard drive. This type of I/O is only available to a synchronous application. Applications that run asynchronously require the creation of an IRP primarily because paging can cause an application not to be handled in a truly asynchronous fashion. Also, this would generally affect the performance of the application and the system as a whole. Yet, synchronous applications are generally handled in the Fast I/O manner. However, file locking can affect the application's ability to be handled in this particular manner. The file system drive handles the determination of whether the request can be handled through Fast I/O or not. When checking for proper conditions, it looks to see if the file in question has any other requests or locks. If there are locks, the I/O is handled through the I/O Manager as an IRP. The Cache Manager thread of the I/O Manager tracks which files are in the cache, but can not track which sections of the files are locked. This functionality is only provided through the other threads of the I/O Manager via an IRP. Therefore, the I/O Manager is sent an IRP to handle the I/O for this particular operation.

In either case, the FILEMON being implemented as a file system driver is able to create and attach objects to the file system device objects. This allows the utility to see all of the IRPs and the Fast I/O requests directed at the drives. FILEMON then records the information on the type of call and the handle associated with the call. FILEMON uses this information to track backwards and associate the particular IRP or Fast I/O with the process that created it. FILEMON then records  start FILEMON in order to use it. Once running, the utility will immediately begin displaying information about the files that it is accessing on the system. Simply watching this tool, even when no other application is open, is enlightening, as you can see in Figure 4.1.

| # | Time | Process | Request | Path | Result | Other |
|---|------|---------|---------|------|--------|-------|
| 5189 | 9:14:00 PM | Explorer.exe | IRP_MJ_CREATE | C:\TEMP | SUCCESS | Attributes: N |
| 5190 | 9:14:00 PM | Explorer.exe | IRP_MJ_CLEANUP | C:\TEMP | SUCCESS | |
| 5191 | 9:14:00 PM | Explorer.exe | IRP_MJ_CLOSE | C:\TEMP | SUCCESS | |
| 5192 | 9:14:00 PM | Explorer.exe | FSCTL_IS_VOLUME_... | C:\NTSRV\Profiles\Administrator\Desktop | SUCCESS | |
| 5193 | 9:14:00 PM | Explorer.exe | IRP_MJ_CREATE | C:\TEMP | SUCCESS | Attributes: Ar |
| 5194 | 9:14:00 PM | Explorer.exe | IRP_MJ_DIRECTORY... | C:\TEMP | SUCCESS | FileBothDirec |
| 5195 | 9:14:00 PM | Explorer.exe | IRP_MJ_DIRECTORY... | C:\TEMP | SUCCESS | FileBothDirec |
| 5196 | 9:14:00 PM | Explorer.exe | IRP_MJ_DIRECTORY... | C:\TEMP | NO MOR... | FileBothDirec |
| 5197 | 9:14:00 PM | Explorer.exe | IRP_MJ_CLEANUP | C:\TEMP | SUCCESS | |
| 5198 | 9:14:00 PM | Explorer.exe | IRP_MJ_CLOSE | C:\TEMP | SUCCESS | |
| 5199 | 9:14:00 PM | Explorer.exe | FSCTL_IS_VOLUME_... | C:\NTSRV\Profiles\Administrator\Desktop | SUCCESS | |
| 5200 | 9:14:00 PM | Explorer.exe | IRP_MJ_CREATE | C:\WINDOWS | SUCCESS | Attributes: N |
| 5201 | 9:14:00 PM | Explorer.exe | IRP_MJ_CLEANUP | C:\WINDOWS | SUCCESS | |
| 5202 | 9:14:00 PM | Explorer.exe | IRP_MJ_CLOSE | C:\WINDOWS | SUCCESS | |
| 5203 | 9:14:00 PM | Explorer.exe | FSCTL_IS_VOLUME_... | C:\NTSRV\Profiles\Administrator\Desktop | SUCCESS | |
| 5204 | 9:14:00 PM | Explorer.exe | IRP_MJ_CREATE | C:\WINDOWS | SUCCESS | Attributes: Ar |
| 5205 | 9:14:00 PM | Explorer.exe | IRP_MJ_DIRECTORY... | C:\WINDOWS | SUCCESS | FileBothDirec |
| 5206 | 9:14:00 PM | Explorer.exe | IRP_MJ_DIRECTORY... | C:\WINDOWS | SUCCESS | FileBothDirec |
| 5207 | 9:14:00 PM | Explorer.exe | IRP_MJ_CLEANUP | C:\WINDOWS | SUCCESS | |
| 5208 | 9:14:00 PM | Explorer.exe | IRP_MJ_CLOSE | C:\WINDOWS | SUCCESS | |
| 5209 | 9:14:00 PM | Explorer.exe | FSCTL_IS_VOLUME_... | C:\NTSRV\Profiles\Administrator\Desktop | SUCCESS | |
| 5210 | 9:14:00 PM | Explorer.exe | IRP_MJ_CREATE | C:\WINNT | SUCCESS | Attributes: N |
| 5211 | 9:14:00 PM | Explorer.exe | IRP_MJ_CLEANUP | C:\WINNT | SUCCESS | |
| 5212 | 9:14:00 PM | Explorer.exe | IRP_MJ_CLOSE | C:\WINNT | SUCCESS | |
| 5213 | 9:14:00 PM | Explorer.exe | FSCTL_IS_VOLUME_... | C:\NTSRV\Profiles\Administrator\Desktop | SUCCESS | |
| 5214 | 9:14:00 PM | Explorer.exe | IRP_MJ_CREATE | C:\WINNT | SUCCESS | Attributes: Ar |
| 5215 | 9:14:00 PM | Explorer.exe | IRP_MJ_DIRECTORY... | C:\WINNT | SUCCESS | FileBothDirec |
| 5216 | 9:14:00 PM | Explorer.exe | IRP_MJ_CLEANUP | C: DASD | SUCCESS | |
| 5217 | 9:14:00 PM | System | IRP_MJ_CLOSE | C: DASD | SUCCESS | |
| 5218 | 9:14:00 PM | Explorer.exe | IRP_MJ_DIRECTORY... | C:\WINNT | SUCCESS | FileBothDirec |
| 5219 | 9:14:00 PM | Explorer.exe | IRP_MJ_CLEANUP | C:\WINNT | SUCCESS | |
| 5220 | 9:14:00 PM | Explorer.exe | IRP_MJ_CLOSE | C:\WINNT | SUCCESS | |
| 5221 | 9:14:01 PM | System | IRP_MJ_WRITE* | C:\NTSRV\Profiles\Administrator\ntuser.LOG | SUCCESS | Offset: 0 Len |
| 5222 | 9:14:01 PM | System | IRP_MJ_SET_INFOR... | C:\NTSRV\Profiles\Administrator\ntuser.dat.LOG | SUCCESS | FileEndOfFile |

**Figure 4.1**    *The FILEMON display fills quickly with information about the various file I/O requests on the system, many of which are related to operating system activities.*

In generating Figure 4.1, EXPLORER.EXE was opened. This caused a series of file accesses as the system enumerated several folders and files. In addition, you will see system accesses to several files of the type .DAT and .LOG. These are the Registry hives being accessed. Files like NTUSER.DAT and associated logs are the user's profile information being queried. Recall that some of these activities are related to Fast I/O, meaning that the information being requested is actually being read from the File System Cache. The type of access is specified in the request column of the display. For example, a Fast I/O request will have the "FASTIO_" in the first part of the description in the request column. Other requests begin with the "IRP" designation, indicating that an I/O Request Packet has been generated and the I/O Manager will be querying or writing to the hard drive or other such media. Recall that this can include the network.

Utilizing the FILEMON is most useful when the filters are applied to make sure that you are zeroing in on the right file activity or a particular process that is in question. The filter conditions are set in the Filter dialog box, which is shown in Figure 4.2. For the Filter dialog box, press Ctrl-F or click on Event and Filter.

**Figure 4.2**    *The Filter dialog box allows you to specify processes or files that may be included or excluded when tracking file activity.*

The conditions include the process name and the file path. In both cases you may specify to include or exclude a particular set of files or processes. One easy and often beneficial filter is to exclude the files in the %SYSTEMROOT% folder. By doing this, you can eliminate the interference from the operating system activity. Of course, you might also miss some of the activity from the process that you are curious about. Knowing at least a little about the application that you are dealing with always helps. Let's take a simple example. We want to track the activity of NOTEPAD.EXE. If you have FILEMON running and open NOTEPAD.EXE, as in Figure 4.3, you will see an abundant amount of activity.

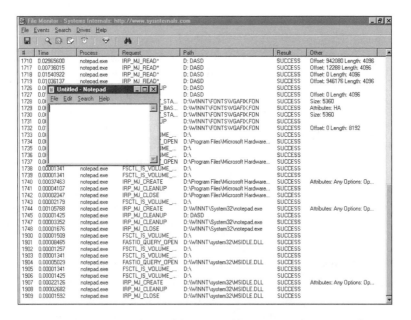

**Figure 4.3**    *Even a simple program like NOTEPAD.EXE will generate plenty of file access activity, even before a file open request is made.*

This activity will include numerous calls into the %SYSTEMROOT%, in our case the D:\NTSRV folder. These calls include references to various DLLs, INI files, and Registry hives. However, if we wish to look more closely at how NOTEPAD.EXE accesses the files on general open and close functions, we can be more specific with FILEMON parameters, as seen in Figure 4.4.

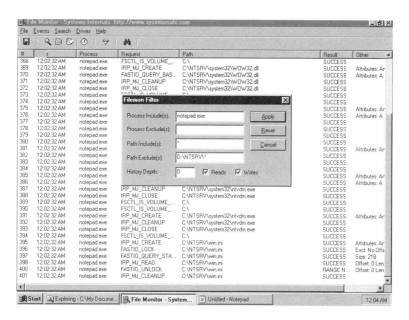

**Figure 4.4**  *By setting the process parameter seen here, we can effectively eliminate the operating system and extraneous calls to DLLs, INIs, and Registry hives made by NOTEPAD.EXE when it starts up.*

The parameters in Figure 4.4 result in a more focused display. Only the information regarding NOTEPAD.EXE and its interaction with the file that is opening and closing is represented. In addition, another feature of the FILEMON can assist in describing the type of access in more detail. This is the Time feature that appears as a clock on the toolbar. This Time feature will alternate and display the time of the occurrence as well as the duration of the occurrence. In Figure 4.3, you can see that the time column—second column from the left—displays the time of day. Clicking on the Clock icon in the toolbar alternates the display after that point to give you the amount of time spent fulfilling the particular request. Notice that this represents a change in the data the FILEMON drivers are collecting. Clicking on the Clock icon does not affect the Time column for previous data points collected and displayed.

Using a duration clock, as opposed to the time of day, can give you an indication of exactly how your application's I/O operations are divided among the files being accessed. For some systems that are accessing logs repeatedly, the duration clock can be of some benefit. Consider a transaction-based system. In order to apply some fault tolerance to the transactions, generate a log file for each transaction and then apply changes based on the transaction log. This is comparable to a database system like MS SQL Server or even the NTFS file system logging mechanism. The transaction record in the log file contains the information required for carrying out the transaction as well as instructions for handling the transaction in different stages, should problems arise.

Examining such a system with the FILEMON can be enlightening. You can anticipate seeing a large amount of activity surrounding access to the log files used for the transactions, as well as in the transaction file or database itself. Seeing this might make you encourage your customers to place the log files on a separate physical disk system in order to significantly improve performance. Of course, you would have hoped that some developer who originally wrote the code would have thought of this to begin with. However, with more complex systems, such details can often be missed or thought to be potentially included later given aggressive time tables for development.

The FILEMON also includes other handy features. The basic search functions are present, allowing you to look for content in any of the columns. The ability to save the captured data is very handy when attempting to diagnose problems that occur sporadically, which are usually the most challenging problems to diagnose. Last, you may specify the drives that you wish to examine. By default, the utility assumes all local hard drives are monitored. You can also include Name Pipes, Mail Slots, Floppy, Removable Media, and CDs.

All in all, this tool offers you the ability to closely track file access and describe in detail the type of files, types of access, and duration of accesses on the file system. This tool, in combination with the disk statistics from the Performance Monitor forms a fine arsenal for troubleshooting and analyzing performance.

# REGMON

The FILEMON utility is very useful and includes information on process access to the Registry hives, but the REGMON goes even further. The Registry is a great labyrinth of knowledge. Within it are treasures both obvious and hidden. Every component within Windows NT and running on the system as an application uses the Registry in some form. REGMON can be used as a spy to track every access to the Registry and leave bread crumbs behind to allow you to find your way back to the treasures. Often you can use the tool to:

Find information to diagnose application configuration problems.

Track down data on driver parameters.

Discover undocumented/unpublished Registry locations.

Track down how/when alterations to the Registry are being made.

## How It Works

The REGMON utility uses some of the same principles as the FILEMON utility; however, the details of the implementation are quite different. When you are monitoring the Registry, you have the same problem that you encounter when you are trying to watch all file activity. You need a central location where you can insert a driver or another type of process that can track and record the activity. In the case of FILEMON, we saw that a File System driver-based filter is used to track the changes. The driver associated itself and its functions with the central I/O Manager driver system. This allowed for the tracking of the file activity. With the REGMON utility, the implementation is different because there is no I/O Manager function that encompasses all Registry accesses. Instead, there is a series of Registry system calls that respond to requests for access to the Registry. One common way to access such system calls is through the Registry API functions. When a system call is passed to the Windows NT handler down in Kernel mode, a system call handler is looked up in a list. The request is passed to this handler and fulfilled. A response is then returned to the application.

As you can see with Registry access, there is no opportunity to implement a simple drive to consolidate and track all of the read/write activity. To solve this problem, the developers of REGMON created a method called *system call hooking*. The method calls for the utility to replace the pointers in NT's list of handlers with pointers to the REGMON functions. REGMON is thus able to intercept all of the system calls that would otherwise respond to requests to read or write to the Registry. The REGMON utility has the ability then to record information regarding the type of request being made and even records the results of that request. REGMON acts as a passive function, simply recording the information and then passing the request on to the Registry call handler that would normally process the request. When the normal handler completes the request, it passes the result back to the REGMON handler, which in turn passes it back to the NT system call handler. Last, the data is returned to the calling application. The implementation of REGMON is quite elegant in its approach. It is both simple and independent of the version of Windows NT being run.

## Note

*For more information on this particular technique, you can look at a couple of articles written by the developers:*

Russinovich, Mark and Bryce Cogswell, "Windows NT System Call Hooking," *Dr. Dobb's Journal* (January, 1997).

"Inside NT Utilities," *Windows NT Magazine* (February, 1999). ◆

This process occurs completely in Kernel mode, so the impact to performance is not too great. However, once you run the utility you will see how often NT actually accesses the Registry. The number of accesses can affect performance in some cases. Generally, the number of system calls per second will be increased. While this will increase the amount of processor resources consumed, it generally will have little affect on most applications.

### The Effect of REGMON on a System

*When I read vendor information about a particular application, I occasionally want to verify some of the vendor's claims regarding their applications, especially their claims about the effects on performance. This is especially true for enterprise level applications that I am considering for major deployment in my client's enterprise. The last thing I want to do is roll out an application that drastically disrupts the performance of their systems or network. In the case of REGMON, I was simply curious about the effect that the application had on the system. It is best to know how your analysis tool will affect the system you are trying to analyze. Remember the Heisenberg Uncertainty Principle? Based on this analysis, you will clearly not want to run this utility on any system over extended periods of time; it is simply not that kind of tool.*

*With REGMON, I performed a simple test. I first created a performance baseline. This was done in the usual manner—using Performance Monitor on a system running Windows NT 4.0 Service Pack 5.0 9128-bit version. The Performance Monitor was configured to log performance data on the processor, memory, physical disk, and the system. The System Performance object has counters for* Systems Calls/Sec *and* Processor Queue Length, *which are used to determine the applications effect on the processor. Several standard NT administrative tools were run—User Manager, Server Manager, and Event Viewer. The User Manager was expected to have the greatest effect on the tests, because the user account information for NT is stored in Registry hives. These tools were simply started and then closed in a serial fashion.*

*continues* ▶

▶ *continued*

*This same test was performed when the REGMON utility was open and collecting information on the accessed Registry keys. Upon comparing the two sets of data, the* System Calls/Sec *were found to be higher on the average by about 47%. The affect on the processor, a Pentium II 266 MHz, was about the same—46%. The* %Processor Time *was around 12.5% in the second trial. Note that the Performance Monitor is reading information from the Registry as well as the tools that we are running. This access, occurring once per second, happened in both trials. The effect of the Performance Monitor was the same in both trials and thus did not account for the differences.* ◆

# Using REGMON

We talked earlier about how the REGMON utility had a variety of uses. Some of these are that Windows NT uses the Registry to store all sorts of information about software, hardware, networking, and services. The more you know about the Registry's contents, the more you know about how Windows NT operates. There are countless times that I have attempted to determine where an application is getting a particular parameter or why a COM/DCOM function is not working properly. This information is, of course, in the Registry. However, finding it is the true challenge in most cases. The REGMON tool offers you the ability to see inside NT's internal network of information.

Once the utility is started, it will immediately begin collecting information, as you can see in Figure 4.5. The display is a simple listing of columns.

The First column is a sequential number. The second column is the process name that is making the request. The third column is the type of request. The type of request has a greater range than you might expect when compared to file access, as follows:

Query Value

Set Value

Delete Value Key

Enumerate Value

Create Key

Enumerate Key

Open Key

Close Key

Query Key

Delete Key

Flush Key

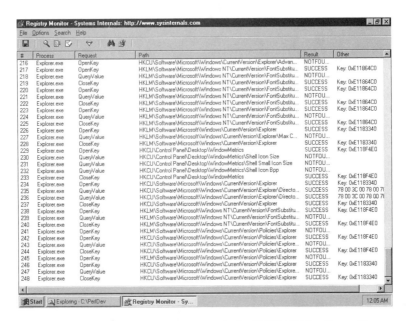

**Figure 4.5**  *As soon as it is opened, the REGMON utility will capture a large amount of information on all Registry accesses.*

Most of these values are self-explanatory; some aren't as clear. Clearly, the Set and Query functions for Value and Key are essentially the same as write and read. The Create Key is used to create a sub-key that did not exist prior to that time. The Enumerate functions are used to obtain a listing or immediate sub-tree structure, which would apply to the keys and sub-keys within the Registry. The delete functions are used when deleting a key. Prior to and just after changes, you will see Flush Key activities, which push the changes out to the hive files on the hard drive. Access to the Registry will take the same form as access to most objects on Windows NT:

- Open Key functions obtain a handle to the specific key and establish the access permissions you will be exercising using this particular handle.

- Operative functions like enumerate, query, create, and delete use the handle to the key that you previously opened. The functions are performed on the opened key or the subordinate values.

- Flush Key functions are performed by the operating system when changes are detected.

- Close Key functions are performed when you are done with the particular handle. Like most objects in Windows, a failure to close an open handle can lead to memory leaks.

This type of activity can be traced in the REGMON utility. For example, Figure 4.6 displays the opening of a key, enumeration of sub-keys, and setting of a value. The REGEDIT32.EXE tool was used to perform these operations.

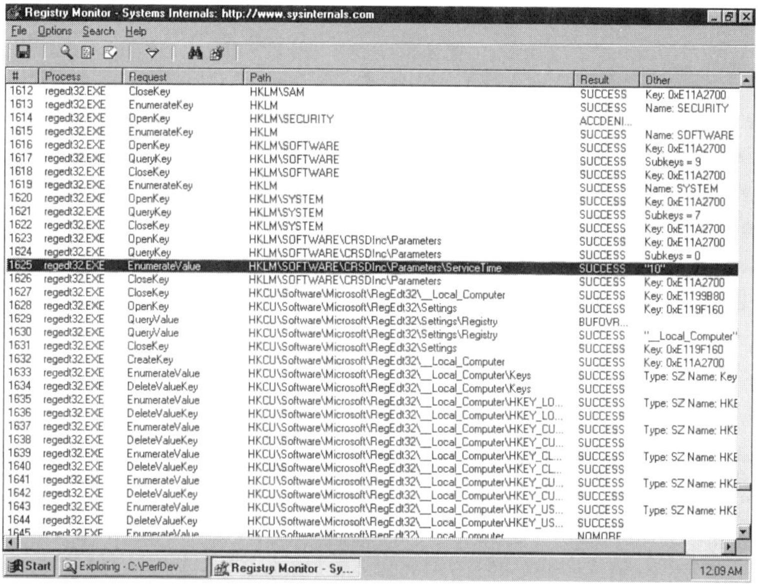

**Figure 4.6**    *REGMON traces the creation and setting of a value entry within the HKLM\Software\CRSDInc sub-key.*

The REGMON display also has a column called *path*, which lists the path of the accessed key. If you place the mouse over a particular entry, the entire path will be displayed. In addition, if you double-click on a particular entry, the REGMON tool will open the REGEDIT.EXE tool to that particular position within the Registry. Now that's service.

**Note**

*The REGMON will run on both Windows NT and Windows 9x. The developers assumed end users would use REGEDIT.EXE in order to provide a common method for accessing the Registry from the REGMON tool. REGEDT32.EXE is native only to Windows NT. Also, the REGMON utilizes a REGVXD.VXD file, which is a dynamically loaded driver, in order to be able to track Registry access on Windows 9x, which is not necessary on Windows NT.* ✦

In the Result column, you will see various messages corresponding to codes returned by the Registry handler. When examining these codes, you need to keep in mind how functions normally access the Registry and Query Values. You will see many "buffer full" and "not found" messages. This is normal for applications using the Windows Registry APIs. When attempting to query a value, for example, open a handle to the Registry key and then query the value with the return buffer smaller than the expected length of the Registry's value entry. The function then returns a buffer overflow message and the length of the value needed to actually read all of the value entry. Call the function again, setting the size of the buffer variable to the value equal to the one returned in the previous read attempt. All of this results in the Registry value being read more than once, with the first return being a failure due to buffer overflow. You will also see various references to "not found" responses.

Many components of Windows NT and software applications are checking for entries in the Registry that are not there. This usually means that the application has some default value programmed into it. When the Registry entry is not found, the default value in the code is used instead. This is not necessarily a problem. However, this does open the possibility for us to discover undocumented Registry entries that affect the configuration of software and the operating system. The final column—marked "Other" in the REGMON display—is used to display additional information that was returned by the various functions. The data here could be the handle to the key, the number of sub-keys enumerated, the value set, or the value returned.

REGMON has the same basic search and filter abilities as FILEMON. You can specify that REGMON collect information regarding only particular processes or particular sections of the Registry. (See Figure 4.7.)

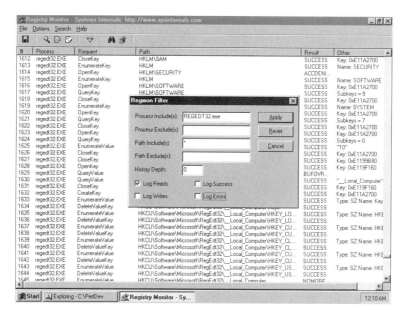

**Figure 4.7**   *In this case, REGMON is configured to collect only data from the process REGEDT32.EXE and only those cases in which information is being read from the Registry.*

## Uses for REGMON

One of the more useful purposes of the REGMON tool is to track problems with COM and DCOM objects. The type of errors that you might see in regard to the COM objects is "File Not Found" and "Could not Create Object" type errors. Other problems arise from poor information in the HKEY_CLASSES_ROOT Registry section. The HKEY_CLASSES_ROOT Registry section is an alias to the HKEY_LOCAL_MACHINE\Software\Classes Registry section. This section contains the information regarding COM objects. Therefore, if you have OLE Servers, ActiveX Servers, or COM objects, they are registered here. That way other applications and functions may call upon them. In addition, your basic file associations are registered in this section and mapped to an appropriate application.

Through repeated registration of DLLs, and removal of software and out of date components, this section of the Registry can become muddled to the point that such components no longer operate appropriately. This can be exceptionally true during the initial development stages. Running REGMON when you encounter problems with COM and DCOM objects and servers can be of great assistance in pinpointing the component and Registry section that is giving you the problem.

Another use for the REGMON utility is tracking installations of other applications. REGMON can save the information collected to a file so that you can examine it at a later time. If you are having problems with your own application or with another commercial application having undesirable affects on some Registry sections, you can use REGMON during the program installation to track the changes that are being made. By doing this, you are able to confirm your suspicions and again pinpoint the exact locations in the Registry that you need to be concerned about.

A final use of the REGMON is performed during the driver initialization of Windows NT. The REGMON tool has a feature that allows you to prepare the REGMON tool to run at boot time. It will start the REGMON before any of the other drivers are initialized during kernel startup. REGMON will then be able to track all of the Registry settings being examined and adjusted during driver initialization and operating system startup. The information will be stored on the REGMON.LOG file on the system drive's root folder. The data will be collected from the boot time until you either start the REGMON interactive application or reboot the system.

Prior to setting the REGMON utility to start during boot up, make sure you have ample space on the hard drive. For Windows NT 4.0 the file will be about 10MB or more depending on how quickly you start the interactive REGMON tool and thus terminate the boot logging process. On Windows 2000, the file will be about 25MB in size. This will be dependent on the number and types of drivers. The size of the file will also depend, in part, on the role of the machine. A domain controller's Registry log file will be larger than a member server's log. Should the disk become full during this process, the REGMON will terminate the logging of data. The crippling of an NT system will be prevented by running this tool. To date, I have yet to have a problem with the system booting even when the disk was purposefully low on disk space. The log file is a tab delimited standard ASCII text file that can be read with any text viewer or imported into a wide variety of applications for analysis. I strongly urge you to do this, at least once on your own workstation, to see the types of entries examined. To set this up you need only to perform the following steps:

1. Start the REGMON tool.

2. Click on Options.

3. Click on Log Boot.

4. Restart the computer.

5. Immediately log in.

6. Start the REGMON tool to terminate the boot logging process.

The REGMON tool will set itself up to log the next boot up of the system. Subsequent system boots will not cause the REGMON tool to collect any information even if the previous collection terminated due to a lack of disk space.

# HANDLEEX and WINOBJ

The previously mentioned tools dealt with examining global accesses to various standard objects on Windows NT. You can use the tools to find out which processes are accessing files or Registry entries. In this section the approach is reversed. We will examine the various processes, getting detailed information about the various handles and objects that they might have opened. In many ways, this approach is more direct than the previous approach. In many cases, you are well aware of the application that you want to examine. After all, you probably wrote it. In the other cases, you are looking at a more global access to various objects. This is more useful when you are not quite sure which process is accessing the files or Registry entries, or if you are examining multiple accesses to those objects. There are a couple of tools that work nicely together to provide detailed information regarding exactly what objects your program is accessing. These tools are HANDLEEX and WINOBJ.

*HANDLEEX* is a graphical program that displays information about the various processes that are running on your system. Much like Process explode and Process View from the Resource Kit, the tool will offer you a listing of processes that you can select from. Unlike the Resource Kit tools mentioned, the HANDLEEX details information on the objects being accessed as opposed to the various pieces of information about the threads.

*WINOBJ* is an Explorer-like tool that allows you to browse through the Windows namespace examining all of the available objects registered on the system.

## How They Work

When a particular process needs access to objects on Windows NT, a request is sent to an Executive Mode Service called the Object Manager. The Object Manager is responsible for keeping track of all of the objects available on Windows NT. This service also provides a centralized standard method for presenting object access, creation, and deletion.

The Object Manager will take care of creating a handle to a particular object, tracking the various processes that are using the objects, and delete those temporary objects when a process is done with them. The Object Manager does not, however, control the object's data or structure—that is done by the object's owner. Think of the Object Manager as a directory or listing of all of the available objects.

Allow me to delve into an analogy. Think of an Internet bookstore. Using your computer's Internet browser, you can see a listing of all the books that the company has for sale. If you see one that you like, you can order it. The Internet company will certainly keep track of the titles that it has available for sale and, for marketing reasons, will keep track of who is placing orders and what books they are ordering. Our little Internet bookstore does not actually write any of the books; it simply keeps a listing of what is available for sale and displays it in a pleasing way. The Object Manager performs roughly the same function. It is aware of all of the base-objects on Windows NT and maintains a listing of those objects that the processes are able to choose from. The details of the Object Manager's dealings are a little more involved.

The objects in Windows NT generally come in two types, Executive and Kernel. The *Executive objects* are the ones that are used by the various processes on the system. The *Kernel objects* are owned and created by the Kernel Services for access by the other Kernel Services. Their primary function is synchronization of the various services. The Executive objects deal with all of the other various components of Windows NT. The Object Manager has a listing—a group of object headers—that describes each of the objects and points to the various Executive Services that control the object body. The header is considered a description of the object, while the object body is the real guts of the implementation. The various other NT services and environmental subsystems can build on the base objects that the Object Manager has to offer, as you can see in Figure 4.8. Environmental subsystems might simply utilize the Executive object directly. However, it is more common to combine the functionality of multiple Executive objects and represent them through DLLs.

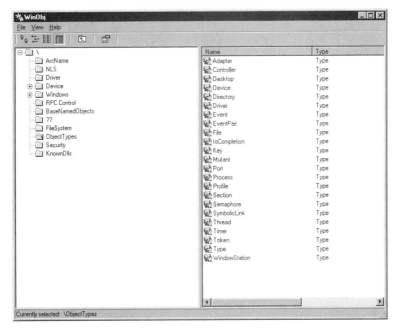

**Figure 4.8**    *The basic objects are the building blocks of the objects actually offered to processes by the environmental subsystems.*

At this point, let's walk through the basics of an object request by an application. The application needs access to some basic NT object, like a file or Registry key. The request is made to a published API and is sent first to the environmental subsystem. In most cases, this will be the Win32 subsystem. The subsystem then will pass the request to the Object Manager using a native NT call. The native NT API is generally undocumented outside of Microsoft, although there are places to acquire some of the information. Making direct calls to the native APIs is usually not a good idea for the reasons of supportability and portability. However, in some cases there can be benefits in added functionality or speed.

*Note*

*For more information on the Native NT API, take a look at the following:*

Solomon, David. 1998. *Inside Windows NT Second Edition*, Microsoft Press. (ISBN 1-57231-677-2).

www.sysinternals.com, which has information on the Native NT API ♦

The Object Manager receives the request and begins processing it. One of the first items in the course of business is to check the security of the requesting process. The Object Manager obtains the access token of the process. The access token or security token is created when the user logs on to the system. When the user starts an application, a copy of the access token is passed to the process. If the application is actually a service, the token of the user account specified in the Control Panel's Services applet is used. Often this is the default Local System account.

The Object Manager takes the information and passes it to the *Security Reference Monitor* (SRM). The SRM then compares the information to the Access Control List and lets the Object Manager know whether the specified token has the rights to access the specified object and perform the requested operation (for example read, write, delete). Assuming the SRM has given the Object Manager the green light, the Object Manager then updates its list of objects. This process is analogous to the Object Manager recording your order for a particular object. Your process ID is associated with the name of the requested object. This way, the Object Manager always knows which processes are using which objects. The application actually receives a handle to the object. The handle points directly to the object on the Object Manager's list of object headers. Using a handle has the benefits of standardizing access to objects on Windows NT and improving performance by avoiding the Object Manager having to look up the object by name each time it is accessed. When a process finishes using the object, the handle is closed. The event is propagated down to the Object Manager, which cleans up the links between the application process and the object.

As you have seen, the Object Manager has a complete listing of the objects and the processes using those objects in Windows NT. The tools mentioned in this section—WINOBJ and HANDLEEX—both query the Object Manager directly to obtain the information about the objects and the processes using the objects. As noted previously, a direct query to the Object Manager is done only using the Native NT API. Thus, these particular applications utilize undocumented access points to acquire their information.

## Using HANDLEEX and WINOBJ

In order to bring the discussions in the previous pages down to earth, we can examine the Object Manager's namespace, which is shown in Figure 4.9.

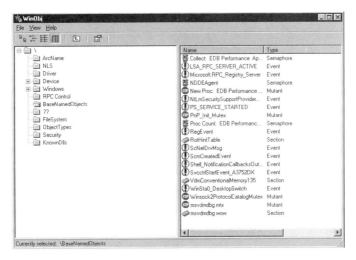

**Figure 4.9**    *The Object Manager's namespace of object headers is constructed in a hierarchical manner to facilitate easy access.*

*WINOBJ* is a simple tool that lays this namespace information out for display. In addition to seeing the structure, you can examine the individual objects. Many of the objects will not be viewable unless you are logged on as an administrator of that system.

> ### Note
>
> *The version of WINOBJ used in this text comes from the* www.sysinternals.com *Web site. Another version of the program with the same name, WINOBJ.EXE, is also part of the Microsoft Windows NT Software Development Kit (SDK). The SysInternals version displays the property information more accurately than the MS version at the time of this writing. Another tool that is part of the NT Resource Kit is called OH.EXE, which displays information about open handles on the system. This is primarily a text-based tool. The last method is to use the Kernel Debugger to examine the system with the* !handle *command. As you will see though, HANDLEEX.EXE is superior in ease of use and clarity of information.* ◆

As seen in Figure 4.9, most of the directories in the display are fairly clear about what they contain, but here we offer a listing of the meanings:

- **ArcName**

   This directory addresses the pointers to the various disk partitions. They are actually symbolic links to the device's section of the structure.

- **NLS**

   These are the National Language Support objects. These are more analogous to pointer tables.

- **Driver**

  This directory includes the drivers loaded on the system.

- **Device**

  This refers to the devices installed on the system. This will roughly correspond to the devices in the Control Panel's device applet.

- **Windows**

  This refers to the Windows stations. Usually one is listed for the logged on user, as well as for the API ports.

- **RPC Control**

  This directory represents the Remote Procedure Call objects. These objects represent communication ports for remote communication.

- **BasedNameObjects, Mutants/Mutexes, semaphores, and section objects**

  The primary function of these directories is to operate as timing mechanisms. Section objects are published as file-mapping objects in the Win32 subsystem.

- **??**

  This refers to DOS devices.

- **FileSystem**

  This refers to File System Driver objects with the notable exception of the Section objects, which are listed under the BasedNameObjects.

- **ObjectTypes**

  Objects are based on an object type, which is also used to group similar objects. Objects based on object types have common properties, but can also have unique properties as well.

- **Security**

  This directory refers to Security objects.

- **KnownDLLs**

  This list consists of primarily Windows NT DLLs and develops when NT first boots up.

Use the WINOBJ to explore each of these primary levels within the Object Manager's namespace. In some cases, you will be able to see more detailed information about the object. This will include information on security and ownership. In other instances, you will not be able to see information due to a lack of permission. Even as the administrator, you might not be able to see some of the information.

The HANDLEEX program provides detailed information on a process and the various objects that it has open, as you can see in Figure 4.10.

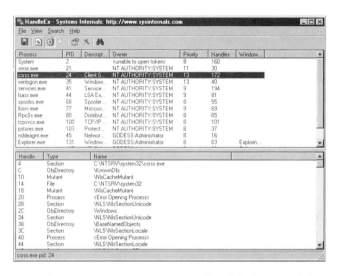

**Figure 4.10**    *The HANDLEEX starts out with a default view of the processes and the related named objects associated with the highlighted process.*

The top portion of the window displays a listing of all the processes on the system. You get to see some descriptive summary information on the processes' PIDs, their names, their description, open handles, base priority of the processes, and if the processes have a window title. Clicking on any one of the title headings will sort the list by that column. In addition, if you double-click on any process you will get some general information about the resource usage of that particular process, as seen in Figure 4.11.

**Figure 4.11**  *Not only do you get more detailed information on the executable, such as its location and version, but you also get information on memory and CPU utilization.*

It is important to notice, in the dialog box shown in Figure 4.11, the two buttons in the lower right corner. The first button is the standard OK button. The other is a Kill button. The Kill command will terminate the process in a drastic and sudden manner. You will not have an opportunity to save information from the program if you select this option. It will simply terminate.

## Note

*I do a lot of troubleshooting on systems. This usually means I am poking around in all sorts of applications and configuration settings on systems. I have purposefully developed a habit of hitting the Cancel button instead of the OK button when exiting dialog boxes. This prevents me from making any undesired changes to the various systems that I am investigating on a server. Unfortunately, in the case of this particular interface, the Kill button is in the very place where I would expect to see the Cancel button. Thus, a slave to my habits, I have terminated a couple of unsuspecting and totally innocent processes. So, if you are like me, you will need to pay close attention to the buttons in this tool. ◆*

On the lower half of the main display for HANDLEEX, you will see a listing of objects. You will have three options for what type of information will be displayed in this pane of the application:

Named objects

Unnamed objects and Named objects

DLLs

By default, you start with the *Named objects*, which are objects that have names associated with them. These will tend to be open files, open Registry keys, links to the Windows Station (user), and Section objects. The *Unnamed objects* tend to be timing objects like semaphores, mutexes, and events. Generally, the Named objects are more illuminating. The other option is to display DLLs that are loaded by the process. Once listed, the DLLs can be queried for more information by double-clicking them or highlighting them and clicking on the properties icon on the toolbar, as you can see Figure 4.12

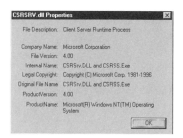

**Figure 4.12**   *You see the basic information just as if you had right-clicked the DLL in Explorer and clicked properties.*

Before leaving our examination of this tool, I would like to mention a couple of other nice features of the interface. One is the ability to search for particular objects or DLLs, depending on which one you are displaying. Another is the ability to save the information in the display as a text file. The information saved is all of the objects/handles or DLLs that are listed for a particular process. Only the information on a single process is saved, not on all of the processes. So, before hitting Save, make sure you have highlighted the process you are concerned with and selected whether you want to display object handles or DLLs.

Overall, HANDLEEX is invaluable when it comes to examining processes and their usage of various objects—not to mention DLLs. On many occasions, I have needed to examine various programs that had gone through several cycles of development. When making additional changes or adding new features, all sorts of issues would often arise such as DLL conflicts, server registration problems, and configuration issues. Sometimes just finding out where a configuration parameter is coming from is a real chore. With HANDLEEX, watching the display while the application is running gives you all the information you need to correct any one of these problems.

## Summary

In this chapter, you were introduced to tools that can assist you in troubleshooting problems and performance issues. Along the way, you learned more about the internal workings of Windows NT. You saw how the FILE-MON and REGMON tools display global information on which files and Registry keys are in use on a system. You also learned more about how the I/O Manager works, and the difference between standard I/O (IRP) and the Fast I/O functionality. You also learned about a technique developed by the REGMON developers called *system call hooking*. You learned about the Windows NT Object Manager's namespace and how to investigate it with tools called WINOBJ and HANDLEEX. In addition, you learned about the Windows NT Native API. I am sure you will find the tools mentioned here as useful as I have. My best advice is to download the tools and have a look for yourself.

# Part II

## Let the Hunt Begin: Finding the Performance Problems

# 5

# General Resource Consumption

Before you start weeding through your code looking for a memory leak or planning a complete rewrite of functions to improve processor utilization, you will want to be sure that the problem is really contained within your application. This chapter will provide definitive methods for isolating your application from the hardware and operating system that is supporting it. We will examine system performance as a whole. Then, we will pick apart and offer concrete indicators of resource problems. We will then analyze the particular resources and the problems that are unique to each one. Special attention is paid to identifying when an application is at fault and when a hardware resource is at fault. Let's not forget the operating system either. Poor configurations of the system can lead to problems with the applications and the users that the OS is trying to serve. We will work to be able to single out the true resource bottleneck and identify its cause.

## Examining Overall System Performance

When examining overall system performance, you will want to examine the entire system prior to making any rash judgments about the actual cause of a problem. We have already seen how memory can possibly have an effect on the performance of the disk. In addition, the network can affect the processor. Processor performance and disk performance can also be tied together depending on your type of hardware. What this all means is that you will want to take a view of the whole system's performance to get the big picture. Zooming in on what you might think is the problem can lead to misinterpretation. When that happens, you can spend a great deal of time working on a solution to the wrong problem. Also, you could be working on your application, trying desperately to get it to perform well, when actually you have a problem with the system's hardware performance. The best way to explain this is with an example.

## Getting to the Source of the Problem

Let's assume that we have some performance issue on a computer we are using for application testing. In general, the application appears to be rather slow in its response. If we were rash, we might think that because this is a network application, the problem is a slow network response or even a slow response from the server component of the application. While this might be true, it is better to analyze the entire system and then zero in on the suspected problem. We start with the four basic building blocks of an application:

Memory

Processor

Disk

Network

Every process on the system will be using at least two of these resources at any time. Consider that, if an application is doing nothing else, it is using memory and thus, potentially the disk. To get a complete picture, we start up good old Performance Monitor and analyze the primary counters for each of the resources, as detailed in Table 5.1.

*Table 5.1    Counters Enabling You to Pinpoint Performance Problems*

| Object | Counter | Description |
|---|---|---|
| Memory | Pages/sec | The frequency at which data is being retrieved and sent to the page file. |
| Processor | %Processor Time | The amount of time that the process is not idle. |
| Physical Disk or Logical Disk | Ave Disk Queue Length | The length of the queue for transaction aimed at the hard drive. |
| Network Segment | %Network Utilization | The amount of the available network bandwidth being utilized. |

Let the analysis begin! Remember that the focus of this particular section is to discover where the problem is. After that has been discovered, the following sections will go into the details of analyzing each particular resource. You should start with the memory because it is the most common resource for applications to use and abuse. Chapter 2, "Windows NT Kernel Debugger," defined the process of paging and the use of the page file on Windows NT. For the most part, if the memory's pages per second are more than 16, you might consider that you have a memory problem. However, this is not always the case. You will also need to figure out if poor disk performance is actually giving you the problem.

### Note

*Keep in mind that throughout the text, when values for concern are indicated, the values must be sustained values. Throughout the operation of the system there will be spikes in performance. The situations that you want to zero in on are when the critical values are reached or exceeded for a suitable period of time. The suitable period of time will be relative to the various counters that you are looking at. In the processor's world even short spikes are significant—on the order of 2–3 seconds—because the processor is operating at the nanosecond level. For the hard drive, which is barely managing milliseconds for the standard workstation, a few seconds are not as significant. Keep the component you are observing and the speed of its expected operation in mind when examining counters and comparing them to critical thresholds. ◆*

After you have examined disk performance, you might consider looking at processor performance. Certainly, a slow system might be related to an overburdened processor. Generally, processor performance above 80% will be cause for alarm. However, hardware or software can cause this. In most cases, we won't worry about hardware. In Chapter 7, "The Web Server," you will see that sometimes there are situations when you will have to dig a little deeper into the relationships between software and hardware. You should have a look at the processor's queue length. This particular counter—Processor Queue Length—is actually found under the Systems object. Understand that this is a measure of the number of transactions the operating system has in a wait state while the processor completes other tasks.

#### Accessing Additional Counters and Objects

*If you really have the desire, you can obtain some additional objects and counters that work with the Performance Monitor to track the activity of Intel-based Pentium and Pentium II processors. There are two places to get these additional counters.*

*The first place is in the Windows NT Resource Kit in the \NTRESKIT\ PERFTOOL\CNTRTOOL folder. Occasionally, I have had problems when adding these counters. They will affect the availability of other extended counters by slightly corrupting a Registry key. You need only to adjust the Performance Monitor's Registry keys to solve this problem. We actually discussed the keys for the counters, earlier in Chapter 1, "Introduction to Performance Monitor," when we were talking about the architecture of the Performance Monitor.*

*continues* ▶

▶ *continued*

*The second place you can find additional objects and counters is from the good guys at* www.sysinternals.com. *Search for "processor." You can download a utility that enables all sorts of additional counters for Pentium II processors. The details might require you to go out and get a good book on processor theory, but hey—if you're interested, it's there.* ◆

When disk activity is the source of your problem, it is more obvious than the others are. Hardware and operating systems both apply various caching and other tricks in an attempt to improve the performance of the slowest subsystem on the computer. Your first indication is usually the little flashing light on the outside of the computer case. However, nothing is ever as simple as it seems. The disk performance can, of course, be related to the memory. It might also be related to the way that the application is reading information or the condition of the file. Fragmentation and disk hardware configuration can certainly play their part.

The disk activity is highly transactionalized, especially in Windows NT where NTFS actually works much like a mini-database system. We will see, later in Chapter 8, "Monitoring Database Systems," how closely these are related. In the mean time, understanding the transactional nature of the disk will be an important factor. For this reason, the disk queue length is an important counter. This will tell us how many transactions are in the disk's queue for processing. This will really be the I/O Managers queue for processing. Any queue larger than two will be considered a bottleneck and a reason to investigate the activity further.

Last, you have the network activity. The network, although often treated as a separate entity, is about as separate from the computer as the ocean is from the shore. The tidal wave might be made of water, but if you are on the beach when it hits, you're going to feel it. Activity on the network, even if it is not directly related to your computer or your application, will affect the performance of the system. The network often calls on the other components of the computer to interpret the traffic. Generally, we can see this interpretive request affecting the processor of our systems. Usually, network issues are related to infrastructure and external system configuration issues. Of course, there are exceptions.

So, we have hit upon each of the main resources that we are concerned with. From our brief discussions, you can see that an overview of the system is a necessary first step. After we have performed this necessary first step, we can isolate one or perhaps two of the components that we are really concerned with, and then move forward in our analysis. Table 5.2 summarizes the counters and the values that we will be concerned with in hunting for the source of problems.

*Table 5.2    Primary Indicators of Problems Per Major System Resource*

| Object | Counter | Indications of Problems |
| --- | --- | --- |
| Memory | Pages/sec | Less than 16 Pages/sec is an indication of an issue. However, this is relative to the application. |
| Processor | %Processor Time | Less than 80% should get your interest. Also, have a look at System: Processor Queue Length. |
| Physical Disk or Logical Disk | Ave Disk Queue Length | Any queue with a length of more than two is a bottleneck. |
| Network Segment | %Network Utilization | Less than 67% is a problem for most networks. |

Now, consider that these values are only guides to lead you in the right direction. They are not intended to be hard and fast rules. Many systems will behave differently. Systems from the same manufacturer are not necessarily made from the same parts—consistency is usually an added cost. This can lead to difference in performance. Also, systems running different components or running different service pack revisions are expected to have different performance behaviors. This brings up the need for performance logs, which can be used as baselines.

## The Procedures for Analysis

The best thing to do for the system that you will be testing on is to first have a benchmark or baseline of how the system behaves under normal conditions. This will allow you to judge exactly how your application might be affecting the performance of the system. Sure, you could look at Table 5.2 and say, "Wow, Pages/sec is above 24 for a whole two minutes. I must have a memory problem with my application. This might be true, but what if the system always runs at about 24 Pages/sec due to another application or service? Perhaps you are running with a low memory configuration or a poorly configured page file. Unless you had a baseline of what the system behaves like normally, you might make a hasty choice. Hasty choices often lead to wasted time. If you have taken the time to performance test your application, you certainly don't want to waste time on a wild goose chase.

In Chapter 1, we thoroughly described how to create a Log file with the Performance Monitor. Prior to any testing of an application or a new version of an application, you should create a new baseline on the machine. If you have an old version of the application installed on the machine, create a baseline running through your normal test cycle with the old application, and then install the new one and test again. Compare the performance logs of the two tests and make a determination on whether you have met your performance objectives.

Now that you have your baseline for performance, you might think that you are ready; but effective analysis takes a little more planning. You must remain objective and scientific when you are analyzing a particular problem. You will want to perform the analysis in the following steps:

1. Get the Big Picture.

2. Hypothesize on the possible bottleneck.

3. Test your hypothesis.

4. Repeat Steps 2 and 3 until you have a solid hypothesis.

5. Make an adjustment and start over with Step 1.

We have already discussed getting the big picture and establishing the baseline for comparison. After you have done this, formulate your hypothesis by looking at Table 5.2 and comparing values with your baselines. You then have to utilize the tools that you were given in the previous chapters to test the hypothesis. Reformulate and retest until you have strong confidence in the root of the performance issue. Then, make a change.

Sounds easy, doesn't it? However, this simple set of steps is actually very difficult to maintain without a certain level of discipline. In any company, especially a software development company, the need to produce is strong. Stopping to perform calculated and repeated steps for performance analysis might be difficult to do, while the guy from marketing and your boss are hanging over you like hyenas waiting for you to throw them a piece of meat. Therefore, with performance analysis you might have to choose your battles with care.

For example, if your application is historically poor on memory utilization, you will want to focus your attention only on the performance tests that indicate memory issues. You might see a processor or disk issue, but you might have to let them go in favor of meeting a deadline. I am not promoting this type of activity. However, we are not all working for Perfect Company, Inc.—we are operating in the real world. This will be amplified if the application you are working with is complex and has a long history already. Previous developers might have made choices based on technology that was present and proven at the time they wrote the code. Trying to fix everything at once is a risky business, and not one that usually results in enhanced performance.

So, in Step 5 when it says make a change, it doesn't mean make a bunch of changes, causing you to spiral into the oblivion of unknown solutions and never-ending repairs. If you have a problem and a hypothesis for the cause of the problem, make a single or very few incremental changes and retest. This might require you to write small sample applications that mimic your primary applications' activities using different technologies. This will allow you to isolate the problem better and make direct comparisons between technologies or methodologies, prior to committing your primary application to a direction. After you decide which solution to implement, retest and compare it both to the previous application and the results from the sample application testing. Making sweeping changes to the application might fix the problem, but it has two other immediate ramifications:

- You don't really know how you fixed the problem.
- The chance that you have introduced other unknown problems is increased.

Consider a problem with memory consumption by your application. To correct the problem, you alter the code to cache more data, increase the physical RAM in the machine by 32MB, double the size of the page file, and reduce the reliance of the application on global variables. Each of these might assist in removing the symptom of excess memory consumption, but which one really fixed the problem? If in the next revision of the program you encounter the same problem, do you then repeat all the actions you took here?

Fixing the problem without understanding how you fixed it is worse than ignoring the problem altogether. Further, how do you know that you even fixed the problem? What if the real problem was a subroutine that failed to close handles to a Registry key causing a memory leak over time? By adding the memory and reducing the memory requirements of other parts of the application, you have only masked the symptom. The problem might occur later on, because the added memory only delays the problem temporarily. This also points out the necessity for thorough retesting of any solution. The other point is that, when you make large sweeping changes, you increase the probability that you will make other mistakes and introduce other problems, or perhaps magnify other problems. The more you handle the fine china, the greater the probability that you will drop it.

The final step in proper analysis is to retest any solution, no mater how small the fix. When any part of the system or the code is altered, there is a possibility that it will affect some other resource on the system. You will need to verify that:

- You have fixed the problem that you intended to fix.

- You have not created another problem.

- You have not amplified an existing, but different problem.

You have to make sure that your changes have not adversely affected other parts of the system. In addition, you want to make sure that you have truly fixed the problem. Your hypothesis of the cause could be solid, yet your solution to the problem can still be incorrect for the circumstances. Starting over with the big picture will make sure that you do not miss anything.

Now that you are clear on how to proceed, we should begin a discussion of the specific resources, and how they affect system and application performance.

## Specific Resources

After you have zeroed in on the particular resource that might be the problem, you will want to further analyze that resource utilization to make a more exact diagnosis of the problem. In this section the general rules for isolating the problem are presented. After you have the cause isolated, you can investigate your code and determine how to resolve the problem.

> **Note**
>
> *The discussions in this section are relatively brief and assume some knowledge of hardware, operating systems, and the techniques for some of the basics of bottleneck detection. This section might review some of the techniques but is intended to expand on the techniques and utilize the tools from the previous sections. If you require more analysis of Windows NT internal architecture and basic bottleneck detection or implementation of hardware solutions to performance and OS tweaks, you might want to read* Windows NT Performance: Monitoring, Benchmarking and Tuning, *New Riders Publishing, 1998 (ISBN: 1-56205-942-4).* ◆

## Memory

Once again, we start with memory. This section assumes that you have performed your original analysis and found some incriminating indication that the memory resource is exceptionally scarce on the system. This might have many causes:

Shortage of physical RAM

Disk issues creating memory issues

A memory leak or memory-hungry application

The shortage of RAM is an easy problem to pinpoint. It is the result of ruling out all the other possibilities. Most people make it their first choice to try and determine if they really need to add more memory. Occasionally, they add more memory and don't worry about why they might have to add memory. With the falling prices of memory, many administrators will take the easy way out and just buy more. They will go down to the local computer store and pick some up, grumbling all the way about how the developers should have coded the application so that it didn't use up all the memory on their systems. Sometimes, we (the developers) are at fault, but not always. Nonetheless, it is often left to the developer to defend his code and his honor. You will need to prove that it is either not your application causing the problem, or that the application, by the nature of what it is doing, must utilize the memory.

With any memory problem the first step is to eliminate a problem being caused by another component. In this case, it is the hard drive.

### Keeping Disk and Memory Separate

Paging is a requirement for the system to offer 4GB of memory to every process on the NT system. Few if any servers will have 4GB of physical RAM for every process. NT simulates this by moving unused code and data out to the page file. This process was described in detail earlier in Chapter 2. Check to see that the memory paging and processing is not slow due to a problem with the disk I/O. When observing and comparing the disk to the memory, you will want to examine the following Performance Monitor counters:

```
Memory: Available Bytes
Memory: Pages/sec
Memory: Page Reads/sec
Physical Disk: %Disk Read Time
Physical Disk: Ave Disk Read Queue Length
Physical Disk: Disk Reads/sec
Physical Disk: Avg Disk Bytes/Read
```

> **Note**
>
> *You are aware of the difference between the Physical Disk and Logical Disk objects. In this case, it is more beneficial to look at the Physical Disk object. Whenever you are unclear about what application is causing a potential memory or disk problem, you start with the Physical Disk object to make sure that you see all the activity affecting the resource. Once you can isolate the activity to an application or subsystem, you can focus on the drive that is being accessed. This can be done by using the Logical Disk object, which will allow you to focus on the counters for a particular partition.* ◆

First, the `Available Bytes` will give you an indication of exactly how low memory is. Remember that Windows NT likes to maintain 4MB of RAM for moving information in around in memory. The `Pages/sec` will affirm that you are having a memory problem when the value is excessive over time. The `%Disk Read Time` will give you an indication how busy the disk is—that is, how much time is being spent reading the disk.

Notice that many of the counters are focused on reads. Generally, when memory is a problem, the applications suffer when they generate page faults. A page fault, as you will recall, is when an application is looking for information within its Working Set and does not find it. When a page fault is generated, the VMM looks in the File System Cache and the PAGEFILE.SYS for the information. Thus, the application is forced to wait while the requested information is moved into physical RAM where it can be accessed. If the %Disk Read Time is low (less than 50%) and the memory response is still slow, you will most likely find a queue developing on the disk. The Ave Disk Read Queue Length will be a clear indicator of a queue forming.

Now, based on whether the %Disk Read Time is high or low, you will determine whether the disk activity is related to reads or writes. If the %Disk Read Time is low—indicating that most of the activity is due to writes—you most likely do not have a memory problem. You probably have a problem with an application performing some type of heavy I/O or some severe fragmentation on the disk.

However, if most of the activity is reads, you will need to determine if the reads are application I/O related or memory related. To see how much of the disk time is being spent servicing the memory paging requests, you need only compare the Memory:Page Reads/sec to the Physical Disk:Disk Reads/Sec. Dividing memory counters by the disk counter, you will get the percentage of reads that are due to the memory page faults. If this is a case of memory being used up too quickly, then the percentage will be very high—if not 100%—indicating that all the disk's read time is being spent servicing the memory page faults. This would point to a memory resource issue. You will then need to figure out if it is a leak and whether it is your application causing the problem. You will also want to have a look at the Disk Reads/Sec. When the I/O is primarily read related, as it usually is, this will be an indication of how many I/O operations are being performed per second.

EIDE disk subsystems and some older SCSI subsystems would get about 30–60 I/O operations per second. With SCSI adapter cards with inboard processors and integrated cache you can expect to get much higher value—in the realm of 1500 I/O operations per second on a good system. More complex systems, such as Storage Area Networks with Fiber connections, can get on the order of 2500 I/O operations per second. Making a determination of how well the particular subsystem you are using should be performing typically requires some simulation testing and building of performance baselines. At this point let's summarize our discussion:

1. Observe key memory and disk counters.

2. Determine whether it is reads or writes to the disk that is in greater percentage by examining the Physical Disk:%Disk Read Time.

   If writes are more frequent, you are more likely to be having a disk problem due to another application consuming a lot of the disk I/O.

3. Investigate the possibility of a disk queue by observing the `Physical Disk: Ave Disk Read Queue Length`.

   If you concluded that disk reads are the problem, you can check to see if a queue is forming the disk. This will be a strong indication that the disk is overburdened with requests.

4. Determine if the reads are due to memory or application activity.

   If they are due to memory, the following equation will result in a high percentage, if not 100%:

   `Memory: Page Reads/sec ÷ Physical Disk: Disk Reads/sec`

   If this relation is solid, the problem is memory and not disk.

5. Observe the `Physical Disk: Disk Reads/sec` to get a determination of how many I/O operations your system is performing.

From the information you acquire following these steps, you can tell what is memory and what is being caused by an inadequate disk subsystem. Although you will usually find that the memory is the problem, you can often find disk issues and repair the problem without too much trouble. Sometimes this requires some new hardware. Sometimes, it is as simple as reconfiguring the page files on the system to reduce fragmentation and decrease contention for I/O operations with other operating system components. Now that you have determined you have a memory problem, you will want to start figuring out exactly where the memory is going.

### Accounting for Memory

You have determined that you have a memory problem, so you need to start figuring out where the memory is going. Initially, you will want to figure out what application or system process is consuming the memory. After you have done this, you will then want to examine the memory utilization of the particular process.

To determine which process is consuming a large amount of memory, you will need to examine a few Performance Monitor counters:

```
Memory: Available Bytes
Memory: Pool Paged Bytes
Memory: Pool NonPaged Bytes
Memory: Cache Bytes
Process: Working Set: _Total
```

> ### Note
>
> *When examining memory counters, you will often see that the values don't always add up to be exactly the amount of memory that you have in your system. Memory allocations are very dynamic. When the various data is being collected, values are changing. Thus, difference can lead to slight variances in the totals, or even variances of the same values between the various tools such as PMON.EXE, Task Manager, and the Performance Monitor. This is just one of those times when close is good enough. ✦*

From the information obtained from these counters, you can determine roughly how the memory is being used. Then, you can get more specific. However, let's see what we have. The Memory: Available Bytes gives us what is left in memory, untouched at that particular time by any other system, process, or application. The Memory: Cache Bytes tells us how much memory is being used by the File System Cache at that particular moment. Finally, we examine the Process: Working Set: _Total. This final counter shows us how much memory is being used by the active processes. This will include kernel operations as well as drivers and user processes. If you add these three counters together, you will get roughly the amount of physical memory in the system. So, you are able to see how the system has divided the memory.

Generally, having an overly large amount of available bytes is not a problem. It is an indication that perhaps the memory is being underutilized and might have been better placed on another system. The Cache Bytes counter will let you know if the memory is being used for I/O operations instead of application processes. While you might have confirmed that you are not using the hard drives to a large degree, you might be moving large amounts of data across the network. In that case, the File System Cache is utilized, just as it is when you are writing to the hard drive. The System Cache will expand to meet the demands of the I/O operations. These operations might be simple file copies of ODBC-type information. The latter is usually the case.

General file I/O (except for loading an initial file) is usually not enough to cause the system cache to expand and maintain a large size. However, the ODBC database commands and objects, such as dynasets, can create large file transfer operations when being built in the local memory. In addition, they will cause the Working Set of the process to grow equally as fast. So, if you have a large system cache, you might actually have a poorly constructed database query, as opposed to a memory allocation problem with your application. Most of the memory will usually be seen in the Working Set: _Total counter. We use the _Total instance to get an overview of how memory is being divided among the various systems. After that has been determined, you might continue by examining the Working Sets' sizes of each of the processes on the system. After you have found the one that appears to have the largest Working Set at the time, you can dig into the specifics of the memory utilization.

---

### Note

*Although the Performance Monitor is an excellent tool for examining performance values, in the case of a quick overview of the memory allocation, you might want to launch the Task Manager and examine the Performance tab. All the information discussed on the previous few pages is available in a simple display on the Task Manager.*

*For more detailed information, you can use PMON.EXE (see Chapter 2). It will display a large amount of information in a text-based, column-formatted display.* ◆

---

You might have noticed that we also included counters for the paged pool and the non-paged pool. These values give you an indication of how specifically NT is dividing up the system memory. The system memory is represented in the various Working Sets and the file system cache values. The use of paged pool and non-paged pool offers you more detail on how that memory is being used. This is especially important to those of you who are writing drivers for Windows NT. User processes and services typically will have sections of these memory pools allocated on their behalf by the NT Executive Services. Excessively large or increasing values for the Pool Paged Bytes or the Pool Non-Paged Bytes are strong indicators of driver memory leaks or even memory leaks in the NT Executive Services. That's right; no one is above making mistakes.

After you have determined which process is using all the memory, you will want to examine it in more detail, which we will do in Chapter 6, "Examining the Application." Our goal here is to be able to break down the performance information and determine the application or process that is consuming the most memory and potentially giving us the most problems. The application could simply require some tuning to more efficiently utilize the memory. Of course, you could potentially have a memory leak.

**Identifying the Leak**

A *memory leak* is more than an application that consumes a large amount of memory. The distinctiveness of leaks is that the application, process, or driver causing the leak does not return its allocation of the memory to the system under any circumstances. When memory is plentiful, Windows NT will allow applications the luxury of keeping unused items in memory. When memory becomes scarce, NT will scavenge all the memory from the various processes if they are not actively using the memory. This will cause the information to be paged out to disk. The leaky process will claim that it is using all its allocations and refuse to surrender any amount of its memory to the pruning process. This constitutes the true memory leak.

Memory leaks can take time. Some leaks, usually related to user applications and services, will consume memory rapidly. This would usually be on the order of hours or days. Others, such as device drivers and Kernel mode services, will consume memory slowly. Drivers and Kernel mode services tend to be rather slim on memory usage to begin with, so when there is a leak, it is a small one that builds over time. These types of leaks will cause problems over weeks or even a month. Identifying the leaks calls for either long logging processes or simulations.

You are already familiar with the logging process. You simply set up a Performance Monitor log to capture all the Process and Memory objects on the system that are suspected to have a memory leaking process. Then, when the system appears to run low on memory, stop and review the log. You will see the Working Set for the errant process growing, while the Available Bytes decreases over time. Again, this could take days or weeks.

To speed things up a bit, you can observe the processes closely and use the CLEARMEM.EXE tool to observe any changes to the minimum Working Set. A leaky application will not respond to the forcible removal of unused memory sections that CLEARMEM.EXE will be exercising. To find the leaky application using CLEARMEM.EXE follow these steps.

1. Reboot the system.

2. Start all processes.

3. Use Performance Monitor to log the size of all the Working Sets.

4. Run CLEARMEM.EXE twice in a row.

5. Use Performance Monitor to log the minimum Working Set of all the processes.

6. Wait for some time, exercising as much of the system as possible.

7. Repeat the last three steps, each time comparing the minimum Working Sets to the initial minimum Working Sets.

By using this process, you should eventually be able to see a particular process growing in size, even if it is by small increments. You will still cut down on the amount of time that it takes to identify the process.

# CPU

The processor's speed is the benchmark of the system's performance. It sets the standard for the users' expectations in many cases. The processor on a system has several duties. In addition to coordinating the activity between the local cache systems, the CPU must service the operating systems as well as the other hardware components. With this in mind, our first duty will be to separate the hardware issues from the software issues. Because we are writing applications, software issues will be our priority. However, understanding the hardware issues will be necessary, so that you can eliminate them and get on with your appointed task of performance tuning your application. After you have cleared up any hardware issues, you will want to analyze the application issues more closely. With applications, especially more complex applications, you will be running Windows NT Services or even drivers. It is often a little more difficult to determine which services or drivers are producing problems, as they are somewhat hidden behind Kernel mode services. Here we will see how to determine exactly where the process cycles are being spent.

## Isolating Software

At this point, you have been able to determine that you have a processor problem. You should have examined the Processor: %Processor Time and the System: Processor Queue Length. You would have found that the processor is busy over 80% of the time. The queue of waiting transactions is over two and thus, indicates a problem with the processor being able to keep pace with the demands being placed on it. Of course, this should cause a question to pop into your mind: Is the processor too busy because too many requests are being made upon it, or is it not holding its weight given the relatively low number of requests being placed upon it? Usually, the case will be that the processor is being overwhelmed, indicating a problem with either hardware requests or application requests being too numerous.

### Note

*If the processor is not performing up to its specifications, you might have a hardware configuration problem. This was found to be especially true of pre-PII systems. The processor requires the use of an L2-Cache for moving information back and forth from RAM to the processor. If there is an overabundance of RAM without a suitable increase in L2-Cache, the Processor performance can suffer.*

*The general rule is to load the system with the maximum allowed amount of L2-Cache, so that you do not have to worry about the ratio of L2-Cache to RAM. L2-Cache maximums are now about 1MB for high-powered workstations. On server models, you can get 2MB or greater for the L2-Cache. Keep in mind that this is for the Intel architecture. Alpha systems have higher capacities and will even employ the use of L3-Caches. ◆*

Applications use threads to place tasks in the processor's queue. Hardware does not use the same type of interface. The hardware uses interrupts to get the processor's attention. Therefore, when we are trying to determine if a particular problem is related to hardware, we will want to track the interrupts. We will also want to track the deferred procedure calls, DPCs, as well. As developers, you already have an understanding that a process has a priority, and that the base priority of the process will determine the range of the thread's priority. Within the realm of priorities, for the various processes and threads on an NT system, there are 32 levels.

The first levels—from 0–16—are for the user processes. The remaining levels are for the Kernel mode processes, which often operate in real-time. However, above the Kernel mode processes are the DPCs, and above that are the hardware interrupts. Thus, when servicing a queue of tasks, the process must first take care of all the interrupts; then the DPCs; then the Kernel mode threads; and then finally the User mode threads. Knowing this, you can easily imagine situations where the interrupts and DPCs can consume all the processor's time. Let's examine the processor just a little closer.

When a piece of hardware is detected on Windows NT, the hardware registers an interrupt with the system. The *Hardware Abstract Layer* (HAL) is responsible for taking care of the registration and matching up the routines with the interrupts when required. When an interrupt hits the processor, all activity stops and the interrupt is interpreted. This means that the microkernel and the HAL work together to identify the component that is making the request and then contact that component to service the request. Some requests can be noted and delayed. The delayed processing is usually done for network cards. When new data is received, the NIC sends an interrupt to the processor, indicating that it needs attention. The processor, microkernel, and HAL determine that this is a NIC and defer processing until other interrupts are handled. This is the nature of the *Deferred Procedure Call* (DPC). The DPC is handled after all of the other hardware interrupts are handled.

*Note*

*On multiple-processor systems, the handling of DPCs is altered. Generally, when a network card is added to a multiple-processor system, the network card is loosely bound to a particular processor. Thus, when that NIC receives information, it contacts that specific processor. When the interrupt is determined to be from a NIC, the processor defers the procedure. However, it might defer the procedure to run on another processor. This is partially dependent on the hardware vendor's implementation of DPC handling routines within the processor. With some vendors, the DPC will get queued on the same processor—on others, the DPC is queued on another. This scenario becomes more complicated when multiple NICs are involved. In Chapter 7, we will return to this discussion and its ramifications for Web servers. ◆*

At this point, it is clear that you will want a method for determining whether hardware or software is impacting the processor. Equally clear is that we will need to use the interrupts in making that determination. The counters that you will want to observe are

```
Processor: %Processor Time
Processor: Interrupts/sec
System: System Calls/sec
System: Processor Queue Length
```

Keep in mind that in a multiple-processor system, the processor counters should be selected for each instance of a processor. Also, note that the System object is global to the system and thus, includes values for all processors, and not just a single processor on the system. This will be important when you begin to make comparisons. If a single processor appears to be having a problem, then examining the following addition counters may offer more insight into the nature of the problem:

```
Processor: %Processor Time
Processor: %Privileged Time
Processor: %User Time
Processor: %Interrupt Time
Processor: %DPC Time
```

Let's return to the first set of Processor counters. Here you are basically observing the %Processor Time and the Processor Queue Length to make sure that during your observation, you are actually experiencing the problem. The other two counters—Interrupts/sec and System Calls/sec—can be directly compared to assist in the determination of whether your problem is hardware-related or software-related. Generally, these two counters will be about equal. Keep in mind that we are looking for sustained values even in this comparison. The occasional spikes in hardware activity will show up. However, if the Interrupts/sec counter is consistently much higher than the System Calls/sec counter, then you are experiencing processor issues due to a hardware problem. Examining the other counters will assist in the determination of which component is creating the problem.

The %User Time counter will represent the amount of time that the processor is spending on non-idle user tasks. This will include the applications and the subsystems. It will also include services and some components of the Win32 Subsystem. (In this section, when we say services, we are talking about Windows NT services that are installed and viewable from the Control Panel's Services applet. We are NOT referring to Executive Mode kernel components.)

The Executive Services' activity will display in the %Privilege Time counter. The %Interrupt Time and %DPC Time can be combined to represent the amount of time that is being spent servicing hardware requests. This is not completely accurate, as some of the processing is actually represented in the %Privilege Time that we must attribute to the software's demand for processing time. However, the results are close enough for a determination. So, combining the first three counters in our list and comparing them to the interrupt and DPC counters again will tell us if more time is being spent servicing the hardware than the software. If the DPC and interrupt values are substantially higher, which would be over 60% of the overall processor time in general, then the cause is hardware. If they are about equal, then the problem is typically software. After you have ruled out the hardware factor, you will then want to break down the system calls and analyze the applications and processes individually.

### Some Causes for Increased Interrupts

*The causes of increased hardware interrupts do not always indicate a problem, although they can. Some of the issues could be as follows*

   *Mis-configured hardware drivers*

   *Faulty, outdated, or incorrect drivers*

   *Hardware about to fail*

   *Loose connections*

*continues* ▶

▶ *continued*

*I have had the opportunity to do some technical training. One company would send the computers to remote locations where they would be set up and installed with software to run the classes. The problem was that, through all the (sometimes-rough) movement, some of the adapter cards would pop loose. Not completely out, mind you, just half way. This would often lead to very high interrupt counts, but the system for the most part would continue to operate.*

*Aside from actual problems, you could simply have a system whose purpose in life is to work tightly with hardware components. A Web server is such a machine. For a large site, the network cards, especially if there are multiple cards, will generate a lot of interrupts and DPCs on the processor without there actually being a problem. Other examples might be customized instrumentation that is connected to Windows NT for monitoring some system—perhaps using an NT workstation to monitor flow and pressures through a water system.* ◆

## Processes and the Processor

Okay, you have now eliminated the hardware from the equation. You need to analyze the various processes on the system to determine what is going on. To start, you would view the `Process: %Processor Time` for each process on the system. This will give you an indication as to which process is using up the processor's time. You might find a single process standing out in the crowd. But, you also might find that there is no single process taking up a majority of the processor's time. In the latter case, you will need to think about the various programs and services that you are running on your system because the processor is generally being overloaded. The other case will show which application is giving the processor the most grief. From there, you have a variety of tools to begin to break down what is going on. The first is the Performance Monitor. You will want to start by observing the following counters:

```
Process: %Processor Time
Thread: %Processor Time
Process: ID Process
Thread: ID Thread
```

This will help you to break down which threads are taking up the CPU time among the ones created by your program. You might then begin investigating the various components that are being accessed by using the APIMON.EXE and the Process Explode program from the Resource Kit.

From these programs, you will be able to determine the API calls that are being made and the DLLs that are being used. This allows you to track the progress of the application and also associate various levels of the Systems Calls/sec counter to activities of your program.

A system call is really a way for an application to get the attention of the processor and the Kernel mode services. The request originates from an environmental subsystem that is running some user process or service. The process will generate some event that results in a system call. The Executive Services have registered themselves, much like the hardware interrupts have done. The various system calls will indicate which services they are trying to reach by indicating the software interrupt level. After the Executive Service is contacted, parameters are copied from the User mode stack down to the Kernel mode stack. Further data that is required might be copied, depending on the method the programmer used to construct the data. If it is in a shared area, the Executive Services checks to see that the area can be accessed. Otherwise, the data will be copied or the system call rejected.

## Disk

Another one of the specific resources to examine is the disk subsystem. The disk subsystem is always one of the slowest, yet most demanded resources on the computer's system. Making sure that your disk subsystem is properly configured is always the beginning point in optimizing disk and memory performance. At this point, we will assume that you have taken the time to make sure that the disks are properly configured for the task at hand. We'll assume that you have an appropriate hard drive controller, such as SCSI, EIDE, or UDMA. In addition, we'll assume that the disk partitions and appropriate advanced disk configurations, such as striping and RAID, have been properly implemented.

> ### Note
>
> *If you haven't gotten the message yet from this text, the disk subsystem has a lot of configuration concerns. These concerns and sample configurations can be seen in the previously mentioned book* Windows NT Performance: Monitoring, Benchmarking, and Tuning. *This book deals more with the administrative side of performance monitoring and system optimization.* ◆

With the disk subsystem, the first thing do is establish the parameters of the system you are using. This implies the use of some of the Resource Kit tools. Then, you can begin to analyze the affect of your application on the disk's performance.

### Understanding Disk Utilization

Disk performance is very much dependent on the type of I/O that is being done and factors such as:

> Sequential versus random I/O
>
> Writes versus reads
>
> Large files versus smaller files
>
> Disk configurations
>
> Buffered I/O
>
> File fragmentation

They can all affect the performance of the disk subsystem. To get accurate readings on the affect of your application or a particular type of I/O on the disk subsystem, you will need to establish a good set of baselines for the performance of the disk subsystem. In Chapter 1, you learned about logging information to the Performance Monitor log, and in Chapter 3, you learned about the Response Probe. In this chapter, you want to put those tools and techniques to use.

The Response Probe can be used in this situation to produce predictable output for the system. You want to first simulate the best conditions, which are buffered reads/writes in a sequential order. This will give the disk the best performance marks. Then, you will want to deviate and begin to get closer to the way that you anticipate your application will be using the disk.

Perhaps you are using a Jet database and want to see how the performance of the system will fair when the database approaches 20MB. This is generally the point at which Microsoft suggests that you consider compacting the database manually to maintain integrity and performance for the MS Jet database. You can create a file of this size and then simulate multiple random reads and writes. You will also want to adjust the Response Probe files, so that the size of the reads matches the record size of the database. This will give you more of an indication of how the system will behave and how a standard disk configuration will react to the type of I/O you are planning. Based on the information you find, you might want to choose a different database system or go with a proprietary database system that you build yourself. When performing this type of analysis, the primary counters to watch will be as follows:

```
Logical Disk: Avg Disk Bytes/Read

Logical Disk: Avg Disk sec /Read

Logical Disk: Disk Read Bytes/sec

Logical Disk: Disk Reads/sec

Processor: %Interrupt Time

Processor: %Processor Time
```

You might notice that two processor counters are in the mix. Disk I/O to some extent always utilizes the processor. You will want to watch the processor, at least a few times, to see if there is any significant affect on the processor's performance.

> **Note**
>
> *Disk I/O and Network I/O devices are generally programmable I/O devices. This means that they rely on the processor to perform some of their work. Of course, some technology is different from others. IDE ISA controller cards are severe in their use of the processor; they can use as much as 40% of the available processor time to perform disk I/O. SCSI bus mastering cards with their own processor and cache will take up almost no time on the processor. Network interface cards (NICs) always consume processor resources. Some vendors are now coming out with cards that have some intelligence and can buffer data/interrupts if the processor is being overwhelmed. ◆*

The `Disk Read Bytes/sec` is the overall measure of throughput for the hard drive. You will want to keep a close eye on this value throughout your testing. This will let you know how much you are affecting you performance. Generally, aside from database applications and perhaps some utilities, the disk I/O performance is not too much of an issue. Later in Chapter 8, when we are specifically discussing databases, we will return to this topic with more vigor.

### Isolating the Application

One of the biggest problems, after you notice some drastic disk I/O, is figuring out what is causing the problem. The Performance Monitor can tell you there is a problem and even point you to the partition, but that is as close as you are going to get. To determine the files and the exact application, you can use the FILEMON utility discussed in Chapter 4, "Freeware/Shareware Tools." This will allow you to identify the files and the application that is producing the I/O problem. Keep in mind, that it is necessary to understand the nature of the problem by reviewing the Performance Monitor statistics. You might see a program that is accessing a very large file, but it might not be the problem. A program accessing numerous and scattered small files or highly fragmented files can be just as damaging to performance.

## Network

The network is the most problematic component of any computer system. The real issue is that the problem is not localized to the machine that you are working on. When reviewing network problems, you must consider the server side and the network components in between the systems, as well as the performance of the networking systems on the local workstation.

### The Network's Effects on the System

We already know that the network components can affect the processor by generating excessive interrupts that the processor has to deal with. Knowing this, we can understand the concern over broadcasts and multiple protocols. A broadcast is a network packet sent out with no particular destination in mind. Every system on the network must react to the broadcast, and thus, must interrupt the processor to interpret the information, even if it is little more than to determine that the packet of information is of no value. Therefore, the health of the network and the general reduction of broadcasts on the network are very important. For the local machine, the reduction of protocols and unnecessary services is a good place to start. Multiple protocols on a workstation or server will do the following:

Use memory resources

Use processor resources

Result in increased reactions to broadcasts

Increase general I/O delays

For the most part selecting a single protocol for the enterprise is very important. From a development perspective, making sure that the size and frequency of network communications is efficient is paramount to an efficient application.

## Tracking Bandwidth

When you are reviewing the performance of the network, you will start by analyzing how much of the bandwidth on the local segment is being utilized. Using the `Network Segment: %Utilization` will show you the amount of bandwidth currently in use. Should you see more than 67% in use, you should start to worry that there is a problem on the network somewhere. Checking the `%Broadcasts` will show you if the traffic is related to broadcasts on the network. More than likely, it is. Broadcast storms, as they are sometimes called, occur when systems are mis-configured on the network but can also come about when server-side applications are poorly written. If you have an application that is going to rely on large amounts of data being moved across the network, you will want to observe the general health of the network and gather some overall statistics about your system performance in general. Much like the Disk I/O, the use of baselines will be important to any analysis of network performance.

### Note

*For more demanding analysis of the networking, you might want to get a hold of a copy of the Network Monitor to collect the packets themselves as well as the statistics about the network's health and performance.* ♦

The exact counters you will want to examine will be dependent on the protocol that you are using. Most sites are using TCP/IP, so that is what we will speak to in most of this text. In the case of TCP/IP, you will want numbers related to the amount of traffic and the efficient packaging of the information for transport. This type of information can be found in the following counters:

```
TCP: Segments Sent/sec
TCP: Segments Received/sec
TCP: Segments/sec
TCP: Segments Retransmitted/sec
```

When you are observing the network interface, you will also want to watch the following processor counters:

```
Processor: %Processor Time
Processor: %Interrupt Time
Processor: %DPC Time
```

Recall that the NIC and the network traffic can have a dramatic affect on the processor. The TCP counters that you see will describe the amount of TCP traffic going in and out of the system on the network. Most of the other statistics we have discussed, regarding the network, have been related to overall network utilization. These counters focus on the individual server or workstation that you are monitoring. When looking for issues related to the transmission of the information on the network, you should look at Segments Retransmitted/sec. This will be an indication of the amount of traffic that is causing problems on the network. *Retransmissions* are packets of data that can not make it to the other nodes on the network and need to be retransmitted. You will usually want to perform a small calculation:

```
Segments Retransmitted/sec ÷ Segments Sent/sec
```

This will give you the percentage of the segments that were transmitted due to previous transmission failures. You will notice that we focused on the receipt and transmission of data and not necessarily the frame sizes. When analyzing the network traffic, your focus will be on the affect the traffic is having on the endpoints, although we cannot completely ignore what is occurring on the network.

When reviewing the traffic, you will usually want to analyze some of the chief components involved in the transmission and receipt of data. In many cases, this communication is between a couple of basic components on Windows NT, the Server Service, and the Redirector.

The *Server Service* is the networking component responsible for responding to connection requests to a system that has some set of resources to share. This is typically a shared folder or perhaps a printer. Certainly there are other types of connections that might or might not involve the components directly. However, the general concept is the same. The *Redirector* is the service that is on the requesting workstation. When a request is made, for example, for a file that actually exists on another server, the Redirector jumps in and routes the communication to a remote system. The remote system's Server Service picks up on the request and processes the information.

To monitor the performance of this communication, you will need to monitor both the Redirector and the Server. Performance issues could be related to either one or both of these services, as opposed to the network in general. The counters that you want to use to monitor this type of communication are

    Server: Bytes Total/sec

    Network Interface: Output Queue Length

    Redirector: Bytes Total/sec

    Redirector: Current Commands

    Redirector: Network Error/sec

The counters with the Bytes Total/sec values give you an idea of exactly how much traffic is being sent and received by the system. The Server's queue is estimated by the Network Interface: Output Queue Length, which shows you how much of a queue there is. The value of Current Commands for the Redirector displays the number of transactions in the queue for the Redirector. Recall that a queue of more than two on any transaction based system is considered a bottleneck. Last, the Network Error/sec counter will give you an indication of problems on the network or with one of the services involved in the communication.

Remember that you should be examining the server side as well as the workstation (Redirector) side of the communications. Usually, errors will be an indication of server timeouts on connections or repeated transmission failures.

Networking performance monitoring is more specialized than the monitoring of any of the other resources. There are many factors and external components that can affect the network operations. We have no way to cover all the potential scenarios here. However, in Chapter 7, we will be covering the communications issues directly related to the Web servers. You will need to remember that, as we have done here, you will need to monitor the components on both sides of the communications as well as any potential issues related to general network bandwidth availability.

# Summary

In this chapter, we walked step-by-step through each of the various resources that a computer system is managing. You learned about some of the issues with monitoring and analyzing each of the various components. In addition, you learned about the objects and counters that you will want to use in your analysis. These counters have been organized for your convenience in Table 5.3. All this was built upon the knowledge of the tools and techniques that you read about in Part I, "Arm Yourself!: Tools for Performance Monioring." Again, the best way to really get to know the material is to try it out. Review the counters for the various computer components and do some analysis on your workstation or server. See how various operations affect the system performance and compare them to some of your applications. This will get you closer to understanding how your programming style affects the performance of the application and the system overall. The next chapter, Chapter 6, will expand on this knowledge to tie it closely with the application operations and investigative tools in Part I.

*Table 5.3    Summary of Problems and Applicable Counters*

| Indications of a Problem | Counters to use in Analysis |
| --- | --- |
| Memory issues: Pages/sec less than 16, regular reboots required, high disk activity. | Memory: Available Bytes<br>Memory: Pages/sec<br>Memory: Page Reads/sec<br>Physical Disk: %Disk Read Time<br>Physical Disk: Ave Disk Read Queue Length<br>Physical Disk: Disk Reads/sec<br>Physical Disk: Avg Disk Bytes/Read |
| Memory issues for drivers: Pages/sec less than 16, blue screens, regular reboots of system required. | Memory: Available Bytes<br>Memory: Pool Paged Bytes<br>Memory: Pool NonPaged Bytes<br>Memory: Cache Bytes<br>Process: Working Set : _Total |
| Processor issues: %Processor Time less than 80%, slow response to interactive user. | Processor: %Processor Time<br>Processor: Interrupts/sec<br>System: System Calls/sec<br>System: Processor Queue Length |
| Processor issues: %Processor Time less than 80%, slow response to interactive user. These counters offer details into hardware causes such as an over-active network. | Processor: %Processor Time<br>Processor: %Privileged Time<br>Processor: %User Time<br>Processor: %Interrupt Time<br>Processor: %DPC Time |

| | |
|---|---|
| Disk issues: Analyzing how the disk is being used. `Ave Disk Queue Length` of less than two is an indication of a problem. | `Logical Disk: Avg Disk Bytes/Read` `Logical Disk: Avg Disk sec /Read` `Logical Disk: Disk Read Bytes/sec` `Logical Disk: Disk Reads/sec` `Processor: %Interrupt Time` `Processor: %Processor Time` |
| General process tracking. These counters are used whenever you are tracking any of the other issues for a particular process or thread. | `Process: %Processor Time` `Thread: %Processor Time` `Process: ID Process` `Thread: ID Thread` |
| Network: `%Processor Time` less than 80%, Network Utilization less than 60%. These counters give you an indication of how much data is actually being sent and received via TCP. Processor counters are present to measure NIC's effect on the processor. | `TCP: Segments Sent/sec` `TCP: Segments Received/sec` `TCP: Segments/sec` `TCP: Segments Retransmitted/sec` `Processor: %Processor Time` `Processor: %Interrupt Time` `Processor: %DPC Time` |
| Network: `%Processor Time` less than 80%, Network Utilization less than 60%, slow interactive user response. These counters look at the another layer of the network communications. Viewing them allows you to analyze the need for adjustments to system parameters. | `Server: Bytes Total/sec` `Network Interface: Output Queue Length` `Redirector: Bytes Total/sec` `Redirector: Current Commands` `Redirector: Network Error/sec` `Processor: %Processor Time` `Processor: %Interrupt Time` `Processor: %DPC Time` |

# 6

# Examining the Application

In Chapter 5, "General Resource Consumption," you dove deeper into the analysis of the system's overall performance. In this chapter, you take some of the more critical resources and delve into more specific analysis and examples. No doubt you are already aware of the critical nature of memory utilization and processor performance, which is what we focus on in this chapter. With a little work, you can relate the performance to what the application is doing. We begin our discussions with the memory resource. The memory resource is the most critical, and probably the most abused, resource on the Windows NT operating system. After all, if you want an application to run faster, you load everything you want into memory. This is not usually the best philosophy for operating a system. In this chapter we examine the memory resource in more detail and discover the common issues related to poor memory usage.

Then, we cover the process. Creating threads is relatively new to the PC programming word, which makes it an interesting and fun programmatic challenge. Multi-threaded applications have the advantage of spreading the work among multiple processors if they are available. Why not create a whole bunch of threads and run the application at full speed? Because you will bring the system to its knees, that's why. We focus on analyzing threads because the thread is the item that is scheduled on the processor for execution. Let's get started with a discussion on memory.

## Memory

You have already seen how critical memory utilization is on a Windows NT system. Let's return to a brief discussion of the systems architecture. Then, we can examine the application's utilization of memory. The details will include not only the application's utilization of memory as a whole, but also how some of the application's actions result in the utilization of other memory by Windows NT's components.

Memory is utilized in a few different ways on Windows NT. Although you might find that the storage of the objects' structures in memory is handled in numerous creative ways, Windows NT creates memory storage in a select number of configurations. The memory utilized by any application can first be divided into *shared memory* and *private memory*. The allocation of each is different and done with different purposes. Next, the Kernel mode operations can pull memory from the paged pool or the nonpaged pool. We have already discussed the difference between these. In this section, we look at some programs' consumption of memory in these areas. During the process, you learn how and why the memory is being used.

*Note*

*Chapter 9, "Pushing the Limits," covers some extreme cases of resource consumption. In that chapter, you can find information on real-time applications, memory monsters, and heavy processor consumers. Although these cases are interesting, in this chapter, we focus more on the mainstream issues. ◆*

By this time, you should already understand that the memory on Windows NT is protected for each process. Each process has 4GB of potential memory on standard Windows NT. This memory utilization on Windows NT is divided into *User mode memory* and *Kernel mode memory*. The Kernel mode memory is not directly accessible from the application or any other application operating in User mode. The Executive Services and functions are controlling the access to these particular areas of memory. The User mode memory is immediately available to the process and the application. Memory that can be viewed or manipulated by other processes is considered shared memory, which we cover later in the text. *Private memory* is the memory that an application requests and utilizes in its own memory space. Allocation of such memory can affect not only the performance of the application, but also the overall performance of the system. We begin with private memory.

## Private Memory

To amply cover the topic of private memory, we first discuss the methods of allocation of memory and then examine the details of an application's private memory.

**Methods of Allocation**
The allocation of memory is a two-fold topic. First, when speaking of the allocation of memory, you can talk about the way the memory is requested. Memory can be either reserved and then later committed or reserved and committed simultaneously. Second, you can speak about the method of delivery. This refers to how the memory is packaged when you request it. This is usually in heaps or sections, which have their particular advantages and uses.

*Using the Reserve and Commit Method*
When memory is requested from Windows NT, the memory is first reserved and then committed. *Reserved memory* simply reserves a continuous range of virtual memory addresses for utilization by the particular process. The physical memory is not allocated at that time. When the memory is needed, the memory is *committed*, which involves allocating the memory to the process. This means that the memory cannot be used by another process, and the memory is either backed by suitable page file space or is guaranteed by Windows NT not to be removed from physical memory. When I say that the memory cannot be used by another process, I am talking about the virtual memory. Memory is allocated by assigning a series of virtual addresses that are published to the application. Of course, if your application is swapped out to the page file, the physical memory locations that the application might have been using can be used by another application. This is all managed behind the scenes by the VMM. Your application knows only that it receives the data or code that it requested; VMM takes care of shuffling it around in physical memory.

Memory can either be committed at the time it is reserved or the memory can be reserved in preparation for utilization prior to being used. Generally, you want to use a combination of these methods when possible. When you are certain that you will immediately use the amount of memory that the application is requesting, you want to reserve and commit. However, if you are aware that you might have sudden and severe memory allocation requirements, you might want to reserve a block of virtual memory addresses in advance. This process allows you to quickly commit memory and have reasonable certainty that the memory you are committing will be contiguous as far as the virtual addresses are concerned. Generally, this works to improve the applications' performance in moving large data sections into memory.

> **Note**
>
> *The level of control that you have over the allocation of memory is dependent on the development platform you are using. C++ developers find that they have very granular control over the methods and allocations of memory within their applications. Visual Basic developers find that the control for many of the structures in Visual Basic is being managed by the VB DLLs and built-in functions, which do the job well enough in most cases. VB developers can still have access to the same Win32 APIs that control the allocation of memory in Windows NT. Traditionally, this has been of only specialized use due to VB's incapability to deal effectively with pointers. ◆*

Let's analyze one application's use of the reserve and commit method of memory application.

> **Note**
>
> *I did not write the application we are about to discuss; therefore, I do not have access to source code. Although this might prevent us from looking at the exact code performing these actions, it still serves as an excellent example of how to use these particular memory functions. Also, it shows how you can tell what an application is doing based on the external tools that we cover here. Finally, it is useful to understand the memory-allocation process and general Windows NT system architecture as outlined previously and in the chapters in Part I, "Arm Yourself!: Tools for Performance Monitoring." ◆*

The application is an enterprise class replication system. The goal of such a system is to provide redundancy for data in real-time by copying any changes instantly to another machine on the network. In addition, the application permits automated fail over should the source machine crash. Speed for this application is very important. It must collect all the changes made to any attribute of any file or folder on the system that you request. Then, it must copy this information across a much slower link, the network. Because the amount of disk changes can be numerous and come in bursts, the application must provide some queuing mechanisms to collect and send the information to the remote machine. With these goals in mind, the application developers wrote the primary collection and queuing component as a Kernel mode driver. This accomplishes the following:

Priority over User mode services applications

Efficient collection of data through tight integration with the I/O manager

More direct use of system memory pools

Because the application was implemented as a driver, the amount of processor time, and base priority for the threads, is increased. This certainly helps the application perform its capture and copy functions in real time. Also, the best and perhaps the only place to put such a driver is in the I/O Manager stack. This allows the driver to collect the information from the source in the form of the IRP (see Chapter 4, "Freeware/Shareware Tools," for a review of the IRP). The IRP can be sent across the network and directly inserted into the I/O Manager queue of another machine. Only the exact changes are sent across the network, as opposed to the entire file, which allows the application to copy every attribute of the files and folders from one system to another. This includes the security attributes as well as other file attributes.

### Note

*The one attribute that is not copied is the date stamps. This fact helps us to understand a little more about the I/O Manager and when the time stamps are applied. The time stamp is not imbedded in the IRP and is placed on the file independent of when the request was made. It is generated when the file gets written. Thus, for the application in question here, the time stamps that are placed on the files are those of the remote machine and not the source machine.* ◆

This particular application is committed to providing fault-tolerant replication of data in a near real-time mode. The key goal is the perfect example of the need for the reserve and commit methods of utilizing memory. The application must be prepared for sudden bursts of data being sent. Also, for the sake of fault tolerance, you want the transfer to occur quickly to reduce the chance of a failure interrupting the transmission.

To account for these possibilities, the application pre-allocates a series of virtual addresses. Should the need arise to utilize the memory, half of the work is already done. The memory is reserved and only needs to be committed to be ready for use. The reservation process—being slightly more intensive than the middle process—saves the application precious time. In addition, the performance of the application is improved because the system has assigned a continuous range of virtual addresses. Although this does not necessarily translate to contiguous space in memory, it does provide some relief for the application and VMM. Where a large number of requests flood into the I/O Manager and the applications driver component, the data can be quickly queued to memory. If additional memory is required, it is quickly committed through one easy function. In this particular application, the amount of virtual addresses reserved is roughly equal to .75 times the size of the physical disk cache that is configured for the application.

**Note**

*In this case, we are primarily discussing the application's architecture from the point of view of its memory utilization method. The application itself has many other nuances for the queuing, storage, and fault tolerance of the data, should there be a failure on the server. Much like other transaction-based systems, such as the mission-critical database, there's a certain degree of transaction logging and transaction committing involved to achieve fault tolerance, in case of a critical system failure. The queuing mechanism utilizes the memory and the physical disk cache to provide this level of fault tolerance.* ♦

You can use the Performance Monitor to analyze the situation to see exactly how the application is adjusting its memory consumption. The following are the counters you should use in this case:

```
Process: Virtual Bytes

Process: Virtual Bytes Peak

Process: Working Set

Process: Working Set Peak
```

These counters help to examine the process. In Figure 6.1, you can see how the application appears when it is first launched.

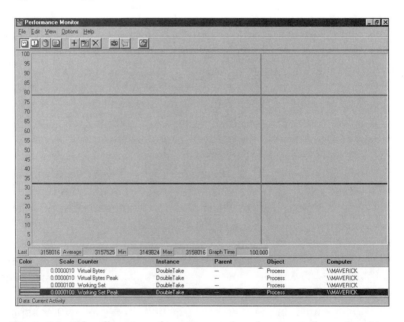

**Figure 6.1** *The allocation of memory needs to be repeatedly analyzed in Performance Monitor to understand how the application is really utilizing memory. Notice how the* Virtual Bytes *far exceed the entire* Working Set *by about 72,500,000 bytes.*

### Note

*When looking at Figure 6.1, keep in mind that the chart display is based on the scale presented in the lower portion of the Performance Monitor display. So, when you look at the values represented by the graph lines, for example, the* Virtual Bytes, *you need to take the value 80 and divide it by the scale, which is .000001. The resulting value is 80MB. If you look at the* Working Set *bytes, you see the value 35. However, the scale for the* Working Set *bytes is .00001. Thus, when you calculate 35 divided by .00001, you get 3,500,000. Notice also that the values for Minimum, Last, Average, and Maximum are displayed on the small area just below the chart's graph pane. These numbers do not require conversion using the scale.*

*When you're looking at exact numbers, working with the Performance Monitor chart display can be a bit confusing. Generally, when you are using the Chart View, you are examining the overall difference of some value. If you were looking for exact figures, as opposed to a simple relationship, you would use Report view. Refer to Chapter 1, "Introduction to Performance Monitor," for discussion on the various views.* ◆

The Virtual Bytes represents the set of virtual addresses that have been put on the reserve list for this particular process. The Virtual Bytes does not represent memory allocated or committed to this particular process. Although Virtual Bytes does not indicate the use of memory, the developer should keep in mind that the number of virtual addresses is finite. If they are overallocated to a particular process, that process might have problems trying to load other DLLs and code into memory. These problems could represent themselves in a variety of ways.

In the case of our particular application, they could represent themselves as a blue screen—a stop error. This brings the machine to a halt. The type of blue screen errors that you might see which indicate memory allocation problems are IRQL_LESS_THAN or IN_PAGE errors. The description of the error shows up in the blue screen. The reason that our application affects the system this way is because it has been implemented as a Kernel mode driver. On the other hand, if it had been written as a User mode service or application, the error would end up as a typical Dr. Watson error.

To avoid such problems, the application developers must have put an appropriate cap on the size of the virtual addresses that the driver can reserve. To do this effectively, the developers have to examine their application utilizing the Performance Monitor. They will have to check the Working Set, Virtual Bytes, Memory: Pages/sec, and Process: Pages/sec. Then, they have to log data using the Windows NT Performance Monitor's Log view during controlled testing. The testing involves increasing the application's load and the number of disk rights. Considering that the application is very focused in its goal and tasks, the code can be quite compact. In addition, there is not the issue of requiring additional DLLs based on different features being launched. This is more of an issue with user programs as opposed to Kernel mode drivers. Thus, for this particular application, the cap for the number of virtual addresses is probably quite high. Now, let's look at what occurs when you begin to place load on the application.

In Figure 6.2, we have changed the playing field by giving the copy application a sudden burst of data to deal with. The application must now move all the data written to the local disk through its buffers, through the network, and finally to the remote system. When this occurs, you can see that some of the Virtual Bytes are quickly allocated to the application's Working Set to provide for these operations.

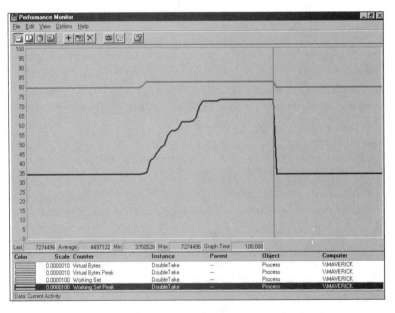

**Figure 6.2**   *The Performance Monitor can record only changes it cannot explain. That's where you come in.*

As exemplified by Figures 6.1 and 6.2, the Virtual Bytes does not appear to be a point of concern. However, recall that the number of virtual addresses is finite within the application. Consuming large numbers of virtual addresses in reservations can result in the application having difficulty loading other sections of its 2GB of User mode address space. If this were the case, the application would have an unusually high amount of paging associated with the loading of DLLs.

Detecting what precisely is "unusually high" is a matter of observing the application under a variety of conditions. Generally, you want to adjust any of the parameters that force the application to increase the virtual bytes that it is reserving. To properly do this type of analysis, you want to utilize baselines, as discussed in previous chapters and previous examples. However, you might also want to alter the programming. You can alter the programming strategy to utilize memory through a simultaneous reserve and commit mode as opposed to reserving ahead of time and then committing memory when needed. Altering the code this way allows you to establish a baseline for the performance of the application using the slower memory allocation method. It gives you an idea of how efficient it is to reserve memory ahead of time and then allocate or commit only when needed. In addition, utilizing this particular method of simultaneous reserve and commit allows you to see how the application will behave in a worst-case scenario.

Using the two-step commit scheme is good for applications that might need large and sudden amounts of memory. However, the method also adds some bulk and necessary logic to the code. Generally, you will use the Virtual Memory functions exported in the Win32 API. This set of functions requires more understanding of the memory allocations that you will require. In addition, you will find that some of the more pleasant benefits of the other functions will be missed. For the sake of keeping the code simple and compact, you do not want to always use this scheme. If you are loading small amounts of transitory data, you want to use the much simplified simultaneous reserve and commit functions in the Windows API. This enables you to avoid adding unnecessary complexity to programming code while still providing an efficient use of the allocation of memory. The more simplified functions for simultaneous reserve and commit utilize objects such as the memory heap—or heap, for short—and the global/local memory allocation functions.

## Using Memory Heaps

In Windows NT, the allocation of memory can occur in groups of memory pages called *heaps*. Heaps are created by system processes and User mode application processes. Some heaps are special and have been named for easy reference, such as the System Heap or the GDI Heap. All processes on Windows NT get a default heap. The default heap is generally 1MB in size and consists of virtual address space. Thus, the memory is not committed, only reserved.

The default heap for a user process can be increased through the heap management functions exported by the Win32 API. These functions allow you to either get a handle for the default heap or create any number of dynamic heaps within the process. A *dynamic heap* simply refers to a heap created within a user process from which the process will be allocating memory. Unlike the default heap, the dynamic heap can be entirely deleted at any time by the user process. The default heap cannot be deleted, although the size of the heap can be altered from the default of 1MB. The heap functions are numerous and have some nice features that allow you to concentrate on coding the application functions rather than worrying about the details of memory allocation. This is a change from using the previously discussed reserve and then commit memory functions. Of course, you lose a certain amount on granularity. When created, a heap can be fully or partially committed, again by using some of the heap functions.

### Note

*The functions that are mentioned here and throughout this chapter can be found in several locations:*

*MSDN*

*Microsoft Platform SDK*

*Microsoft Technical Articles (Web, TechNet)* ◆

Although the Windows NT Performance Monitor can give you an idea of how the memory is being allocated, if you want to see how the heaps are created and being divided, you need to use another tool. In Chapter 3, "Windows NT Utilities," you saw how an NT Resource Kit tool called the Heap Monitor can show you how the heaps are being utilized. This gives you an idea if you have programmed the heaps to be utilized or if you are simply wasting address space by creating them.

Keep in mind when creating your dynamic heaps that it is usually good to give the heap a name. Otherwise, when the heap is created, you cannot tell the difference between multiple heaps unless you can recognize them by the address where they are located. Programmatically, this does not matter much because you will be using a handle to access the heap. However, if you are trying to analyze the application's use of memory heaps, as we are here, having heaps with names makes analysis much easier.

When analyzing the heaps, you have to utilize several methods, depending on the level of detail that you want. Generally, your goal is for the sizing of the heap and the de-allocation of the heap (when necessary) to be appropriate.

First, you want to have a rather granular view of the memory allocations of the process that you are dealing with. This is best done in the Process Explode, PVIEW.EXE program. As seen in Chapter 3, this tool allows you to view the exact allocations of memory on a per process basis. It also gives you the information on the various DLLs that have been loaded by the program.

*Remember that some of the memory will not be in User mode, but in Kernel mode. In addition, some of the memory represents shared memory, as indicated in the Pool Charges section of the Process Explode screen. ♦*

Next, you want to use the Heap Monitor, HEAPMON.EXE, from the Windows NT Resource Kit. This tool allows you to track the allocations of the memory from the heaps. As a refresher, let's look at the Heap Monitor view of a VB 6.0 application in Figure 6.3. Here you can see that heaps are created and utilized by the VB 6.0 compiled application.

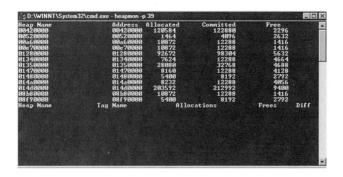

**Figure 6.3** *The Committed column indicates the size of the heap, whereas the Allocated and Free columns indicate the amount of memory utilized by the process.*

Within Visual Basic, you do not specifically know how memory allocation functions are using memory or heaps. These functions are typically accessed through the Windows API, which is what Visual Basic is doing behind the scenes. As I pointed out earlier, although you can access the Windows API functions from within Visual Basic, this is not usually a method used in regard to memory functions within Visual Basic. In this case, the normal programming methods for Visual Basic are simply to use declared variables and some user-defined structures. Visual Basic takes care of the memory allocations and heaps structures for you.

The application in question is a database frontend. The application collects information from an access database, which allows a user to view data and input additional records into the database. In addition, it allows for browsing through all records as well as the production of formatted reports. For this particular example, the application is used to browse system records for the selected individual records for editing.

Exercising the application causes the memory heaps to be exercised, which prompts Heap Monitor to update the display. Inverted lines indicate the changes. You can then compare the changes to the Process Explode's display of the process' memory utilization. This assists in determining from where the heaps are allocated. Recall that the process has a default heap that is initially 1MB in size. Shared memory heaps do not usually appear by name, with a few exceptions. In our Visual Basic application, the dynamic heaps are all created without utilizing naming conventions. Thus, all the heaps are listed based on their starting point in memory. As other features of our particular application are utilized that call upon various components—both the internal Visual Basic functions as well as external objects and functions from other OLE type servers—more heaps are allocated. For example, the application utilizes Microsoft Access object queries to achieve some of the listings.

In addition, the reporting utilizes Crystal Report® objects. In the preceding case, when we accessed the browsing and reporting methods, additional heaps were generated by Visual Basic and the supporting applications. Generally, multiple dynamically allocated heaps are good for small, discrete memory requirements. However, multiple heaps are poor performers when compared to careful utilization of the default heap for the process. The default heap, although starting at 1MB, is permitted to grow in size if memory allocations exceed the size of the heap. In addition, compilation options often allow you to set the size of the default heap for the application if you can calculate the size needed.

If you are observing the heap utilization when you have multiple heaps and notice that the heaps are 40% free on the average, you should consider using the default heap. In addition, when creating multiple heaps, you want to carefully examine the page faults for the application. Again, it is good to have a copy of the program that uses the default heap and a copy that uses the multiple heaps to compare. Any excessive increases in page faults are an indication of a poor implementation of the multiple heaps and a potential shortage of Virtual Address space.

### Global Allocations

Use of the Global and Local allocation functions is perhaps the highest level of memory manipulation. These memory functions have been around since Windows 3.1 and continue to be useful in the 32-bit world. The other allocation methods, although having more granularity in allocation of memory, have not completely replaced the functionality of the Global Allocation functions. These functions allow the user to access various heaps, generally named *shared heaps* and the default process heap, to claim memory. When examining the use of memory by these functions, you can use the same tools you used for the heaps. The only difference is that the functions are encapsulating some of the heap allocation functions within their own routines.

## Shared Memory

We have talked about the User mode memory, which is generally private memory. Private memory is visible only to the process that requested it. Other User mode processes will not be able to read or access the memory in any way. This is part of the protected memory model that is one of the core features of Windows NT. However, applications need to communicate with one another and share information. In addition, repeatedly loading DLLs and other code is a strain on the memory of any system. Shared memory is allocated by the Executive Services. It is allocated as section objects or mapped file I/O objects. These objects, when created, are named so that other processes can see the information. By default, Windows NT creates executables and DLLs in read-only section objects. This allows multiple processes to access the same DLL in memory without complications or having to reload the DLL. The system maintains two pools of memory for shared access, the Memory Page Pool and the Memory Non-Page pool.

When reviewing an application's use of the system pools, you can utilize the Process Explode program, PVIEW.EXE, to review the information for the application, total process, or the individual DLLs that it has loaded. High utilization of the shared memory can point to poorly constructed DLLs or badly organized functions within the DLLs.

## Note

*In this text, when discussing DLLs, I include ActiveX components, or OLE servers, and COM objects. DLLs started out as methods of treating shared code that can be used by multiple programs. However, today DLLs, as well as COM objects, are used for a different purpose—to modularize the code. Sometimes, it is done so that other programs can utilize particular functions. Other times, it simply serves as a method of distributing the program and its functions across multiple machines. Each instance has a different goal. One method shares functions for easier access, and another is for distributed computing. Thus, the coding for each one is different. Because the code is different and is created with a different goal in mind, the analysis should be different as well. Any analysis you perform must consider the goal of creating the COM object or DLL.*

*If you're writing a DLL for use locally, that is, for a workstation without any consideration of sharing the functions of the DLL or distributing the computing demand, the functions that you place in the DLL should be small and concise. The functions also should have a program-wide scope and be reused heavily.*

*In this case, if you place too many functions inside the DLL, it becomes large, increases paging, and generally results in a slower program. However, if the DLL is primarily a COM object built to distribute these functions across a network to multiple workstations, the functions that you place inside the COM object might be more numerous. You want the COM object to be self-contained so that the code can be updated efficiently. In this case, the DLL might be larger and contain functions that might not be used as often.*

*You will generally find that the COM object is paging slightly higher at times, but you might find this acceptable. On the other hand, in the case of the DLL running locally on a workstation, you would not find this acceptable. The bottom line is, when performing analysis on the types of DLLs and their effect on the performance of the system, you want to remember the purpose of the DLL, OLE server, or COM object. ◆*

You can perform further analysis on the process by using the Performance Monitor. You need to track the following counters for the user process running your application:

```
Process: Pool Paged Bytes
Process: Pool NonPaged Bytes
Process: Working Set
Process: Virtual Memory Bytes
Process: Page Faults/sec
```

These counters give you an idea of how the memory is being used and if it is being used effectively. Of course, you should always be leery of any application that continues to increase its system space, paged or non-paged pool, during the course of its operation. More than a 20% increase past the original start time is cause to believe that the application may have some sort of memory leak. This is especially true of device drivers, which spend much more of their time in the Kernel mode. If you suspect that a memory leak exists, you might want to examine the Process: Handle Count. If this value continues to increase, your application is allocating handles to objects and not relinquishing them.

More detailed information on allocation of memory can be seen in the PMON.EXE tool from the NT Resource Kit. This, in combination with the Process Explode and the Performance Monitor counters previously mentioned, should give you an adequate description of where the memory is going.

When reviewing the system pools and the page file utilization, it is important to keep the memory allocations in perspective. The application you are using is utilizing some shared resources on the system. If the resources run scarce, the entire system will begin to suffer.

## Processes and Threads

In this section, we turn our investigation toward the utilization of the processor. You need to understand the particular functions that affect and access the processor. In particular, you need to understand how to track processes and threads.

At the core of any program's operation are the *process* and the *thread*. The application cannot get anything done without them. These are the primary interfaces into the CPU via the Windows NT Microkernel. Understanding the process and the thread as well as the Microkernel's methods for dealing with them is key to being able to effectively analyze the processor's activity. First, you need to be able to isolate the process on a system giving you the problem. You have already seen this in Chapter 5, "General Resource Consumption," when you isolated the application calls from the interrupts. Then, you need to analyze that process and determine why or how it is consuming the processors' time.

## How Windows NT Runs Threads

Before you can review the actual activity of the processes and threads, you need to have a little more detail on how the threads get run. This allows you to better understand what you are seeing and make some assumptions about the data.

The first part of the discussion begins with how threads get scheduled on the processor. We discuss in detail the various states the thread goes through on its way to having the opportunity to execute code on the processor. We also discuss how threads can be interrupted on various levels rather than what the causes of these interruptions are.

We also discuss thread priorities. Of course, it is difficult to discuss scheduling without at least mentioning the priorities. However, initially, all you need to understand is that threads are assigned priorities and that some priorities are higher than others. Also, know that Windows NT examines priorities to determine which threads go on the processor and when. In the section "Priorities," however, we get into more detail about what the priorities really mean and how they relate to the performance of your application.

## Scheduling

A *process* is generally a container for the thread. The thread inherits some of the properties from the process and facilitates the execution of code on the processor. Thus, it is the thread that you are usually more concerned about when talking about processor operations.

The thread is scheduled to run on the processor by Windows NT's Microkernel—specifically the dispatcher or scheduler functions of the Microkernel. When a thread gets scheduled to run on the processor, it enters a queue. The Performance Monitor can display the current number of threads in the ready queue through the System: Processor Queue Length counter.

### Note

*Note that the* Processor Queue Length *counter is contained within the System object as opposed to the Processor object. This is because the* Processor Queue Length *is a measure of the entire queue, not just a queue that is associated with the single CPU. This is true even in a multiple processor system. When evaluating this particular counter, you need to keep in mind how many processors are currently installed on the system. Generally, when discussing the lengths of queues, you usually become concerned that there is a bottleneck when the number of items waiting in the queue is more than two. However, if you have multiple processors on your system, the potential* Processor Queue Length *value could be higher than average. This is because the* Processor Queue Length *is a measure of the queue for all processors. Thus, you do not have to be concerned until the value is greater than the sum of the processors multiplied by two.* ◆

A thread has several states as it progresses through the execution of code on the processor. The states are outlined in Figure 6.4. Changes from one state to the next are controlled via the Microkernel as well as the functionality of the processor code.

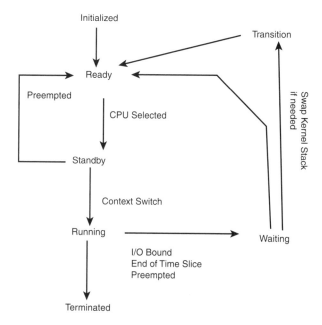

**Figure 6.4**    *The thread can be transitioned to different states based on the requirements of other threads on the system.*

The transitions occur for any of the following reasons:
- The thread has reached the end of its time slice (or quantums).
- The thread has become I/O bound.
- The thread has been pre-empted by a higher priority thread.

Each thread is given a time slice, or quantum, within which to perform as much work as possible. On Windows NT, the size of the quantum varies depending on the architecture of the system. The number of quantums that a thread has to complete its work is dependent on whether you are running Windows NT Server or Workstation and if the thread had been previously waiting for a chance to run.

> ### Note
>
> *On Windows NT Workstation, a thread starts with 6 quantum for a time slice. On Windows NT Server, the thread starts with 36 quantum. The idea is Windows NT Server is attempting to make sure that the thread can complete as much work as possible when it is given a chance to run. Consider that the server is typically responding to user requests. You don't want the server to be responsible for the client thread not getting the information requested; thus, you make sure that, more often than not, the server can fulfill a request within a single time slice before returning to a wait state. ♦*

Threads can receive changes in the number of quantum they receive based on what is usually called a *boost*. The thread boost occurs when a thread returns from an I/O bound state or when a thread has not been able to run for a period of time. When a thread becomes I/O bound, it stops running because it is waiting for input from some external source, such as the keyboard or hard drive. When the data is received and the system is notified via an interrupt, the thread is given a boost in priority and quantum in an effort to allow it to immediately react to the data. *Priority* is simply an organization of the importance of a thread or process. We cover this topic in more detail shortly.

The other condition, where a thread has not been running for some time, occurs when other threads with higher priority continually grab the processors' attention. If NT permits the condition to continue, the thread with less priority may never have a chance to execute. Thus, a priority and quantum boost is given to the thread. In the Performance Monitor, you can see this condition shown in Figure 6.5.

When analyzing your program, you want to look for these conditions among your program threads. Having this type of activity occur on a regular basis is an indication that the threads are not being utilized correctly in the program. The problem can be one in which a thread of lesser priority has information that a thread of higher priority is waiting on. The higher priority thread drops into a wait state, but other high priority threads continue to monopolize the CPU. Thus, the lower priority thread never has a chance to complete the work and feed the high priority thread the information that it needs. Windows NT then attempts to resolve the problem by boosting the lower thread. This should allow the work to complete, but is not a guarantee. When using multiple threads in your application, you need to be aware that this condition can exist. Although it usually does not stop the system from running, you can slow the system down—especially the execution of your application.

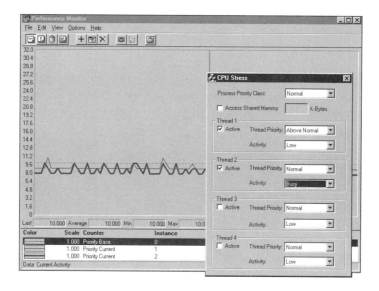

**Figure 6.5**    *The thread is given a boost to allow it to complete,*
*as seen by the sudden peaks.*

The last reason for the thread to transition off of the processor is the pre-empting of the thread by a higher priority. The thread priority is based on the process's base priority when it is first launched. The priority of the process affects how the Windows NT Microkernel schedules the thread and can affect performance. The next section examines the priorities in an effort to first describe what the priorities mean and then relate the various priority levels back to performance.

*Priorities*

On Windows NT, priorities are assigned to every thread or interrupt on the system that can be scheduled. The priorities for system and application threads are used to determine when they will get processor time. Table 6.1 shows the various priorities.

*Table 6.1    Priorities on a Windows NT System*

| Thread Priorities | Process Base Priority | | | |
|---|---|---|---|---|
| | Idle | Normal | High | Real Time |
| Idle | 1 | 1 | 1 | 16 |
| Lowest | 2 | 6 | 11 | 22 |
| Below Normal | 3 | 7 | 12 | 23 |
| Normal | 4 | 8 | 13 | 24 |
| Above Normal | 5 | 9 | 14 | 25 |
| Highest | 6 | 10 | 15 | 26 |
| Time Critical | 15 | 15 | 15 | 31 |

The thread priority is based on the process's initial priority. Generally, the thread operates within the range of base priorities of the process. Recall that the base priority of the process is generated upon the creation of the process. So, this initial priority that can be set programmatically determines the process's overall base priority and thus, the priority range within which the threads will operate. Earlier we discussed the boost that a thread gets when the thread was determined to not have been running or to have received only input from an external source.

Usually, most programs run at the normal process priority. However, you might have a program that requires a more aggressive operation cycle. In those instances, you want to increase the priority of the process and allow the thread to have a higher maximum priority.

Other threads that have a higher priority can pre-empt threads that are running on the processor. In addition, threads can be pre-empted by hardware interrupts, as you saw in Chapter 5. Although this scheme helps in the efficient scheduling of threads, there is the potential, as I pointed out earlier, for the thread to have a problem getting an execution time at all. The scheme of priority boosting and pre-emptive operation allows the Windows NT system to operate smoothly.

Using the Process Explode, you can view the priority of the various processes and threads running on the system. Within the Process Explode, you can view the information but you cannot adjust the priority of the process or the thread.

At this point, you understand what the priority of a process or thread is. You know that the thread's priority can be shifted, programmatically or by the Windows NT Microkernel. You understand the reasons for these various shifts in priority. So, tracking shifts in priority can assist us in determining what the Windows NT system, and the programs it's servicing, are doing. It is also an indication of how programs are reacting to other influences, such as hardware interrupts. You have just a little further to go to effectively track and utilize the data regarding our processes and threads so that you can judge the performance of our application. Let's continue our discussion of processes and threads by examining how to analyze the various priorities in wait states of the threads that actually perform the work on behalf of our applications.

## Tracing Thread/Processes in Performance Monitor

At this point, you have isolated the processor activity down to the software, as opposed to the hardware. Now you need to do some real analysis on the process to determine how it is using the processor's time. Isolating the system down to a particular process is easy. You simply open the Performance Monitor and select the Process: %Processor Time for each of the processes on the system. Then you can switch the Performance Monitor over to the histogram style in Chart view. Identify the process with the highest peak, and you are there. After you have done that and determined which process is causing the problem, you want to analyze the process in question. Again, we start with the Performance Monitor and the following counters:

```
Process: %Processor Time
Process: %Privilege Time
Process: %User Time
Process: ID Process
```

Recall that the ID Process is necessary to make sure that the instance of the Process does not restart on you. When that happens, the ID Process value momentarily drops to zero. When reviewing the process, you will observe the %Privilege Time and the %User Time; these counters give you an indication of where the process is spending most of its time. When reviewing process and thread activity in Chart view, you should adjust the update time. The default update time for Chart view is 1.0 seconds. You should adjust this down to 0.1 seconds, which is about as fast as the Performance Monitor can handle. The screen updates quickly, so if you want to analyze anything, you need to be ready to adjust the Chart options to Manual Update. The quickest way to put the update on hold is to perform the following keystrokes: Ctrl+O, M, Enter. This puts the Chart update on manual mode. The processes are generally containers for the threads, which carry the program instructions to the processor via the Microkernel. Examination of the program processor utilization must include an examination of the threads.

In the Performance Monitor, you can identify and examine the various thread activities. Initially, you want to isolate any problems to the thread that is causing the problem. In the Performance Monitor, you can examine the same counters for the thread that you had already monitored for the overall process:

```
Thread: %Processor Time
Thread: %Privilege Time
Thread: %User Time
Thread: ID Process
Thread: ID Thread
```

As you can see, you want to track the ID Process and the ID Thread when you are examining the threads, so that you are aware if the process or the thread is stopped and restarted. As with the process, if the thread is terminated, the ID Thread value drops momentarily to zero. When you are examining the system, you can then identify which thread is causing the problem. Then, examining the code, you can figure out which thread it is. This allows you to track what you have done to keep the thread so busy.

The last section covered threads and their various states of operation. The transition between the states can speak to the operation and efficiency of your code. In addition, it can give you information on the potential causes for excessive context switches. A *context switch* occurs when a different thread is moved onto the processor or when a thread requires information from another thread. It is best to avoid the second case when you program. This can be achieved through careful planning and the use of appropriate prioritization of the threads. Threads that need to complete prior to other processes should be given a higher priority to facilitate the completion of calculations or input of data prior to another thread requiring the information.

To view the context switches, you can use the Performance Monitor's System: Context Switches/sec. When reviewing the context switches, adjust the update time for the Performance Monitor to 0.1. This allows you to view the information more accurately. Generally, for a system doing very little, the number of Context Switches/sec is around 120. This is another one of those values that you need to track if you want to see the effects of your particular program. Putting this value together with the observation of the thread state transitions details the efficiency of your thread execution and prioritization. To review the thread state transitions, use the Performance Monitor. For the Thread object, use the following counters:

```
Thread: Context Switches/sec
```

```
System: Context Switches/sec
Thread: Thread State
Thread: Thread Wait Reason
```

To determine the percentage of the context switches directly attributed to your particular application's threads, use a combination of the Thread: and System: Context Switches/sec. Observing just the System: Context Switches/sec can be deceiving as the scope of the object is the entire system, which includes multiple processors. The Thread State and the Thread Wait Reason are both integer numbers corresponding to a description. In Tables 6.2 and 6.3, the descriptions are matched up with the various states and wait reason values.

*Table 6.2    Thread States*

| Counter Value | State Description |
| --- | --- |
| 0 | Initialized—The thread is being created. This is typically brief. |
| 1 | Ready—This thread is prepared to utilize a processor; however, there is no processor free to handle the thread. Threads in this state are counted against the System: Processor Queue Length in the Performance Monitor. |
| 2 | Running—The thread is actively utilizing a processor. |
| 3 | Standby—The thread is in transition. It is to be processed on a processor. This transition is the context switch from the ready queue to the running state on the processor. |
| 4 | Terminated—When the thread has completed its operations, it drops into the terminated state. This does not imply that the thread object is being destroyed. Whether the thread is destroyed or maintained is left to the original process and programmer. |
| 5 | Wait—The thread enters a wait state when the thread has requested synchronization of data with an external component or subsystem. |
| 6 | Transition—The transition phase occurs after a wait state. If the kernel memory containing the needed information for the execution of the thread has been swapped out of memory, the thread is given a designation of transition while the information is swapped back in. When the memory is present, the thread enters the ready state. |
| 7 | Unknown—This occurs when the Performance Monitor is unable to ascertain the exact state of the thread. This can happen when the thread is moving from one state to the next. |

*Table 6.3    Thread Wait Reasons*

| Counter Value | Wait Reason |
| --- | --- |
| 0, 7 | Waiting for the Executive |
| 1, 8 | Waiting for a free memory page |
| 2, 9 | Waiting for a memory page to be paged into memory |
| 3, 10 | Waiting for memory pool allocation |
| 4, 11 | Execution Delay |
| 5, 12 | Suspended condition |
| 6, 13 | User Request |
| 14 | Event Pair High |
| 15 | Event Pair Low |
| 16 | LPC Receive |
| 17 | LPC Reply |
| 18 | Virtual Memory |
| 19 | Page Out |

These reasons are only valid when the thread is in a wait state. When reviewing the various states in the Performance Monitor, it is best to review them in Report view, rather than Chart view.

Using this information, you can determine how often threads are waiting and why. You can look at the thread wait reasons; they give you an indication of the nature of the problem, which sometimes is with a different component. Memory again plays its part. If excessive paging is occurring, the information the threads need may not be readily available. This results in wait reasons of 19, 18, 1, 8, 2, 9, 3, and 10. Again, if your threads are unorganized, you tend to wait on information from the other threads. Also, the use of shared memory can present a problem for multiple threads utilizing the same information. Both the unorganized thread functions and the shared memory can result in synchronization problems, reasons 14, 15, 4, and 11.

When creating multiple threads, it is usually recommended that you have no more than four threads per process. Also, you should have a distinct reason for the creation of a new thread. Your code should utilize the thread in a consistent manner. Although it is good to have a thread working in the background on tasks, it is not good if the foreground application is not properly programmed to handle delays in receiving information from the background thread. If your display is completely blank while the background thread is retrieving data, your extra thread has done little but allow you to update an empty display.

# Summary

In this chapter, you spent some time getting into more detail regarding particular resources, memory and processor. Starting with memory, you learned how applications can allocate memory and the effects of such allocation. You learned something about how the various choices can affect the overall performance of your application. You also looked at how to analyze the effectiveness of your choices for memory allocation utilizing some of the Resource Kit tools, as well as the Performance Monitor.

Our discussion of the processor resource delved heavily into the analysis of processes and, more specifically, threads. You learned how the Windows NT operating system schedules threads and how priorities work into the scheduling. You learned about thread wait states. This information, combined with the information about priorities, enabled you to see how you can use the Windows NT Performance Monitor to analyze how your application is performing on Windows NT in regard to the processor. You also saw how you can use this information to determine if you are encountering performance issues related to other components, such as network interface cards.

As with most of the information supplied in this book, I recommend that you apply it at your next opportunity. I suggest taking a couple of applications and analyzing the process and thread priorities and wait states. Try to relate this back to what the application and the rest of the system was doing at the time when you made your observations.

*Part* **III**

# *The Specialist: Analysis of Specific Application Scenarios*

# 7
# The Web Server

The Web server has been getting a lot of press lately. The Internet and Web services are a new generation of systems that administrators and developers have to deal with. For Internet services, it is a very exciting time; but it is also a time of constant and rapid change, as well as untried technologies. Trying out new technologies and programming methodologies is always interesting and often entertaining. However, without historical data to help us make determinations on programming methods or styles, we are left to use our own performance analysis tools to help us make those choices. In this chapter, we utilize tools and techniques that should assist you in analyzing the performance of your applications on a Web server.

We start by looking at the general resources the Web server might consume and how to monitor its overall behavior. The tools we will use are the same ones we have been using for general program analysis on Windows NT. However, in the case of a Web server, we have to apply these tools in a different way or look at the presented data with a new point of view. Understanding how to monitor the basic system is necessary before you can focus on the reaction of the system to running your code. After we have this information well in hand, we can concentrate our analysis on particular resource issues for Web services. One of the important resources on a Web server is the memory cache.

We will spend some time analyzing the Web server's caching system. *Caching* is how most Web services attempt to speed up the delivery of Web content. As with many operating systems, the hard drive is the slowest component. The Web server attempts to compensate by utilizing a memory cache independent of Windows NT's own file system cache. For most Web services, the cache utilization and size are reactions to the load being placed on the Web server by the Internet or intranet users. Thus, we need to spend some time discussing how clients affect the load on the Web server.

The next section focuses on how the community of users browsing your Web site affects its performance. Clients can affect the Web server's performance in a variety of ways. The number of clients affects the load on a server. But there's more. The clients' patterns of usage on the Web server can affect the system. Because the usage pattern of the client is directly affected by the system architecture, design of the Web pages, and the supporting code, it is important for the developer to analyze the performance of the system over time. In addition, the client's selection of a browser can sometimes affect the system. Given that there are multiple ways of making connections and displaying information, we also should spend some time looking specifically at how to analyze the type and the efficiency of our connections.

In the final section of this chapter, we look at the connectivity methods and, specifically, how the coding selections made by the developer affect the performance of the system.

### Note

*Although the rules and issues presented here apply to any Web server, sometimes I speak of particulars of running Web services on Windows NT. The system I primarily use for my analysis and examples is the Microsoft Internet Information Server (IIS).* ◆

Prior to talking about the analysis, we should discuss the methods for analysis in this particular case. Up to this point, we have looked at applications that are generally self-contained on a single workstation. So, our analysis has been specific to this narrow and somewhat monolithic mode of operation.

In the case of the Web server, we are analyzing the effects of multiple users and multiple browsers on the system's performance. Thus, some of the techniques and approaches to analysis must be adjusted to better suit the particular type of system we will be analyzing. For starters, limited studies of your own system are going to yield very little information. In other words, to check performance, you cannot simply load the Web server on your workstation or test system and analyze your single connection to it.

When analyzing the Web site or any other enterprise-type application, you need to analyze the system over an extended period of time in a close-to-production situation. Often, this means you are monitoring the production system on a regular basis so that you can anticipate what coding changes might do to performance of the Web server. You need to analyze your production Web server constantly anyway. Why? Because these systems' performance is always at the whim and fancy of the people connected to it, the users. The users' patterns of operation or functions that they use might change at any time. These changes in usage patterns might be dependent on conditions or influences that you know nothing about. It might be that the business you wrote the software for is simply doing better than you anticipated, which can be both good and bad. At any rate, you need to be on top of how the programming changes you make affect the system, and, more importantly, how the changes in the user usage patterns affect the system.

Some seemingly simple changes to your Web site can alter the way the users perceive and access the Web site, changing their navigation patterns completely. Such a relationship, though difficult to completely study, is certainly worthy of attention. If you can anticipate how the users will react to your system, you can build your system to guide the users in a direction you want them to go. This should greatly affect your ability to build an excellent application as well as ensure that the hosting systems perform to the best of their capability. It comes down to a commitment to perform constant analysis on your system and applications, in order to discover improvements and vulnerabilities. In the Web system, users can be unpredictable in their usage patterns and relentless in their demand for system responsiveness.

To summarize, in our pursuit to analyze a Web server, we begin with looking at the overall resource consumption. Observing how the Web server utilizes memory and caching mechanisms is next. Then, we look at how the users affect the system. Finally, we analyze the connectivity methods and some programming choices.

# Resource Consumption on the Web

Like any other large system package, the Web server has its particular issues and primary resource consumption areas. When examining any Web system, you want to start by looking at the overall system. This is similar to the approach we took when examining the overall system performance for applications in Chapters 5, "General Resource Consumption" and 6, "Examining the Application" However, you need to examine the Web server's specific components once you have a clear understanding of the system's overall performance behavior. Any Web system uses all of the system resources on a computer, but in particular ways. Let's look at each one briefly and then focus on the particulars. We begin with the physical disk resource. The Web server's utilization of the disk is fairly unique to this type of system. Next, we have a look at the memory cache, primarily due to its relationship to disk performance. The caching system on a Web server has a primary goal of augmenting the disk subsystem. Finally, we discuss the processor and the networking component collectively.

## Disk Performance on a Web Server

First, you must consider the disk operations. A Web server is almost completely a read-only system. Now, you can argue this point, indicating that the input pages and business connectivity systems make the Web server more like a traditional read-write system, but I disagree. In any major system where you have a Web server connected to a major business system, you want to separate the physical systems. For example, if you have a Web server that collects simple survey information from users visiting the site, you might have a database that holds the resulting data. The best-suited database is an enterprise class database, such as MS SQL Server or Oracle for NT.

The systems you run the database server on have drastically different resource requirements from the Web server. Databases are routinely heavy memory users, gobbling up memory left and right to satisfy user requirements. In Chapter 8, "Monitoring Database Systems," we examine these types of systems and their resource consumption. Web servers use memory more sparingly, although they too can utilize a lot of memory when many users are connected to the system. You might get the idea that these types of systems (databases and Web servers) do not necessarily play well together when they are on the same computer, which is one of my points. You will usually want to separate systems that are expected to receive heavy use so that each computer can be best configured to handle the types of tasks that it will be performing. A serious enterprise Web server will not be running additional system-like SQL database software. The system will be dedicated to Web services. With this in mind, the Web server is anticipated to be alone on the system, resulting in the disk operations being primarily read operations. Thus, you want to focus on the read operations of the system to get an idea of how the system is performing.

### Finally, a Use for Disk Striping

*For those who never thought that there would ever be a good use for plain old disk striping, here it is. Disk striping, called RAID 0, is the distribution of data on multiple disks. Disk striping by itself is not fault tolerant like its brother, disk striping with parity—RAID 5. Vanilla striping simply reads data from across multiple hard drives and potentially multiple controller cards, which accomplishes increased disk throughput. The NT system is permitted to access multiple drives simultaneously when reading data. This means increased response to the Web server's requests for Web pages to be loaded.*

*Because the Web server is primarily a read-only system, this really can help the Web server's performance, even on low-cost hard drives with relatively inexpensive or old technology controller cards. Of course, it is understood that you have your Web server pages and code stored on a separate machine in some type of source code control system with adequate fault tolerance measures in place as well as regular backups. If you are basing your business on such a system, I expect you to have a redundant server in place as well. This type of configuration makes your Web system completely read-only with no reliance on critical data fault tolerance.*

*With this in mind, the disk configuration needs only to consider speed of data retrieval. Issues of fault tolerance and disk write performance are irrelevant. Disk striping meets the needs of speed as well by being inexpensive to implement.* ✦

When analyzing the disk issues related to the Web server, you want to pay close attention to the size and usage of the file system cache, as well as the Web server's own cache. Talking about cache naturally leads us into a discussion of another resource—memory.

## Memory Usage on a Web Server

Memory on a Web server is used in a couple of different ways—one is for running the system code and the other is for caching information to compensate for disk performance. Despite the Web server's unique use of memory, the memory on Web servers is not seen as a highly critical resource when compared to other enterprise class system services, such as database servers. This is primarily due to the relatively small size of the code and data that needs to be cached. However, in the near future this could change.

Every system needs enough memory to run its functions effectively; however, the Web server is not a particularly greedy system. Every Web server has some type of caching system to make up for the relatively slow speed of the disk subsystem. Later, we pay some special attention to the analysis of the caching system of a Web server. For now, watching the Process: Working Set Size, Process: Virtual Bytes, and the Process: Page Faults/sec should be sufficient to have a handle on the Web server's use of memory. Note that in all cases where we utilize the Process object, you want to use the Web services as the instance—for example, Internet Publishing Services for IIS. When you are analyzing a Web server's functions, make sure that you include all the relevant processes. This includes services that have to do with indexing and other maintenance functions that are not necessarily part of the Web-page delivery system, but nonetheless affect the overall performance of the machine.

## Processor and Network Resources on a Web Server

The next resources that we should discuss are closely tied together—the processor and the network. Overall, the Web server is not a processor-intensive system. However, you might recall that the network interface card relies on the processor to handle almost all the communication between the card and the system. Thus, the processor's capabilities affect the performance of the network in as much as it is able to respond and process hardware interrupts. For this reason, we'll discuss these resources collectively as opposed to individually. When examining the networking resource on a Web server, it is always really important to watch the following:

```
Processor: %Processor Time
Processor: %Interrupt Time
Processor: %DPC Time
System: Total DPCs/sec
System: Total Interrupts/sec
```

You have seen the first few counters before. We used them to determine if the processor activity was related to hardware or software. In this case, we assume that the determination was already made and that we are specifically analyzing the performance of the network card on a Web server. Of course, it could be any system that has very high volumes of network traffic, not necessarily just a Web server. The two System object counters give us totals for the entire system.

### Note

*The last two counters in the list, the System objects, have special significance on a multiple processor machine. The value of the counters is a total value for the entire system, which means for all of the processors simultaneously.*

*When performing an analysis on a multiple processor machine, you want to make sure that all the counters examined for the Processor object are done for each individual processor. Despite Windows NT's best efforts, the processors are rarely utilized uniformly. Analyzing each individual processor gives you a better idea of exactly how the work is being distributed. In some cases, it is possible to adjust the parameters of the system's hardware to achieve a better distribution of the workload specifically related to the handling of interrupts. We return to this topic shortly, after we have discussed some of the underlying concepts.* ◆

The counters and objects are all related to the processor, but we are really analyzing the effects of network traffic on the processor. When looking at the network traffic, you want to have some idea of the amount of traffic to compare against the resource utilization of the processor. You generally start with the `Network Segment: %Network Utilization`. This gives you a gauge of how busy the network segment is. Collecting information on this counter and the previously mentioned counters for the Processor object is important to establish the trend of utilization of these system resources. A production system always requires constant analysis. In addition, any system that you are using for simulation or testing should be analyzed in the same way. This allows you to predict how your changes might affect the production system when implemented. Later, in the section called "Connections," we examine the network more closely.

Now that we've covered the general resource utilization for a Web server, we need to get a little more focused. We begin our more intent analysis with a concentrated look at how the Web server utilizes memory to the various caching systems. Understanding this caching system is useful in understanding other issues, such as the users' effect on the Web server and connectivity choices the programmer makes when developing code for Web servers or browsers.

# Cold Hard Cache

In this section, we focus on memory utilization. The analysis and control of the various caching mechanisms are important to a Web server. Caching allows the system to respond quickly as it does not have to rely on disk I/O when retrieving critical information. Of course, as a developer, controlling the number of objects and the flow of the code can assist in reducing the load that the system has to carry in the cache. When looking at the Web server's memory utilization, we must keep an eye on the following general resources:

Service Memory (Working Set)

System Memory

System Cache

Service Cache

In the following sections, I discuss these general resources and point out ways to analyze how the Web server utilizes each one. In addition, information is provided on Performance Monitor objects and counters that can be useful in your analysis. When appropriate, various programming choices that can affect the particular resources are presented.

## Service Memory

First, you need to get an idea of the size of the Web services' Working Set. The Working Set usually includes, at the least, the code for the service. However, it also usually includes a good portion of some of the resources for the caching system for the Web services. In IIS, the Working Set also contains the IIS Object Cache. The Object Cache contains all the information on the loaded or frequently loaded objects. These objects are usually comprised of objects the programmers have created—such as connections to other systems, file handles, or other customized objects. You probably realize that, as you build new objects and connectivity to other support systems, you affect the overall size of the Web server's Working Set. For best performance, you want to ensure that the Working Set of the service fits into physical memory. In the IIS world, the service is called INETINFO.EXE.

The size of the Working Set depends again on the various components you have running. According to Microsoft, the IIS code is about 400KB. Although this might be normal for the code, it is unlikely that you will see a Working Set this low. The basic elements that make a Web site great are the objects that use lots of memory, thus, increasing the size of the Working Set. In the simplest of Web sites, you will see the Working Set size around 5MB. This size increases depending on which users are connected to the system and, mostly, on what those users are doing. Again, you need to monitor the site over time to get an idea of the type of activity that occurs on your site and the objects that get loaded. We discuss the actual details of the Object Cache shortly. For now, to get a grasp on the size of your Working Set, you need to log the information about the Working Set over time. In addition, you want to have a concept of the amount of paging. The following are the counters that you should collect for this situation, as well as others that will be mentioned shortly:

```
Process: Working Set: [Web service instance]

Process: Working Set Peak: [Web service instance]

Memory: Available Memory

Process: Page Faults/sec: [Web service instance]

Web Service: Current Connections

Internet Information Services Global: Objects
```

The first four counters are clearly common to all Web services; the last two are particular to IIS. You should keep an eye on the `Available Memory` to make sure that the system is not undergoing any major strain due to the activity of the Web services. The `Page Faults/sec` gives further indication of memory pressure as the system trims the Web services' Working Set, and any other services on the system, to curb overall memory utilization. When this happens, you either need to reduce the size of the Working Set through some creative coding or increase the physical memory.

Additionally, you have the option of reducing the utilization of memory from other components on the system. The `Web Service: Current Connections` lets you know how many connections there are, giving you a general indication of how busy the Web site is. The `Internet Information Services Global: Objects` lets you know how many total objects are loaded into the system's Object Cache, which is held in the Working Set of IIS. The number and size of these objects are the chief concerns of the developer. Keeping the number of objects low and compacting them as much as possible are key to keeping the memory requirements of the Web services to a minimum.

> **Note**
>
> *Keeping the number of objects to a minimum can be tricky. Depending on the scripting choice and the Web services you are using, you should reuse the same object as much as possible. With IIS, for example, the connection pooling can be configured so that a small set of connection objects is created to service the multiple connections to external systems. Such mechanisms should be researched and utilized to their fullest extent if you hope to keep the Web server running as efficiently as possible.* ◆

## System Memory

Next, we look at the system memory. When speaking of the system memory, we are chiefly referring to the memory pools the system controls. The `Pool Paged Memory` and the `Pool Nonpaged Memory` counters are of primary concern. The use and consumption of these pools varies widely depending on your Web server system. The IIS system tends to operate primarily in Kernel mode, and through programmer choice, much of the memory utilization occurs in the nonpaged pool. Keeping such threads and some critical information in the nonpageable memory pool guarantees that the data is in physical memory at all times. This is good for the performance of the service;

but if abused, it can lead to problems keeping the operating system, as a whole, functioning normally. The size of the pools is controlled by the operating system and is primarily based on the amount of memory in the system. To increase the size of the pools, you usually must increase the amount of physical memory in the system.

> **Note**
>
> *You can increase the size of the nonpaged memory pool and the page memory pool manually, although Microsoft strongly suggests that you leave it to the system to calculate. But, if we always followed rules, we wouldn't be programmers, right? So, using the Registry editor of your choice, you can adjust the following parameters to the values that you prefer:*
>
> ```
> HKEY_LOCAL_MACHINE
>     \SYSTEM
>         \CurrentControlSet
>             \Control
>                 \Session Manager
>                 \Memory Management
> ```
>
> *For the* `nonpagedpoolsize`, *the maximum permissible value is 128MB, no matter how much memory you have on the system. When increasing this value, I suggest incremental changes of 1MB until you get to a suitable size. If you want information on how this particular calculation is performed, a Microsoft Knowledge-based article, "Q126402: PagedPoolSize and NonPagedPoolSize Values in Windows NT," roughly explains the calculations.*
>
> *When you are viewing the Registry key, you might notice two subkeys that refer to session manager. The first has a space, "Session Manager"—this is the one you want. The other subkey, "SessionManager," does not apply to the topic at hand.* ◆

## System Cache

The system cache, or file system cache, is used by the operating system to improve data retrieval from the hard drive. Quick response time to requests for data is an objective of the Web service, which makes the optimization of the system cache a chief concern of the Web master. Making sure there is ample memory for the system generally is the big issue. Looking at the effectiveness of the cache is also important. The efficiency of the cache gives you an indication of the quality of the organization of your code and pages. In addition, it gives you signs that perhaps your disk subsystem's structure needs to be better organized.

### Note

*Recall that the file system cache is where the most recently read items are stored. Due to the importance of this, you have some options for setting up the bias for the server service. Normally, on an application server, you set the bias in the Control Panel's Networking applet as Maximize Throughput for Applications. In the case of the Web service, this is the default recommendation as well. There are some exceptions.*

*If you are watching the Working Set of the Web services and have ample memory to handle these services, you should consider changing this setting to Maximize Throughput for File Services. This favors giving more in memory to the file system cache. Again, you want to monitor the system over time, and whenever you make changes to Web content, make sure you are supplying the system with the appropriate memory for the Web services' Working Set. Be careful that altering this setting does not cause an increase in paging for the code contained within the Working Set.* ♦

To check on the file system cache, you start by looking at the size of the cache over time as the system is utilized. The cache is monitored using the Performance Monitor counters, or you can look at the Task Manager. In addition, you can use the Resource Kit Utility PMON.EXE. For the Performance Monitor, you want to look at the following counters:

```
Memory: Available Memory
Memory: Cache Bytes
```

These counters give an indication of the size of the cache and the amount of available memory. If the available memory is around 4MB, you are generally short on memory. You either need to add physical memory or reduce the memory requirements of other components. Logging this information over time is important. You should compare it with the other counters mentioned thus far in this chapter. Analyzing all the counters together and comparing them reveals the effects of one on the other.

To check on the file system cache performance, I first must explain a few memory items. Generally, when you are providing information to the network interface, the system utilizes a method called *Direct Memory Access* (DMA), which you are probably familiar with. DMA enables the system to move information directly from the cache, which is simply a section of memory allocated for a specific purpose, to the *network interface card* (NIC). To access the appropriate locations in memory, the system employs

the *Memory Descriptor Lists* (MDL). The lists track the address relationships between the files and the physical address locations in memory for the
file system cache. Because the Web server is primarily moving the information out through the network card, the Web services and related components take full advantage of the MDL in the file system cache.
Understanding this process allows you to use the Performance Monitor to
track the performance of the Web services' use of the file system cache. The
following are other counters you can use to track the Memory Descriptor
Lists:

```
Cache: MDL Reads/sec

Cache: MDL Read Hits%

Memory: Cache Faults/sec
```

These counters tell you how often the information is being found in the file
system cache. The MDL Reads/Sec value should be observed over time.
Typically, the cache is highly utilized when the Web site consists primarily of
static pages. If you are dynamically creating a lot of pages, the importance
of the file system cache begins to decrease. Dynamically generated pages are
not found on the hard drive or held in memory but are re-created upon each
access. Although these certainly have a place in the world of Web content,
overuse of dynamic pages can cause substantial reductions in the responsiveness of the Web site. Thus, watching the number of MDL Reads/sec can, over
time, tell you if you are decreasing your utilization of the file system cache
and potentially reducing your performance.

> **Note**
>
> *Reducing the reliance on the file system cache is not always a bad thing. However,
> it does mean that you need to think of your Web site differently. If you are using
> more dynamic pages, you need to be sure to consolidate the code that generates
> those pages effectively. You will most likely see an increase in the size of the Web
> services' Working Set. This is due to the increased necessity to keep information
> loaded in the Working Set as opposed to the file system cache. The Working Set
> contains the code and objects that you will use to generate the dynamic pages.
> Also, if you have shifted your use of dynamic pages, you definitely want to make
> sure that the Server Service bias in Control Panel, Networking is set to Maximize
> Throughput for Applications. This favors giving memory to Working Sets instead
> of giving memory to the file system cache.* ◆

The MDL Read Hits% lets you know how often the MDL reads hit their mark in the file system cache. If this counter is low, below 70% or so, see if you haven't altered your reliance on the file system cache by using more dynamic content. Make adjustments to the system to compensate for this. However, if you are expecting your site to have primarily static content, this counter should actually approach 100%. The more dynamic content that is present, as well as the more that the dynamically generated content consists of requests by users, the lower this value will be. With a primarily static site, if the counter is lower, you also should look at the organization of the Web site. A low value for a primarily static Web site could be caused by any of the following:

> An extreme number of Web pages
>
> Heavy use of large graphic files
>
> Heavy use of animated objects
>
> Lack of memory
>
> Use of dynamic pages

Essentially what occurs is that the memory resources required to maintain the objects in the cache exceed what the operating system will allow based on current physical memory and the memory requirements of other processes.

Generally, the textual content of a Web page is not enough to cause a problem. However, when you add other, more graphical content, you begin to see issues with the organization of the pages. Use of graphical content and other large objects should be considered carefully for their impact on the Web sites responsiveness. Developing common themes and the reuse of particular graphical images often increase the availability of the objects in the cache. Use of large varieties of images leads to a reduced availability of the objects in the cache; if you are not careful, it can result in a cluttered and unfocused look to your Web site as well. Graphical and animated content often produces a greater impact on the users' experience at your site. Thus, the use of such objects is often desirable. Simply choose your images and animations wisely. Also, as you add the graphical objects to the content of the Web site, monitor the site's use of memory. If you want to have the objects in the content, it is likely you will need to increase the physical memory of the server to compensate. When the content simply will not fit in the cache of the system, you will have to rely on the performance of the disk subsystem.

I mentioned earlier how disk striping assists in reading pages into memory to be displayed from the Web site. Disk access is very important for reading the Web pages and pulling objects from the hard drive. The file system cache is a major concern, but you still want to make sure you have superior disk access. You can never fit everything in the file system cache or the Web services' Working Set. As Web content continues to evolve into more visually stunning images, sounds, and animations, the performance of the disk subsystem will grow in importance because more requirements will exceed what can be installed on a system. The disk is always going to be a factor in the performance of the Web site. Keeping the disk defragmented and in good condition is a standard maintenance rule. If possible, make sure that the Web pages are separated from the operating system files or the PAGEFILE.SYS file that the operating system utilizes for virtual memory.

## A Sample Disk Configuration

*The disk subsystem configuration and the placement of the PAGEFILE.SYS are always important to the performance of the system. In the case of the Web server, we have talked about how you want to separate the Web pages from the rest of the operating system. Also, we have discussed utilizing the disk striping for improved disk subsystem performance. Let's look at how we might configure a Web server for maximum disk performance for both the Web services and the operating system.*

*For this example, consider the following scenario: When we order our Web server, we elect to have five hard drives included in the system. In addition, we have a dual channel SCSI controller card. The first thing we want to do is install the Windows NT operating system on one of the hard drives. Due to current limitations with the Windows NT operating system, the largest partition we make is 4GB. In our case, we have purchased five 8.4GB drives. Thus, we have 4.4GB space left on the first drive.*

*For fault tolerance reasons, we mirror the operating system partition onto the second drive. Then, we create a new partition on the remaining space of both the first and second drives. We create a PAGEFILE.SYS on each one of these second partitions on the first and second physical drives. The remaining three drives are connected to the second channel of our SCSI controller card. Lastly, we format the remaining three drives as a stripe set and put our Web services and HTML pages on this partition.*

*So what have we accomplished? The Windows NT operating system is on two partitions—the original drive and the mirrored drive—and is protected by this mirrored configuration. Because the operating system is primarily read from the disk, the mirror configuration improves performance. When you use Windows NT's mirroring, the operating system will read from either the primary partition or the mirrored partition. Thus, read performance for a mirrored configuration is increased. The page file performance and memory performance are enhanced by creating multiple page files on multiple physical disks. In addition, putting the page files on partitions by themselves as opposed to putting them on the same partition with the NT operating system reduces fragmentation of the page files. The operating system can almost always access the page file because there's more than one and they are on different physical disks. The operating system functions have been separated from the Web services. This is done by putting the Web content on the stripe set, which is connected to a different channel on the SCSI adapter card. This means that the system can always access the operating system code and the Web services code simultaneously. ◆*

## Service Cache

The service cache is used by most of the Web services to cache particular objects. This cache is normally part of the Web services' Working Set. In IIS, the service cache is called the IIS Object Cache, a particular section of memory that is held in the service's Working Set where recently used objects are kept. When observing the Object Cache, you want to watch the following counters:

```
Internet Information Services Global: Objects

Internet Information Services Global: Cached File Handles

Internet Information Services Global: Directory Listings

Internet Information Services Global: Cache Hits

Internet Information Services Global: Cache Hits%
```

The `Objects`, `Cached File Handles`, and `Directory Listings` all are used to describe what is in the cache. The `Cache Hits` and `Cache Hits%` let you know how effective the IIS Web server is in providing the right object at the right time. The `Directory Listings` is primarily used for FTP servers; usually this value is relatively small compared to the others. The `File Handles` refers to all the open file handles in use by the Web services. Some are related to the Web pages directly; others are related to the services' operation.

To separate this out, you should observe the Web server when there are no user connections made. Rebooting the server accomplishes this nicely and ensures that no extraneous objects are left in the cache. Then, you will have a reading of the minimum amount of objects that the Web server needs to run. Next, you should monitor the system as users make connections and use the site. The values for the `File Handles` and `Objects` will demonstrate how the values can rise due to your particular code choices.

**Note**

*The IIS service Object Cache can be controlled via the Registry. By default, the size of the IIS Object Cache is 10% of the memory available on the server. This default value is used if there is no corresponding value entry in the Registry:*

```
HKEY_LOCAL_MACHINE
    \System
        \CurrentControlSet
            \Services
                \Inetinfo
                    \Parameters
                        \MemoryCacheSize
```

*If the cache hits% appears to be low and you have a corresponding increase in the* Process:Page Faults/sec, *you might consider increasing this value by 5MB from the default. You need to stop and restart the service (not the Web site but the service executable INETINFO.EXE listed as the World Wide Web Publishing Service in the Control Panel's Services applet). After making this change, observe the performance of your system. If you don't see a decrease in the amount of paging and an increase in the number of cache hits, you should increase it again. If you increase it past 20MB, you should consider that you have either a memory leak or a lack of memory on the server that cannot be compensated for by such adjustments.* ◆

The Objects counter is more than just a superset of the File Handles and the Directory Listings. The Objects counter has information on other objects you have created, ASP objects, and connectivity objects associated with a more complex Web site. Continuous monitoring of the values and Web pages being accessed will give you excellent information on how well your code is being executed.

**Note**

*With many Web services, including the Microsoft IIS, you can purchase or acquire shareware utilities that track the utilization of the Web pages. Combining this utilization with the Performance Monitor data can be very powerful in determining exactly which pages or code is producing the greatest strains on resource utilization. One such product comes from Microsoft's Site Server. Others are certainly available.* ◆

# Tracking the Effects of the Clients on the Server

In the previous two sections, we talked about how the users' use of the Web site and selection of connectivity methods can greatly affect the overall performance of the Web server. In this section, we do not cover details on how to develop an attractive and smooth flowing Web site, but we do discuss the impact of language choices and programmatic technologies. Usually, you would look at the applications supporting the data pages. The applications are generally a function of the type of Web server you are using. Many of the applications are server based, such as ASP, PERL, and CGI. Others are more client based, such as Java. Keep in mind that monitoring the applications has many variables, the least of which is the server software you are using. The server software, however, can have an impact on the tools and the type of monitoring you can achieve. For IIS, you will chiefly have *Active Server Pages* (ASP) and the ISAPI to monitor. Other Web services might use these languages and support systems as well as others. In this section, many of the examples speak to the IIS system.

When monitoring the client systems, usually you must pick the objects that you will have available. For IIS, the objects include ASP and ISAPI at the least. Looking at a few examples, here is what you might look at when observing the ASP activity:

```
Active Server Pages: Requests Failed Total

Active Server Pages: Requests Not Found

Active Server Pages: Requests Queued

Active Server Pages: Requests Rejected

Active Server Pages: Requests Succeeded

Active Server Pages: Requests Timed Out

Active Server Pages: Requests Total

Active Server Pages: Requests/sec
```

These counters serve as the basis for reviewing the activity with the ASPs. Examining the list, there are a few points to make about the counters. The `Requests Failed Total` is usually a point of concern. Within that grouping, you want to examine the `Requests Not Found`, `Requests Rejected`, and `Requests Timed Out`. The `Requests Timed Out` and `Requests Rejected` counters can indicate that the server is not living up to its performance end of the bargain. This could be due to the amount of memory available for the Working Set of the Web services. For that information, review the previous section in this chapter. For the Requests Not Found counter, you need to look for broken links in your logic, syntax errors, and potential problems with the disk. The Requests Total is just what it says and gives you a value to compare the failures with. Generally speaking, you do not want more than a five percent failure rate (Requests Failed Total/Requests Total). The Requests Queued is much like other queues. A value of two or greater is generally a sign of a problem with the performance of the system.

Generally, there are two problems. The first is related to the lack of memory on the system. The memory we're talking about is the memory allocated to the Web services' Working Set. So, you should review the information on the Working Set and determine if that is the problem. If the delays persist, you must examine the logic of your code. Problems here are usually related to communication with other systems. This could be a query to a business logic system or database system. If there are connectivity problems or there is a problem with the performance and responsiveness of this particular component, you will run into a problem with queued requests and potentially with requests timing out. The Requests Queued can be high without a problem with the timeouts. The queue might spike, but should be relatively low on the average.

Another possible scenario deals with ISAPI calls. The Internet Service API is a set of functions that can be utilized by standard programming means to facilitate the use of some functionality built within the IIS and Windows NT itself. With Microsoft's IIS Web system you can use the following counters to monitor the performance of the ISAPI calls:

```
Web Service: Current ISAPI Extension

Web Service: Maximum ISAPI Extension Requests

Web Service: Total ISAPI Extension Requests
```

For an idea of how much activity is being spent utilizing the ISAPI extension to feed Web content, refer to these counters. They are also related to the size of the nonpageable memory pool that you observed earlier. Using the ISAPI extensions can improve performance greatly as much of the operation is performed in the Kernel mode by the Executive Services. This does, however, place additional requirements on the system's memory pools. You need to observe the pools with more vigor if you are using the ISAPI heavily. To compensate, high volume sites might have to adjust the nonpageablepoolsize parameters in the Registry.

**Note**

*When observing the applications, it is valuable to generate scenarios in the testing environment. In the Internet Information Server Resource Kit, you can find a utility called the Web Capacity Analysis Tool (WCAT). This tool provides a method for simulating user connections and Web content utilization, much like the Response Probe does for standard Windows NT testing.* ◆

# Connections

In this section, we discuss the network interface. This particular component of the Web server is very important, but usually outside the scope of a programmer's development efforts. The programmer writes code (possibly for services) that works at the application level. Thus, most of the control of the network interface is left to the operating system. We can't completely ignore the networking because the operating system and the network affect the total responsiveness of the Web server. The following are some of the basic counters you want to track when watching the overall performance of the Web server:

```
Web Service: Bytes Sent/sec
Web Service: Bytes Received/sec
Web Service: Bytes Total/sec
```

Here, we are looking at the transmissions rates for the basic Web service, IIS. These counters give you an indication of the overall throughput of the Web server. These counters really only carry value when compared to the other components for the Web services. You use these as the basis for how busy and how well the server is handling the business. Then, you use them as a basis for tracking how other components—such as the Object Cache, Working Set, Processor, and memory—handle the situation.

In addition, whenever you analyze the network component, you will want to have a look at the processor. We have discussed on several occasions examining the processor's interrupts and DPC levels. These values indicate how much time is being spent servicing the network interface cards, as opposed to the code running on the system. Normally, this should not be a problem for any type of Web server. However, complexities arise when multiple network interface cards are added to a system, especially when there are multiple processors on a system. Chapter 5 examined the general effects of the networking and hardware on the processor.

## Summary

In this chapter, we analyzed a Web server's use of resources on a Windows NT system. We began by breaking down how a Web server would use the memory, disk, processor, and network. You first learned how to generally analyze the Web server's performance. Then, you discovered how to analyze each of the major resources in detail. You saw how to examine the various cache systems that are utilized where Web service is installed on a system. In addition, you learned how to analyze disk performance and even received some tips on disk subsystem configuration. Next, we looked at the effects of the clients on the Web services. In this discussion, we brought together our knowledge of the various resources to look at the system utilization from the perspective of an application running on the server or a remote client Internet browser. Finally, we looked at analyzing the load over the network of a Web server. Throughout the chapter, we also pointed out some detailed information that can be used with Microsoft's IIS Web server system.

# 8

# Monitoring Database Systems

The database server system is one of the more complex components within any company's computing enterprise. Unlike the Web servers that we studied in the last chapter, the database server system is much more of an interactive system. Web servers generally deliver information, whereas the database server system is responsible for collecting information. In fact, the database server system is usually responsible for manipulating the data, indexing the data, and presenting the data and reports in response to user requests. The foundation of the database server system is primarily the storage of information. This information is often critical to the operation of the company for which it was developed. Thus, the database server system must also be designed with fault tolerance and data recovery in mind. The enterprise-class database server system must collect the information, report the information, protect the information, and do it all as quickly as possible. Clearly, performance of the database server system is important to everyone.

In this chapter, we dedicate ourselves to analyzing database server system performance. We begin by offering an overview of how the particular system we're analyzing is different from others that we have studied so far. To supply users with information quickly and effectively, you must understand the nature of the database server and the key resources it uses.

Next, we look at how to analyze the overall performance of the database server system. You'll be exposed to new uses of the tools we have already used, such as in Chapter 7, "The Web Server," where we used the Performance Monitor to examine the IIS Web server operation. As in previous chapters, particular objects and counters are mentioned with explanations of their use as well as when the value indicates a problem.

> **Note**
>
> *Throughout this chapter, I refer to particular components and occasionally give examples of how some components operate or have additional functionality built in. Generally, I use the Microsoft SQL Server version 7.0 as an example. The Microsoft SQL Server performance objects and counters that we use with the Windows NT Performance Monitor will have some corresponding component within other database server software. This includes Sybase and Oracle for Windows NT. Each database server system has its own set of strengths and weaknesses, but in general they have common goals; thus, the tools and techniques used here can be globally applied.* ✦

After we have examined the database server system in general, we get more specific by examining one of the more important resources to the database system—memory. In this section, we look at the database server system's utilization of memory and how it uses it much like the Web server to compensate for disk performance.

Of course, having discussed memory performance in detail and its link to disk performance, next, we analyze the disk utilization. In this section, we examine closely the disk performance and, perhaps more importantly, suggest some disk subsystem configurations for improved database performance.

In the case of database server system performance, the construction of the database tables, indexes, and stored procedures directly affect the overall performance of the system. Although this is true of any program or Web page, for database systems, the impact is magnified. Therefore, we must spend some time discussing techniques for analyzing user connections, query structures, and table indexes. This section in particular focuses more on the Microsoft SQL Server than other sections. The tools covered in this section are specific to Microsoft's database server solution. However, as we point out, other vendor solutions most certainly have similar tools to provide the same functionality and analysis benefits.

You have the game plan. Now let's get down to business.

# How the Database System Uses Resources

Let's begin our discussion by looking at how the database server system differs from other enterprise computing components in its utilization of system resources. The speed at which the database server can retrieve information is key to the user's perception of its overall performance. Always keep in mind that the user's perception of your system's performance is the real judge of the efficiency of the system. For database systems, retrieving information typically involves some use of a cache. Caching is done both on the operating system level as well as the database server software level. Each database server system differs in its methods for caching data and procedures.

As you might recall, *caching* is a mechanism of allocating physical memory for the purpose of holding recently used data in hopes of improving responsiveness and reducing reliance on the disk subsystem. Memory is the key component to observe, whether you are looking at the database server system by itself or examining how the system is responding to user requests from your client applications. Therefore, memory performance analysis is a constant activity for the system administrator of any production database server system. In the next section, we devote much of our time to analyzing the memory performance and the database system's use of that memory. For now, let's consider how a database server system uses memory and what might affect the system's utilization of this resource.

For most database server software, because the memory is so critical, the software makes special arrangements for its use. For example, in the case of Microsoft's SQL Server, the database, upon installation, immediately allocates a certain amount of memory for use whenever it starts up. The actual amount of memory allocated depends on the amount of memory on the system and some of the configuration options for the software. Information about the exact numbers is recorded in the SQL Server documentation. This preallocated memory is held within the database server software's Working Set. Remember that the process' Working Set is the memory that the process utilizes to perform its operations. Within the Working Set, the database server software generally divides up the memory into various sections for data caching, procedural cache, and general thread memory. In this case, we speak of thread memory as the memory required to allow one of the database system service threads to be created and run on the system processor.

Unlike other software components, the database server software does not allow the Working Set to be adjusted by Windows NT with the same flexibility as other applications. Instead, the allocation of this memory is controlled through the database server system's software configuration. In some cases, this is a directly configurable item. In other cases, the allocation of memory is calculated by the database server software based on other indirect allocations of memory like the following:

The number of user connections

The number of object locks

The number of open objects

In the section "Analyzing Database Server System Memory Performance," we utilize some tools to analyze exactly how the database server system is dishing out this memory. For now, you should understand that procedural cache is used to store the procedures or code that is being run directly or indirectly by clients accessing the database server system. The data cache is used to hold temporary data or data sets in response to user requests.

> ### Note
>
> *Throughout the introduction and first section of this chapter, I have already mentioned the users more than I have in any other chapter in this book. This is because the user has more power to interfere with the proper operation of the database server system than with almost any other system in the computing enterprise. Without appropriate programming or applicable training to guide their activities, users can directly affect the performance of the database server system by generating unreasonable queries or creating programming procedures in client databases that are not properly configured to take advantage of the indexes in the database. In the section "Analysis Tools in Microsoft SQL Server," we discuss user actions in more detail. For now, though, understand that when you're analyzing memory, you need to analyze the user interaction as well.* ♦

Much of the use of memory is dedicated to cache, a method of enhancing the throughput for the disk subsystem. Clearly, this must mean that the database server system relies heavily on disk I/O.

As stated in the introduction to this chapter, the database server system is primarily one of information storage and retrieval. The information, of course, is being stored on the system's hard drive. Other software components utilize the disk, but not to the extent that the database server software does.

The Web server, as we saw in the previous chapter, is primarily based on reads from the hard drive. We have seen that the Web server's performance is based in part on the disk subsystem's capability to retrieve this information. We also saw that the Web server utilized memory in the form of a cache to hold the most commonly requested Web pages. The database system not only has to read the information quickly but often is updating the information on the hard drive as well. Thus, the caching mechanisms are much more complex in the case of the database server than they are for the Web server. In addition, the database server routinely has much more information. If you look at the information the Web server must provide to the requesting users, you will see that, in general, the size of the data is relatively small. Consider that your standard Web page is somewhere around a few kilobytes in size. In comparison, the database server contains data of enormous proportions, potentially on the order of a terabyte. Also, the database server must be a fault tolerant system. Storing information of a critical nature requires a system that can withstand any type of failure.

In addition to withstanding a failure of the system or the surrounding network, the database server must be able to store data and retrieve data dependably. Thus, day-to-day, second-by-second, the database server must be writing and reading information without corruption and without data loss. These stringent requirements force the database server system to implement fault tolerant mechanisms for every right to the database. Anyone who has worked with a database system will recognize this technique as transaction logging. Transaction logging, although providing additional fault tolerance for every read and write, produces a further burden on the disk subsystem. Based on our discussion so far, you can see that the disk subsystem performance will be one of the focuses  of our analysis.

At this point, you should have a clear understanding of the resource requirements for the database server system. Memory and disk are the most important resources to analyze. In most cases, you should analyze both of them at the same time, keeping in mind the reliance on one another. The database server system uses the memory to augment the disk performance. However, the Windows NT operating system uses the disk to manage the memory utilization. It is time to begin our analysis.

# Reviewing Database Performance

To begin our analysis of the database server system, you first need to gain an overall view of how the system is doing performance-wise. This is consistent with the way we presented performance information for Windows NT and Web services in the last chapter.

Using Microsoft's SQL Server as an example, let's examine a basic set of Performance Monitor objects and counters provided with the software upon installation. These particular counters offer you a general look at the SQL Server's performance. We use these counters as an example in this particular case. Keep in mind that there are corresponding counters within other database server software:

```
SQLServer: Buffer Manager: Buffer Cache Hit Ratio

SQLServer: General Statistics: User Connections

SQLServer: Memory Manager: Total Server Memory(KB)

SQLServer: SQL Statistics: SQL Compilations/sec

SQLServer: Buffer Manager: Page Reads/sec

SQLServer: Buffer Manager: Page Writes/sec
```

When examining the counters that Microsoft has supplied for their version of the database server, you might notice that most of them have to do with cache, which is memory. Again, this is an indication that memory, and more specifically, the caching of data, is very important to the overall performance of the database server system.

The User Connections counter is used as a basic indication of the amount of requests being made on the database server. User connections are different from the number of logged on users. A single user can maintain multiple connections to the database server system. Each connection requires memory resources to maintain. The amount of memory per connection will be dependent on the database server system that you have selected. In the case of Microsoft SQL Server, it depends on the version of the database system as well.

The Total Server Memory counter shows how much of the memory SQL Server is actually using out of the memory it has reserved for its Working Set. Keep in mind that other database server software provides its own set of counters that can be used to measure similar features and performance.

Even in the event that you do not have software-specific performance objects and counters available for use, you still need to be able to analyze the particular software's performance and resource requirements on Windows NT Server. You simply have to treat the database server system service like any other process on Windows NT. You want to gain an overall picture of the requirements the database software is placing on the entire system. To do this, you can use the following familiar counters:

```
Process: %Processor Time:[database server instance]

Process: Working Set: [database server instance]

Process: Page Faults/sec: [database server instance]

Physical Disk: %Disk Time

Physical Disk: Ave Disk Queue Length

Memory: Available Memory

Processor: %Processor Time

System: Processor Queue Length

Network Segment: %Network Utilization

Processor: %Interrupt Time
```

In the preceding list of counters, the database server instance refers to the process that is responsible for most of the database server functions. Utilizing these particular counters gives you an overall view of how the system is reacting to the demands being placed on it by the database server component. The counters focus on the processor, memory, network, and disk resources. Although the network is an important piece of the overall performance of retrieving data from a database server, the network is routinely not the cause of exceptional delays.

In addition, heavy network utilization is typically a symptom and not a problem in and of itself. A heavily utilized network is more of an indication of inappropriate queries resulting in large data sets. It could also be an indication of a poorly designed database or client application. Nonetheless, the counters referring to network utilization are important for a complete picture of the system's performance. Bear in mind that the `Processor: %Interrupt Time` is an indication of how much time the processor is spending responding to hardware requests like those sent by the network interface card. Thus, when this counter shows large values coupled with heavy overall processor utilization, it is an indication of a network issue that requires further analysis.

When examining the memory and disk counters, remember that they are tied together. On Windows NT, the page file is used to back up memory. When a process does not find what it needs in physical RAM, it generates a page fault, and the data is read from the hard drive. The database server systems add an additional layer to this process. The database software attempts to provide information in memory prior to the user requesting it.

This method of caching serves the same purpose as a Windows NT page file caching. It reduces the reliance on disk performance in favor of the faster, more efficient memory access. With this in mind, a disk queue length of more than 2 should warrant further investigation into memory and disk performance. If the `Available Memory` is above 4MB, you can consider that the problem is related more specifically to disk utilization instead of increased pressure from a memory shortage. Always consider the need to analyze the entire operating system and all applications running on it—not only the database server system you are focusing on. If the `Available Memory` is close to or below 4MB and you have a large disk queue length, think about analyzing memory resource utilization intently. At this point, let's have a closer look at analyzing the memory utilization of a database software system.

## Analyzing Database Server System Memory Performance

We begin our detailed analysis of memory by going through the same steps we went through in Chapter 5, "General Resource Consumption." First, we look at the system's overall utilization of the memory resource. This, of course, is done by looking at the system's paging. Similar to Chapter 5, we start with the following counters:

```
Memory: Available Bytes
Memory: Pages/sec
Memory: Page Reads/sec
```

You first need to identify the database server processes that are running on the system. This is typically very straightforward. In the case of Microsoft SQL Server, you have two processes running on the system. The first, most important service is the SQL Server Service. Routinely with database server systems, there are other services running that are responsible for scheduling tasks and other minor maintenance operations. Make sure that you have properly identified the main process that is responsible for responding to user requests and manipulating the databases. You need to check the vendor's documentation for the particular database server system that you are running to determine which services you need to be monitoring. Generally, you can use the following counters after you have identified the service that you want to monitor:

```
Process: ID Process: [server process]
Process: Working Set: [server process]
Process: Working Set Peak: [server process]
Process: Page Faults/sec: [server process]
```

You will examine these counters in addition to the ones mentioned previously in regards to memory. The first counter listed is the ID Process. You want to make sure that the particular process does not stop and restart anytime while you are monitoring the system. As in the past, observing the process ID allows us to make sure that the process has been running consistently through the duration of the analysis. This is especially important when you're logging data as opposed to observing it interactively. You might recall this particular technique from Chapter 1, "Introduction to Performance Monitor," and Chapter 5.

The Working Set counter indicates the current memory utilization of the server process. This is the primary indication of the amount of memory the database server service is using It is useful to compare this value to the Working Set total for the entire system. By dividing the Working Set counter of the database server process by the total of all processes, you get the percentage of the database server's consumption of the entire system's memory resource.

The Working Set Peak counter tells you what the peak utilization of the memory resource is for the database server service. If the peak is not much higher than the Average Working Set value, this indicates that the system is being well utilized, and there is no problem. However, if this condition is present along with a general lack of memory, the system might be undergoing some serious memory resource shortage. You want to investigate whether there is a particular process within the database server system consuming most of the memory or if this situation is being created by another process on the system. Usually in these cases, you want to use the performance objects and counters provided by the vendor of the database server system. If the Working Set Peak is much higher than the average, you should consider that this is a particular query or process with a onetime affect on the system. However, it still warrants further analysis. You need to collect information on the processes and users connected to the system as well as the memory utilization on the system.

Collecting information on user connections and user-generated queries is usually done by utilizing some type of trace utility. In database terms, a *trace* is when the system is instructed to examine and record the activity from a particular user's machine. All the information regarding this activity, both the queries and the results, is reported in a log file. Often, collecting information in this way can greatly affect the system's performance. You need to keep this in mind when you're doing any kind of tracing through the database server system. For example, Microsoft SQL Server allows you to trace the incoming queries and operations for any particular user or machine. However, such action has a toll on overall system performance. Again, we see that benchmarks created from Performance Monitor logs are key to understanding the performance counters in production and different conditions.

> **Note**
>
> *Even with Microsoft's own product, SQL Server 7.0, associating particular processes with particular resource utilizations with a SQL Server can be a bit of a chore. So, it usually takes a little more effort to acquire this information. Isolating the SQL Server in a separate network is the best way to start. Once in an isolated network you can control the number of connections and queries being run. At this point, you can collect information in a controlled environment, run tests, and determine exactly which processes, queries, or actions are affecting the SQL Server. ◆*

Although we examine the overall memory utilization—or the memory utilization by specific database server system software—you must also consider the other factors that contribute to memory utilization on a database system. Some of these factors are the following:

Database schema

Database indexes

Database queries

You can see that the performance of the database server starts with the construction of the databases. Proper construction, testing, and use of indexes greatly affects the overall performance of the database server. Each database server system has its own methods of assisting in the creation of appropriate indexes, tables, and queries. Continuing with our example of Microsoft's SQL Server, this system has a Profiler and several wizards that assist in the development of appropriate indexes and the testing of queries against those indexes and the underlying tables. Later in the section "Analysis Tools in Microsoft SQL Server," we take a closer look at the tools provided with SQL Server to perform analysis of the effectiveness of indexes and queries.

Remember that we are primarily analyzing memory from the point of view that it is enhancing our overall disk performance. Now that we have sufficiently covered the analysis of memory performance, we can move to analyzing the disk performance.

## Utilizing Disk Space

In our discussions of database server system's memory utilization, we have commented several times that memory usage is ultimately tied to disk performance. This is true of Windows NT in general but even more so with database server systems. The need to retrieve and store data rapidly and efficiently is paramount to the performance of the overall system. However, much attention must still be paid to fault tolerance. Otherwise, the database server system is not going to be worthy of a place in the business computing environment.

Primarily, you should be concerned with overall disk utilization. We have already examined several utilities you can use to detail the disk performance or cost in relation to your basic queries and stored procedures. In this section, we pay some attention to the disk utilization and performance analysis in general. Usually, when examining disk performance, you are concerned primarily with disk reads. However, in the case of database server systems, you have to be concerned with writes as well as reads. The following lists some basic performance counters that you can use to begin your analysis of the disk performance:

```
Physical Disk: % Disk Time

Physical Disk: % Disk Read Time

Physical Disk: % Disk Write Time

Physical Disk: Avg. Disk Queue Length

Physical Disk: Avg. Disk sec/Transfer

Physical Disk: Disk Bytes/sec

Physical Disk: Disk Transfers/sec
```

The first three counters have to do with the amount of time the disk is spending on various operations. You, of course, have the overall Disk Time followed by the division of Read Time and Write Time. This allows you to judge whether your disk is involved with reads or writes at a particular time. The counter representing the Avg. Disk Queue Length is your primary indication of whether the disk is a bottleneck or not. As we have repeatedly discussed throughout this book, any queue with a length of less than 2 is considered to be a suspected bottleneck.

The next two counters, Average Disk sec/Transfer and Disk Bytes/sec, permit you to determine what kind of I/O your disk is being subjected to. With sequential I/O, the hard drive generally operates at a low Average Disk sec/Transfer and has a high Disk Bytes/sec when compared to average disk activity. However, when the disk is busy with random reads or dispersed among reads and writes to various disk locations, you will see the Average Disk sec/Transfer increase while the Disk Bytes/sec decreases.

### Evaluating Disk Counters

*Disk counters are more complex and difficult to evaluate than some of the other system performance counters. This is due to the complexity of the components involved. The disk counters not only give you an indication of the performance on the physical spindle, but they also serve as an evaluation of the drive, the adapter card, the bus, and the technology used. Offering numerical values for the counters as guides is often of little use. Disk evaluation requires the monitoring of a particular disk subsystem over time and under particular conditions. Simulation of such conditions can be done using the NT Resource Kit Response Probe tool. When evaluating disk performance, you will want to vary file size, read type (random versus sequential), and the number of threads performing actions. The data should be logged. You can then compare the logs to data in the production environment to determine how stressed the disk subsystem has become.* ◆

Constantly collecting disk activity is important to interpret the information collected during any kind of specific process activities. More than simply monitoring disk activity, you should specifically test your disk subsystem and configuration under specifics to get a baseline for the performance of your disk subsystem. This is very valuable in assisting with the interpretation of the type of activity that is occurring within the disk subsystem.

### Note

*Prior to monitoring any disk activity using the Windows NT Performance Monitor, you need to activate the disk performance counters. To activate these counters, all you have to do is open a command prompt and type:* `diskperf -y`.

*When you reboot the Windows NT system, the disk performance counters are active. Remember that if you're using a software-based RAID array, you must use the command* `diskperf -ye` *to use the disk performance statistics directly. On hardware RAID array configurations, you only need to use the* `-y` *parameter.* ◆

The last counter, `Disk Transfers/sec`, is one of the more important counters for database server systems. We have already discussed how disk performance is directly related to the overall performance of the database server system. Given the average amount of data being transmitted back and forth to the hard drive by the database server system, the more critical counter for evaluating the disk's performance is the number of I/O transfers per second. In most situations, you will use a high-performance disk controller card, most likely a RAID array controller card.

These cards typically have on-board cache and high throughput values. In addition, the use of multiple spindles through the RAID system permits you to have an exceptional transfer rate for the data. Most database queries and writes involve few or single rows being read from tables.

Therefore, the input and output to the disk is usually limited by the number of I/O operations per second that the disk subsystem can perform.

### Note

*Generally, if you're dealing with a good SCSI controller card, you will have in the range of 75 to 150 I/O operations per second. This is usually a single drive on a system. However, rarely will you have your database server systems running on such a configuration. Most of the time, you will have an array controller card with some type of on-board cache and processor built-in. Such controller cards are capable of around 2000 I/O operations per second.*

*Occasionally, you'll have the opportunity to build a disk configuration with more advanced technology such as in a Storage Area Network (SAN). These systems are usually connected through a gigabit fiber-optic connection to an external disk array. These systems are capable of more than 3500 I/O operations per second. Larger configurations are capable of even better performance. In other words, database servers rely on the performance of the hard drive, and you should pay attention to this need before you install software. When it comes to the disk configuration for your database server system, being cheap will cost you in the end.* ◆

You might have noticed in the preceding counters that we used the Physical Disk object in all cases. This is because, in general, the performance of the database server system depends on overall disk performance and not the performance of the particular logical partition that the database server system is located on. Thus, you always want to examine the Physical Disk object rather than the Logical Disk object.

When examining all of the counters for disk performance, you want to compare this data with information from other available utilities that come bundled with the database server software. For example, the tools we already presented are available in Microsoft's SQL Server. Collecting and comparing all of the data at once allows you to detail the exact affect of your software, queries, and stored procedures on the system's performance.

**Note**

*Database server system performance always seems to be under scrutiny. Any delays in presenting data in response to the user queries or updating the database have a very dramatic impression on the user's perception of the quality and efficiency of the software. For this reason, you need to perform some serious load testing of your database server applications. There are a variety of tools available for you to perform such analysis. In the case of Microsoft's SQL Server, you can obtain a utility called LOADSIM, which can be found in the BackOffice Resource Kit. It provides a method for testing large numbers of simulated user connections to database server systems using relatively few workstations. ♦*

At this point, it is beneficial to look at the disk configurations that are applicable for database system service. Database systems performance can be enhanced through appropriate adjustments to disk configurations. You need to remember some basic rules when developing a disk configuration for the database server system.

First, most database server systems utilize a log as well as a database. Separating the log and the database files onto two different physical disks and, if possible, different physical data channels, greatly enhances the performance of the system and permits the operating system to perform multiple I/O simultaneously.

Second, never have the log file or the databases share a physical disk with the operating system. Also, you do not want a page file to exist on the same physical disk as one of the databases or log files. Remember that the disk performance is paramount to the overall database performance, so you don't want the database server services to have to contend for disk time with any other systems.

Third, for a serious database server system, make sure that you have a serious disk subsystem. This means you need a quality RAID array controller with on-board cache. If you intend on having a large database, you want to consider an external RAID array connected through a fiber-optic channel. Such systems offer full redundancy, RAID 5, and have throughput on the order of 1GB per second.

Fourth, for larger systems, you want to consider separating other components besides just the transaction logs. You can separate the tempdb database from the rest of the system. With Microsoft's SQL Server, it is possible also to separate other database objects, including tables, from the rest of the database. This allows you to physically relocate various database objects so that heavily used objects can be separated from the rest of the databases and logs. This enhances the capability for concurrent disk I/O.

Also, for these large systems, consider placing individual transaction logs on their own hard drive and potentially their own controller. Sometimes, this can understandably be difficult to achieve because this increases the cost of hardware. However, considering the results of a poorly performing database server system, I would much rather spend the money.

These are only suggestions. In the case of your particular database server, you need to work with your systems administrator to properly configure the system ahead of time. If you're developing commercial code to work with a database server system, do extensive load testing to make appropriate recommendations for hardware and disk subsystem configurations. Take these suggestions into account and use them creatively to come up with the most efficient and cost-effective system possible. Again, knowing your application and how it works gives you a big advantage when it comes to creating and configuring the appropriate system.

Analysis of the database server systems' memory and disk performance can give you some strong indications of where your problems lie within the database system or client programming. However, to correct the problem, you must look deeper inside the database server system. This involves utilizing the tools provided by the database server system vendor. Continuing with our Microsoft SQL Server example, let's look at some of the tools provided with this enterprise-class database server system.

# Analysis Tools in Microsoft SQL Server

When you discuss monitoring the performance of a database server system, it is difficult to separate the services and tools offered within that server system from those offered in the operating system. Although the operating system can provide tools to analyze the particular process's resource consumption, it cannot see inside the internals of the database system software. This is where the vendor tools come into play. In the case of Microsoft's SQL Server, we have a variety of tools for analyzing queries and looking at the performance impact of stored procedures and queries. Some of these tools are as follows:

Profiler

Index Tuning Wizard

ShowPlan

These tools provide the additional information that the operating system tools cannot provide. The Profiler can analyze queries and stored procedures that run on SQL Server. It records information regarding the various amounts of resource consumption. That information can be displayed or written to a file or SQL table. The Query Analyzer allows you to run individual queries or stored procedures and review the performance impact in other tools such as the Profiler and the Performance Monitor. In previous versions of Microsoft's SQL Server, the Query Analyzer was referred to as the ISQL/W tool.

The Query Analyzer, the Profiler, and the Index Tuning Wizard, when used together, make an excellent troubleshooting and performance tuning arsenal. It is the Index Tuning Wizard that can actually interpret the Profiler's output and make recommendations or corrections to table indexes.

Finally, ShowPlan can be used to display information on how SQL Server is attempting to optimize and run queries that you have created. Reviewing this information can give you insight into how to better construct tables and queries as well as identify problems with particular stored procedures or queries that you are running. Let's take a closer look at some of these tools.

## Profiler

Within SQL Server, you use the Profiler to collect performance information about the I/O, the CPU, and a multitude of other objects within SQL Server. When the Profiler is run, it records information in a .TRC file. Let's look at how the Profiler runs when analyzing a particular query.

To start the Profiler, you first need a query, table, and location where you're going to store the information. Next, you start the SQL Server Profiler, which is located in the SQL Server Enterprise Manager. Select Tools and then SQL Server Profiler. True to Microsoft's form, there are at least three ways to start the SQL Server Profiler. You can also launch it from the Start Menu.

> ### Note
>
> *As stated, we use the SQL Server version 7.0 in this chapter. This particular version is much different from the SQL Server version 6.5, including changes to its interface. However, version 6.5 includes most of the tools and utilities discussed here.*
>
> *The primary user interface for SQL Server version 7.0 is based on the Microsoft Management Console (MMC), a new standardized interface for most of the Windows NT and Windows 2000 tools and utilities. Microsoft has indicated that the Microsoft Management Console will be the default interface for most of its enterprise-level software. Sometimes, finding familiar tools in the older versions of Microsoft's software is a little difficult when you start using the MMC.*

*Instructions for the examples in this particular chapter discuss only the keystrokes and menu mappings for version 7.0 of SQL Server. For further information on the corresponding menu items in version 6.5 of SQL Server, please consult Microsoft's online help or the SQL Server Administrators Guide.* ◆

After launching the SQL Server Profiler, you want to execute the following steps to perform the analysis:

1. Create a new trace by clicking File, New, and Trace.

2. Give your trace a name.

3. Click the Capture to File check box. Select the location where you will store the information and click OK.

4. The new profile, or trace, as it is called, is now displayed and active. If there are any current connections to the database server, they are displayed, as seen in Figure 8.1.

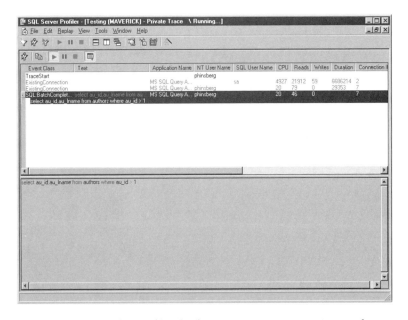

**Figure 8.1**   *The Profiler displays any current connections and queries that are running against the system. You either want to place the system in an isolated environment, as I have here, or adjust the filter for the trace to filter out extraneous data.*

Now that the Profiler is prepared and recording information that you need to start the Query Analyzer, you can generate some activity to analyze. The Query Analyzer is started from the SQL Server Enterprise Manager by clicking Tools and then SQL Server Query Analyzer.

5. Create a query to be analyzed.

6. Run the query (CTRL+E). Make sure that you have not disabled or paused the Profiler prior to running the query. If the Profiler was disabled when you ran the query, you need to close the Analyzer window and restart it. This is because the data that the query generates will be held in the data cache by the SQL Server system. Thus, when you re-run the query without first restarting the Analyzer window, the data will be presented with very little effort on the part of the system.

7. Return to the Profiler.

The Profiler will record all of the information regarding the query you run. Figure 8.2 displays the output from a sample query.

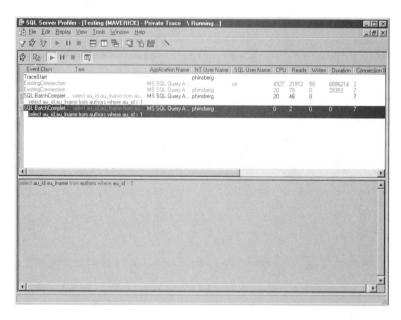

**Figure 8.2**    *This query was quite simple, but still displays all of the information that a more complex query would.*

In this display, you can see most of the critical calls on the default display for the Profiler. Of course, you get to see the query that was run. Also, you can see columns indicating resource utilization for the CPU and the disk. The CPU column records the amount of time in milliseconds that the SQL Server service used to fill this particular query. The Reads and Writes columns are records of the time in milliseconds that was spent on behalf of this query reading or writing to the physical disk. By utilizing these numbers in conjunction with Performance Monitor data, you can determine the amount of resources SQL Server uses on behalf of this particular query. In our example, the query was relatively simple and finished without utilizing much of the system's resources. However, when things have gone wrong—either when the databases are not designed correctly or the query is written poorly—resource utilization can be quite high. These are the situations you are looking for. They are also the situations that SQL Server Profiler can be most useful in resolving.

Recall that we configured the Profiler to store the information in a file as well as display it on the screen. You can now use this information stored in the file with another tool, the Index Tuning Wizard, to enhance the performance of the query, the underlying views, and the supporting tables involved in this particular query. For better results when using this information with the Index Tuning Wizard, as well as attempting to analyze complex queries or multiple sets of queries, you should have the Profiler store the information in a database table as opposed to the standard file format.

To have the Profiler store the data into a database table, you only need to adjust the properties for the trace. If the trace has already been created, all you need to do is stop the trace and select File and Properties. In the resulting dialog box, Trace Properties, you can see the options to capture the information to a file or capture the information to a table. Notice that it is possible to capture the data both ways at the same time. After you have selected the Capture To Table option, you need only select the database and table that you want the information to be sent to. Storing the data in a table has the additional advantage of enabling you to use the Query Analyzer to look at the top users of CPU and physical disk by running a simple query.

Now that you have the data stored in either a file or a SQL table, you are free to use the Index Tuning Wizard with the data that you have collected. This tool turns the raw data into information and actual changes to the tables and indexes within our database.

> **Note**
>
> *In this particular case, I have used the Profiler to simply collect information recorded in a file so that I can use it with the Index Tuning Wizard. However, the Profiler has many other uses in the realm of troubleshooting, in addition to performance analysis. The Profiler has other options and functions that allow you to customize the tool to the task you are attempting to perform. I strongly suggest that you read the online help files and practice with this tool repeatedly and under various conditions, as it is invaluable to troubleshooting and optimizing your database system. ◆*

## Index Tuning Wizard

Usually after you have completed work with the Profiler, you want to use the Index Tuning Wizard for further analysis on the database queries. The Index Tuning Wizard in Microsoft's SQL Server can review the information from the Profiler and present suggestions or corrections to the queries you have run. The Index Tuning Wizard is launched from within the Profiler tool. You simply click on Tools and then Index Tuning Wizard. Then, you follow the dialog presented by the Wizard. Let's walk through a few of the steps required to run this utility:

1. Select the server and database you will be analyzing. This should correspond to the server and database you were using when you ran the queries and collected the information in the Profiler. The selection of both of the option boxes on this particular dialog typically results in the best performance gains.

2. Select the option I Have a Saved Workload File. This option tells the Wizard you will be using data from the Profiler.

3. Use a workload file as generated from the Profiler or instruct the Profiler to store the information in the SQL Server table. In either case, indicate the file or table where you have stored the information. You then see a dialog box in which you must select the tables you need to involve in the analysis. By default, all of the tables are selected.

4. To avoid wasting time, select only the tables that are related to one another in this dialog box, if you are clear on the relationships between them. Of course, if you don't know the relationships, select all of the tables to make sure that every table is considered, which can add considerably to the amount of time it takes to perform the analysis.

The results of the analysis performed by the Index Tuning Wizard are a series of suggestions and reports. The Index Tuning Wizard can perform some of the changes for you. The primary suggestions it makes are to create indexes on critical portions of the tables.

When you are doing this type of analysis, keep in mind that it is very important to run the analysis several times before committing to any changes. This allows you to vary the types of queries, the data sets that you query for, and size of the result sets. This is important in making sure that the Index Tuning Wizard provides you with appropriate information as opposed to simply optimizing a single query.

We have now utilized Microsoft's SQL Server tools to perform tracing, analysis, and tuning of our tables, indexes, and queries. Still, there will be those cases where these tools will not suffice for detecting problems and correcting performance issues. No tool is capable of considering all cases in all situations. This leads us to the next tool in our arsenal for performance analysis on SQL Server.

## ShowPlan

The ShowPlan tool allows you to see how SQL Server's Query Optimizer examines and determines how to actually run the query that you designed. When creating a query in SQL Server, the query is not always run in the same way that the user had intended. The SQL Server Query Optimizer intervenes and determines the best method for running the query against the database.

**Note**

*In SQL Server version 7.0, Microsoft has placed a good deal of emphasis on the improvement of the ShowPlan tool, especially in the area of graphical display. The tool still has the same goal as in SQL version 6.5. It has simply been expanded and improved. The SQL Server online help provides more details on the enhancements to the new ShowPlan utility.* ◆

Running ShowPlan is done within the Query Analyzer. Prior to executing a query, you simply press CTRL+K or select Query, Show Execution Plan. Then, when you execute your query, the system records and displays the information about how the SQL Server Query Optimizer has executed the query. In addition, it displays the costs. The costs in this context have to do with the relative amount of effort and resources that SQL Server must utilize to complete the requested query. The query is broken down into sections for easy analysis. The costs associated with each section of the query are displayed, as seen in Figure 8.3.

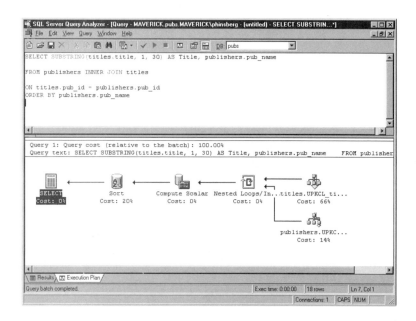

Figure 8.3 *Although the SQL Server Query Analyzer displays
information in a text-based format, the graphical tool
is much more informative and intuitive.*

As you can see in Figure 8.3, various graphical icons represent the portions
of the query or stored procedure that will be executed. Each of these particular sections of the query can be highlighted to display additional information about the exact cost of that particular portion of the query. In Figure
8.4, you can see the additional information that is displayed when you highlight one particular section.

The Query Analyzer's ShowPlan functionality displays the type of operation being performed, the Row Count and Estimated Row Size, the I/O Cost,
the CPU Cost, and the Overall Time Cost. Finally, it displays information
about the Argument that was being run and the Overall Subtree Cost. All of
this information can be used to determine the overall affect of running the
query on the SQL Server. If you couple this information with Performance
Monitor data, you can relate the query's performance to the overall database
server system's performance. In our case, we performed a simple query that
involved an inner join between multiple tables. The relative costs are also
presented as percentages that allow you to see exactly which section of the
entire query was costing you the most in overall system effort.

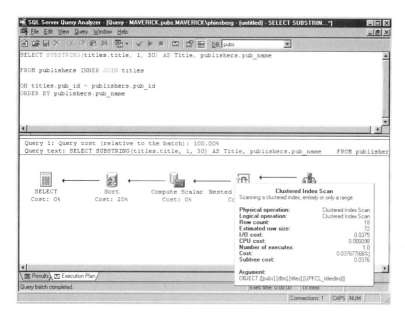

**Figure 8.4**   *The information is nicely displayed when you simply hold the mouse over an icon that represents a section of the query. Sections are logical separations of operations that are performed to satisfy the overall query.*

## Note

As anyone who has worked with SQL Server or database server systems can tell you, there are many ways to get the same information from the same tables. The ShowPlan utility is excellent for providing the information you need to select the best method for retrieving data. However, this particular utility requires practice for you to use it effectively. I suggest that you examine multiple queries that are currently in use and employ a variety of different mechanisms such as joins, multiple tables, clustered indexes, and non-indexed columns. This provides you with a background for judging which query and query structure provides the best performance while returning the same information. ◆

## Summary

In this chapter, we returned our critical eye toward the database server system. For any company, this complex and often mission-critical component of the computing enterprise requires constant monitoring and a good understanding of the internal database structure. We utilized our standard Windows NT tools to first examine the resource utilization of the database server system. As always, we started off with the big picture by examining processor, memory, disk, and networking performance. From there, we focused on the critical areas for a typical database server system, which are memory resource utilization and disk subsystem utilization. We analyzed the memory performance and gained an appreciation for the link between memory and disk subsystem performance. We then analyzed the disk subsystem and learned more about how database server systems, specifically Microsoft's SQL Server, utilize hard drives. In addition, you were presented with some disk subsystem configuration tips for use with any database server system. Finally, we delved into analyzing database indexes and queries utilizing specific tools within Microsoft's SQL Server. Although we tended to focus on Microsoft's database product in this chapter, you should be able to translate the techniques and tools to whatever database server system you are using. At this point, you should attempt to utilize these tools on test databases, or you can control the activity on the database. This helps you learn to identify particular scenarios and problems with database systems and client software.

# 9

# Pushing the Limits

This chapter takes a slightly different perspective than the preceding chapters. In this last chapter, we incorporate all of the knowledge and tools that we have learned about in the previous chapters. You need to combine your architectural knowledge of Windows NT, your programming knowledge, and the performance analysis techniques. In this chapter, we deal with the extremes of application resource consumption or performance demands. In the examples and cases in this chapter, we assume that you've taken every possible step to make your application utilize fewer resources and run more efficiently. Despite these efforts, the requirements for your particular application have still exceeded the norms for application performance. Your application might include heavy number crunching, involve computer-aided drafting, make extensive use of multimedia, or need to operate in real-time mode. Any one of these requires the use of every available resource on the system. The demands for memory, for processor performance, and for networking throughput remain higher with these types of applications than with other standard enterprise applications. In these cases, basically, you must do something out of the ordinary. Given the specifications for these applications, you have no choice but to use the various tools to figure out a superior configuration for the workstations or the server so that they are best equipped to meet the demands of your application. In this chapter, we use the tools that we have established in previous chapters to determine the best configuration for your application.

We begin by discussing applications that require excessive memory. These types of applications routinely are those that either work with large files or perform heavy calculations across a vast array of variables. Usually, applications that work with large files are heavy multimedia applications dealing with three-dimensional objects, movie-making techniques, or engineering diagrams. The files tend to be exceptionally large, and every effort must be made to keep as much of the application in memory as possible. This, of course, improves the performance when you are working with a particular file within the application. Other types of memory-intensive applications are your serious number crunching applications. These are typically financial applications utilizing a series of stored values to project far into the future.

In addition to these applications, you have your scientific applications that take in vast amounts of data to perform simulations or statistical calculations. In any one of these cases, the amount of data and the requirements to maximize performance to best serve the user cause the developer to make some hard decisions about resource utilization. Most of the time, it comes down to gobbling up memory resources or presenting the user with substandard response times to requests.

The next class of applications you need to consider is made up of the real-time applications. These types of applications must perform their actions in a real-time mode. An example is an application that is connected to some kind of instrument that collects data. Consider an application running on Windows NT workstation that is connected to a device that collects and sends information about the pressure, volume, and temperature of crude oil running through a pipe. The application must collect, evaluate, and respond to the information it is collecting second by second. In this case, allowing your application to be paged out to disk, having the application's threads preempted on the CPU, or having excessive paging by other applications due to lower resources creates serious performance problems and potentially dangerous situations. This type of application requires additional configuration of the NT workstation.

Finally, we consider another type of application that utilizes a different resource—the network. We already covered Web services in this regard. However, non-Web service applications can have different needs related to the responsiveness of the networking components. Generally, this refers to the Server Service and the Redirector. Consider a server that is collecting and recording data in a close to real-time fashion over the network to LAN- or WAN-based clients. This might be a financial data server similar to those used for stock exchanges.

In the preceding situations, you can see that we're dealing with applications that have specifications that reside outside the norm for your standard business or consumer application. These types of applications need more than simply analyzing the performance. They require an adjustment of either the application or, more commonly, the application and the underlying system. Again, this involves all of the tools, techniques, and knowledge that is contained in the other chapters of this book.

# Memory Maximizers

We have already mentioned several applications that might require some pretty heavy memory resource allocation. In this section, we point out a few tips for reducing the overall memory requirements by other operating system components, and we try to figure out the exact requirements for your particular application.

First, you want to reduce the memory requirements of any of the other applications running on the system. In some cases, you can remove the application or service altogether. Many services on Windows NT workstations and servers aren't necessarily required. However, in some cases, you must use caution, as disabling a particular service can have ramifications for other services or general functionality. The following services can be disabled on Windows NT workstation:

Computer Browser

Messenger

Scheduler or Task Scheduler

Spooler

Also, consider the critical nature of any other services that can be applied based on standard configurations within your own enterprise. Remove anything that you don't require specifically for your application or the operation of the core operating system. It might seem a little picky to stop individual services at this point, but we're dealing with a situation that is beyond normal. We're dealing with an application with special requirements, and we must do everything in our power to deal with those requirements. Disabling services that you might not necessarily need is a first step.

Prior to disabling services, you need to understand how their removal affects the operation of your system. The Computer Browser, for example, is used to make browsing the network more efficient. Yet, in the case of an application that is on the extreme edge of resource consumption, browsing the network might not be valuable to the operation of your application, but the resources that the Computer Browser consumes might have exceptional value. So, there is a trade-off. We shut down the Computer Browser, making it more difficult to browse the network servers' shares from that workstation. In return, we receive a little more memory below more processor time. In the specific case of the Computer Browser, you receive an error in the event log regarding the fact that this service has been disabled.

Another service you can disable is the Messenger service. The Messenger service is used to capture and display messages sent across a network. Such messages are usually sent using the NET SEND command. The messages and potentially other alerts are not displayed on this particular workstation. The Scheduler or Task Scheduler takes care of executing commands scheduled using the command scheduler. Disabling the services prevents any commands scheduled in this way from running.

> **Note**
>
> *The Task Scheduler replaced the standard Scheduler service on version 4.0 of Windows NT Workstation and Server. This was done in Service Pack 2 of Internet Explorer 4.0. Undoubtedly, this change will also show up in other service releases. It could also appear in the next release of IIS or in Service Pack 6 for Windows NT 4.0. ◆*

The Spooler service is used, of course, for printing purposes. Although the disabling of this particular service on a workstation does not prevent printing to a network server that has been appropriately set up, it does prevent local printing.

Last, we have the catch-all, the extraneous services. These types of services are perhaps antivirus software, specialized hardware services, time synchronization services, and other enterprise application services. You need to evaluate the necessity of each one of these on your particular workstation. Leave only those that are necessary for the proper operation of the system and, in particular, your application.

In addition to disabling some or all of these services, you should evaluate the server service's bias for memory utilization. By default, the server service is configured so that memory is maximized for file sharing. This prevents memory from being given to your application's Working Set in favor of supplying the file system cache with additional memory. Because the memory resource is such an important resource for your application, you should alter this option so that the server service is set to provide the memory to applications instead of the file system cache. This is set in the Control Panel's Networking applet.

Due to your application's increased memory requirements on the system, you also want to maximize the page file. This can be done for appropriate disk configurations. For example, you might want to get an additional controller card and hard drive dedicated to the page file of this particular

Windows NT workstation or server. This gives the system full and continuous access to page files. In addition, if the page file is intended to be less
than 400MB, consider partitioning the disk drive so that there is a single
logical partition of 400MB, formatted as FAT. The FAT file system is faster
and has less overhead than NTFS when the partition is less than 400MB.

You probably want to figure out what the exact memory requirements
are for your particular application. With most applications, especially those
we're considering in this particular chapter, you should provide the users
with some recommendation for the amount of physical memory they need
to build into their workstations. To do this, you need to examine not only
the Working Set of the particular process as it is running, but also the
overall memory utilization by the system as you would expect it to be configured for your application. You should look at the following counters:

```
Memory: Available Bytes

Paging File: %Usage

Paging File: %Usage Peak

Process: Working Set: [your process]
```

You also need the total combined size of the page files on the system that
you are examining. If your Available Bytes value is less than 4MB, you
know that you are not meeting your memory objectives. You can calculate
the amount of physical RAM required to keep your applications in memory
by performing the following calculation:

```
% Usage Peak X total size of page files = required RAM
```

You want to perform repeated tests exercising various functions of your
application before you commit to a particular number. You also should keep
an eye on the Working Set of your particular process to make sure that the
scenarios you are running are affecting your application process. You will
also want to periodically observe the Working Set for the other system
processes to see if your applications and the tests you are performing are
having an affect on them as well. When you have such exacting requirements for memory, you might also consider altering the memory configuration of the system. For example, you can alter the size of the pageable
memory pool and nonpaged memory pool. These values can be altered in
the following Registry key:

```
HKEY_LOCAL_MACHINE
    \SYSTEM
        \CurrentControlSet
            \Control
                \Session Manager
                    \Memory Management
```

You might be thinking of actually decreasing these values; however, if you have sufficient memory and your application is utilizing a lot of the Win32 API or has been implemented as a driver, you should increase the size of these values. Increasing the size of these memory pools enables your application to be held more often in physical RAM rather than paged out. However, this is not a recommended course of action for a standard workstation running multiple applications. This particular technique is useful for real-time applications, which we discuss next.

# Living in Real Time

Real-time applications are those applications that must be running as fast as possible. For an application to be running as fast as it can, it must be almost completely held in physical RAM so that no disk paging occurs. We have already discussed how you can make sure that your system has sufficient RAM for your application to primarily be held in physical RAM. Now, let us examine some of the ramifications of establishing a process with a very high priority.

When an application has a process priority that is much higher than the normal application, you risk interfering with the standard operation of the operating system. For this reason, you want to examine the various thread states of the processes on your system. This way, you can determine if your application is creating situations that interfere with the operating system. In Chapter 5, "General Resource Consumption," we examined the thread states with the Performance Monitor by examining the following counters:

```
Thread: ID Process: [your process]

Thread: ID Thread: [your process]

Thread: Priority base: [your process]

Thread: Priority Current: [your process]

Thread: Thread State: [your process]

Thread: Thread Wait Reason: [your process]
```

By examining the threads for your particular process, you can determine if they are being serviced and if they are monopolizing the processor's time. If the system appears to be running slowly, you might also consider reviewing the Processor: %Processor Time counter.

For any real-time based application, you should seriously consider writing and implementing the critical data collection portions of the application as a Kernel mode driver. When written in this manner, the threads for your particular process are serviced more often and with higher priority. In addition, being implemented as a Kernel mode driver allows the operating system to better manage any other components in concert with your driver. Keep in mind that a driver should have a focused purpose and be compact.

You need to have the response and analysis modules running as a service in User mode with some quick method for examining the data. Implementing a Kernel mode driver requires some care, as errors cause the entire system to halt. In addition, Kernel mode drivers utilize system memory pools differently than standard services or User mode applications. Thus, you want to re-evaluate the size of your paged memory pool and non-paged memory pool.

As with the memory-intensive applications, make sure that your system is not running any extraneous services, drivers, or user applications. Unlike tuning a system overall, you want to configure your system and its services so that they are responding specifically to the needs of your application or driver.

With such an application, additional attention must be paid to hardware interference, meaning that you must pay attention to the processor's %Interrupt Time. You might recall that the processor services both the application and the hardware. The %Interrupt Time indicates whether the hardware or software is utilizing the CPU's time. For this reason, make sure that you do not have unnecessary hardware connected to the system. Also, the disk subsystem should not be reliant on the processor for the majority of its operation. This typically means that you need a bus mastering PCI board, preferably SCSI. In addition, if at all possible, this machine should not be connected to a network. Network interface cards remain highly processor intrusive.

As you saw in Chapter 7, "The Web Server," with the Web services, network traffic can burden the processor. Also, the interrupts and, potentially, the DPCs have a higher priority than even the real-time application or the operating system. This means that hardware interference interrupts could degrade your application's performance. Considering the importance of the application, this could be devastating.

Lastly, consider the effects of collecting data and storing it to the disk subsystem. Perhaps you need to optimize the disk subsystem to make sure the least amount of time possible is being spent storing any data. In any case, the data that is immediately collected should be stored in memory. You might want to employ some type of caching system within your application to improve the data storing process. Because your application can tell when it is busy and when it is not, it might be best to provide a cache functionality within your application. Again, this reduces the effect of the disk subsystem on the overall performance of your application.

With a real-time application, perhaps even more so than with other types of applications, it is very critical to thoroughly test the application and its performance. You need to run through repeated test cycles and a wide variety of scenarios to properly test the system and the application.

---

**Note**

*Using the Windows NT Performance Monitor to monitor the real-time type of application can be a trick in itself. Consider that the real-time application is operating at such high priority in comparison to the User mode applications like the Performance Monitor that you could have some problems appropriately collecting data. In Chapter 1, "Introduction to the Performance Monitor," we showed you how to turn on the error checking for the Performance Monitor. This is one of those cases where you want to detect every error that the Performance Monitor might generate.*

*In addition, you should seriously consider creating your own performance counters within the application so that you can more appropriately track its performance. You might need to adjust the base priority of your application downward temporarily to allow the Performance Monitor to properly collect data. In this case, you need to use the Performance Monitor in conjunction with some type of statistical package to extrapolate the actual performance of your application.* ◆

---

# Pushing the Network

The final section in this chapter is about networking. Networking on any system remains the most complex performance tuning problem and the most difficult to solve. When it comes right down to it, when you try to figure out some networking problems, you sometimes have to make an educated guess based on information about the end points of the network and an understanding of your system's architecture. When we discussed the Web services in Chapter 7, we talked about how networking performance was important and also how it has a variety of components with many variables. In this particular case, we talk about standard connectivity to a server from a workstation.

There are many cases in which there is a need to have very specific parameters set for the networking components on a server. You might be moving large files across a network. You might have many users connected simultaneously to a particular server. Alternatively, you might have many small files being sent to a particular machine on the network. In these cases, as in most, you are treating the server system primarily as some kind of data repository for files. This means that you deal with the Server Service on the server machine and the Redirector on the client machine.

## Server Service

In any of the aforementioned scenarios, the Server Service needs to be running at its optimal level. First, let's examine the Server Service in the Performance Monitor. When you're looking at the Server Service performance, start with the following counters:

```
Server: Context Blocks Queued/sec
Server: Pool Nonpaged Failures
Server: Pool Paged Failures
Server: Server Sessions
Server: Work Item Shortages
```

The first counter in the list, Context Blocks Queued/sec, is your general indicator of whether there is a bottleneck with the Server Service. As we have repeatedly mentioned throughout this text, any queue of a level less than 2 is considered a bottleneck.

### Note

*There are exceptions to the "less than 2" queue length indicator. These exceptions occur when you have multiple processors on your system. In the case of the server service queue, the queue is maintained for each processor. Thus, with a single counter, you are getting a value that represents all of the queues for all of the processors. On a dual processor system, you could see a value of about 4 and not need to be concerned. The critical value is determined by multiplying the number of processors on the system by 2. ◆*

The next two values have to do with memory pools. If you are seeing failures that continually increase while the system is running, perhaps you should examine the system's memory counters. If there do not seem to be any other causes for the memory problems, consider adjusting the pool sizes manually. This requires editing the Registry directly. As in the section "Memory Maximizers," the values you need to modify are found in the following:

```
HKEY_LOCAL_MACHINE
    \SYSTEM
      \CurrentControlSet
      \Control
        \Session Manager
        \Memory Management
```

The values under the Memory Management subkey are all set to zero if the Windows NT operating system is dynamically defining these values, which is the default. If you are having a problem with the memory failures, make sure that you do not have a memory leak in any of the system pools. Detecting memory leaks was discussed in Chapters 2, "Windows NT Kernel Debugger," 5, and 6, "Examining the Application." Also, keep in mind that the size of the nonpaged memory pool is limited to 128MB, regardless of the amount of physical RAM.

The Server Sessions counter offers you a benchmark for how busy the system is. This counter displays the number of current sessions on the server. This counter should always be included when you are examining the server service.

The Work Item Shortages counter indicates when you have a work item shortage on the server. A work item can be considered a holding place for an incoming request from a workstation. The requests take the form of a *Server Message Block* (SMB). The SMB is stored in the work item until the Server Service can process the request. If there are no more work items, the SMB is rejected. The number of work items available to the Server Service is based on the Control Panel's Network applet configuration for the Server Service. In addition, the amount of memory installed on the computer is considered by the system when calculating the number of work items that will be made available. You can manually adjust how many work items are available for the Server Service by modifying a couple of Registry entries. The Registry key for the Server Service is located at the following location:

```
HKEY_LOCAL_MACHINE
    \SYSTEM
      \CurrentControlSet
      \Services
        \LanmanServer
        \Parameters
```

The following are the values you should consider adjusting:

```
InitWorkItems

MaxWorkItems
```

Both of these values have a range of 1 to 512. First, you need to examine the current value of each of these counters. Then, you want to adjust the `InitWorkItems` value, which is the starting point for the available number of work items. Although the number of work items is a dynamic range between the two parameters, you can still experience problems if the system must constantly increase the number of work items from the starting point. Thus, if you are receiving a number of work items shortages when you start utilizing the server, but experience no further shortages for extended usage, you should increase just the `InitWorkItems` parameter. However, if you continually see shortages throughout the usage of the system, increase both the `InitWorkItems` and the `MaxWorkItems` parameters.

Unfortunately, there are no rules for setting the `MaxWorkItems` parameter. I suggest that you start by increasing the value by 2. Then, examine the system over time while you exercise your applications and review the results. There is a cost in increasing the number of work items. However, this cost is relatively insignificant to the overall affect of not having enough work items available for the number and frequency of connections. This does not mean that you should ignore the cost in memory. As you alter the `MaxWorkItem` parameter, you want to track the changes to the amount of paging as well as the amount of available memory on the system.

---

**Note**

*It is important to keep in mind that many of the counters for the networking component, Server Service, and Redirector can indicate problems unrelated to the network. For example, the* `Work Item Shortages` *can indicate that you have a general lack of memory, rather than an excessive number of network connections that has overburdened the system. Recall what we discussed in earlier chapters that, with almost every problem, you should start with the basic four areas, which are the default counters for processor, memory, disk, and networking. Such problems can also be detected by examining the Redirector on the client and the connection.* ◆

## Redirector

The Redirector is basically the workstation service. When a request is being made from a workstation, it is the Redirector that takes this request and packages it into an SMB. The SMB is then sent to the Server Service on the server system. Clearly, the Redirector and the Server Service have a symbiotic relationship. A problem with the Server Service can be detected by examining the Redirector on a workstation. Let's have a look at the counters you use to examine the Redirector:

```
Redirector: Current Commands
Redirector: Network Errors/sec
Redirector: Server Disconnects
Redirector: Server Reconnects
```

The Current Commands counter is the queue for the Redirector. Thus, like all other queues that we have discussed, a value of less than 2 describes a problem. Before taking any action, you need to examine the other counters. You should also consider going over to the server that you are connected to and examine the Server Service counters on that machine. A strong indication that you need to examine the server is the presence of nonzero values for the other remaining three counters on the list.

Each of these counters represents varying degrees of networking problems. The Network Errors/sec counter represents the most severe of the errors. If you receive many of these, you are having a serious connectivity problem between your workstation and your server that could extend beyond either of the machines and be part of the network.

The Server Disconnects counter represents connections that potentially have been disconnected due to timeouts. After so much time of inactivity, the server disconnects a client. The Server Reconnects counter indicates how many times the Redirector had to reestablish a connection to the server to complete your request. The causes for the original disconnects, which forced the reconnects, are determined by examining the other two counters. Keep in mind that the Redirector maintains a connection for about 10 minutes even after you are no longer using it. After that time, the connection is declared dormant; although you might still see your drive connected or have some other indication that you have a connection, the physical connection is not made unless some request is made to that object on the workstation that re-activates a connection.

If you are not receiving any errors or excessive disconnects from the Server Service on the corresponding machine, any key that you have in the current commands for the Redirector could be based on your workstation's configuration. In this case, consider adjusting the number of available commands that can be placed in the queue.

> **Note**
>
> *Much like the system queue for the processor or the system service queue, the redirector's queue is dependent on the number of network cards in the system. Therefore, you should consider there to be a bottleneck only after this has reached a value of less than two times the number of network cards.* ✦

Adjusting the available commands simply increases the size of the queue and is controlled through the Registry. You can adjust the number of commands by altering the following Registry key:

```
HKEY_LOCAL_MACHINE
    \SYSTEM
        \CurrentControlSet
            \Services
                \LanmanWorkstation
                    \Parameters
```

The value that you alter is `MaxCmds` and has a range of 0 to 255. The initial value is based on the configuration of the workstation and the amount of memory installed on the workstation.

Finally, the number of network cards installed on the workstation should also be considered. I suggest that, if you consider changing this parameter, you should increase it by 2, re-examine the situation, and determine if this is a suitable value. Readjust if necessary and remember to analyze after each adjustment.

# Summary

This particular chapter was dedicated to extreme cases of application resource consumption. It served as the culmination of our knowledge and techniques to perform analysis and system configuration in those times when the demands of our particular application exceed the norms of application resource needs. We covered the applications that require excessive memory. With these applications, we needed to make sure that we correctly identified the amount of memory so that we could suggest an appropriate configuration. In an effort to squeeze the most out of our system's installed memory, we offered a few tips.

Next, we discussed the real-time application, which basically pushes the limits of the system's overall performance. We found that the real-time application requires a fine balance between itself and the operating system, because such applications can interfere with the operation of Windows NT. Generally, when we're dealing with real-time applications, we want to pull out every trick in the book to maximize the system's performance and reduce any interference from other software, services, or hardware.

Lastly, we discussed some additional networking issues. In Chapter 7, we covered the Web services, but here we focused more on general connectivity. You learned how to examine the Server Service and the Redirector service. You now understand their relationship and ways to adjust both to achieve the best performance for transporting data.

As was said, this chapter consideres the techniques that have been discussed throughout the book. Throughout the book we looked into the internals of Windows NT and learned to examine the operation of the drivers and system. We have seen how this knowledge of the architecture and operation assisted us in analyzing our own applications. We've looked at how our applications are critical in terms of their resource consumption. We have become familiar with a variety of tools both native to Windows NT and external. Some of the tools have been from Microsoft. Other tools were developed by programmers like yourselves who sought to better understand their own applications and the operating system they were running. We spent a good portion of our time developing our understanding of the operating system and its tools. Then, we applied these tools in Chapter 5 and 6. We continued applying our knowledge to more specialized situations in our analysis of the Web servers in Chapter 7 and database server systems in Chapter 8, "Monitoring Database Systems." Finally, we used our newfound knowledge to examine some extreme cases in this chapter.

Despite all that we have covered, there's still more. You should make every effort to discover and examine the tools made available to you for your particular development platform. For example, Microsoft provides many tools and white papers with their Visual Studio development environment. Other vendors supply their own tools that are just as effective for their environments. And perhaps most importantly, you should always take time to do performance analysis on your applications. Finding and dedicating that time is usually the most difficult part of performance analysis.

# *Index*

## I-J

# New Riders Professional Library

Michael Masterson, Herman Knief,     *Windows NT DNS*
Scott Vinick, and Eric Roul:     (ISBN: 1-56205-943-2)

Sandra Osborne:     *Windows NT Registry*
    (ISBN: 1-56205-941-6)

Mark Edmead and Paul Hinsberg:     *Windows NT Performance: Monitoring,*
    *Benchmarking, and Tuning*
    (ISBN: 1-56205-942-4)

Karanjit Siyan:     *Windows NT TCP/IP*
    (ISBN: 1-56205-887-8)

Ted Harwood:     *Windows NT Terminal Server and Citrix*
    *MetaFrame*
    (ISBN: 1-56205-944-0)

Anil Desai:     *Windows NT Network Management:*
    *Reducing Total Cost of Ownership*
    (ISBN: 1-56205-946-7)

Eric K. Cone, Jon Boggs,     *Planning for Windows 2000*
and Sergio Perez:     (ISBN: 0-7357-0048-6)

Doug Hauger, Marywynne Leon,     *Implementing Exchange Server*
and William C. Wade III:     (ISBN: 1-56205-931-9)

Janice Rice Howd:     *Exchange System Administration*
    (ISBN: 0-7357-0081-8)

Sean Baird and Chris Miller:     *SQL Server Administration*
    (ISBN: 1-56205-955-6)